Coffee House
to Cyber Market

Coffee House to Cyber Market

200 Years of the London Stock Exchange

Elizabeth Hennessy

EBURY PRESS

First published in Great Britain in 2001

1 3 5 7 9 10 8 6 4 2

Copyright © Elizabeth Hennessy 2001

Ebury Press
Random House, 20 Vauxhall Bridge Road, London SW1V 2SA

Random House Australia Pty Limited
20 Alfred Street, Milsons Point, Sydney, New South Wales 2061, Australia

Random House New Zealand Limited
18 Poland Road, Glenfield, Auckland 10, New Zealand

Random House (Pty) Limited
Endulini, 5A Jubilee Road, Parktown 2193, South Africa

The Random House Group Limited Reg. No. 954009

www.randomhouse.co.uk

Papers used by Ebury Press are natural, recyclable products made from wood grown in sustainable forests.

A CIP catalogue record for this book is available from the British Library.

ISBN 0 091 87096 8

Designed by Ruth Prentice
Picture Research by Juliet Brightmore

Printed and bound in Italy by Graphicom

Contents

1 On 'Change Alley, 1698–1798   6

2 'A Centrical Situation', 1798–1815   20

3 A Two-Way Traffic, 1815–40   34

4 The Wheel of Fortune, 1840–65   46

5 The Stock Exchange Investigated, 1866–90   62

6 High Noon, 1890–1914   78

7 War and Peace, 1914–29   98

8 Dark Days, 1929–45   114

9 The Birth of the Modern Market, 1945–65   132

10 The Stock Exchange Tower, 1966–79   152

11 Big Bang, 1979–86   168

12 Equities Powerhouse, 1987–2001   187

Further Reading   202

Index   203

Acknowledgements   208

On 'Change Alley
1698–1798

*I*N JANUARY 1698 A BROKER NAMED JOHN CASTAING began to issue 'at his Office at Jonathan's Coffee-house' a list of prices under the title of *The Course of the Exchange and other things*. It came out regularly on Tuesdays and Fridays, and the first edition, on a single sheet of paper measuring ten inches by four, gave prices of foreign exchange in fourteen centres including Amsterdam, Rotterdam, Antwerp, Paris and Dublin. Gold, ducats, silver staters and pieces of eight, and stock and commodity prices were also quoted; the latter included tobacco, salt, coal, paper and 'Low Wines'. Stock prices were given for Saturday, Monday and Tuesday for 'Bank Stock, India, African, Hudson Bay' and other items including a blank ticket for the Million Lottery at £6. 15s.

Castaing's publication, which was later issued from Garraway's coffee house, was the first in an unbroken succession of published share prices culminating in the *Daily Official List*; it is also among the earliest evidence of the existence of organised trading in marketable securities in London. Even in the sixteenth century there had been some buying and selling of shares of such few joint-stock companies as existed, but this was mostly carried out in private negotiation between individuals and did not require a specialist group of dealers, although shares were occasionally traded at public auctions 'by inch of candle', that is, with bids accepted during the burning of a length of tallow candle. By the time John Castaing was publishing his list, the situation was very different. There had been a dramatic rise in the numbers and capitalisation of joint-stock companies and there was an increasing number of people with sufficient wealth and financial sophistication to trade in stocks and shares. Before 1690 there were only some fifteen joint-stock companies, with a total capitalisation of £0.9 million; by 1695 there were about 140, with a capital of £4.5 million – one of these was the Bank of England, founded the previous year with capital of £1.2 million.

The selling or purchasing of their stocks and bonds was one activity of the stockbroker. The other, and much more important, was trade in the public debt. Like the trade in shares, this was not a new phenomenon: European royalty, including Queen Elizabeth I, had been borrowing from financiers for centuries. The inception of a permanent National Debt was in 1693, when one million pounds was raised partly by a tontine and partly by the sale of annuities. This was repeated the following year under the same act which established the Bank of England.

In the same year, 1694, the first of a number of lottery loans took place. The loan of a million pounds, divided into 'tickets' of ten pounds each, was serviced by funds provided by Parliament to pay dividends to all the ticket holders over a period of sixteen years, plus a sum divided among the prize winners; at the end of the sixteen years all payments ceased and there was no repayment of the capital. This and succeeding lotteries gave rise to the term 'the Funds', which at first referred to the sums provided to service the loans and was later transferred to the government loans themselves.

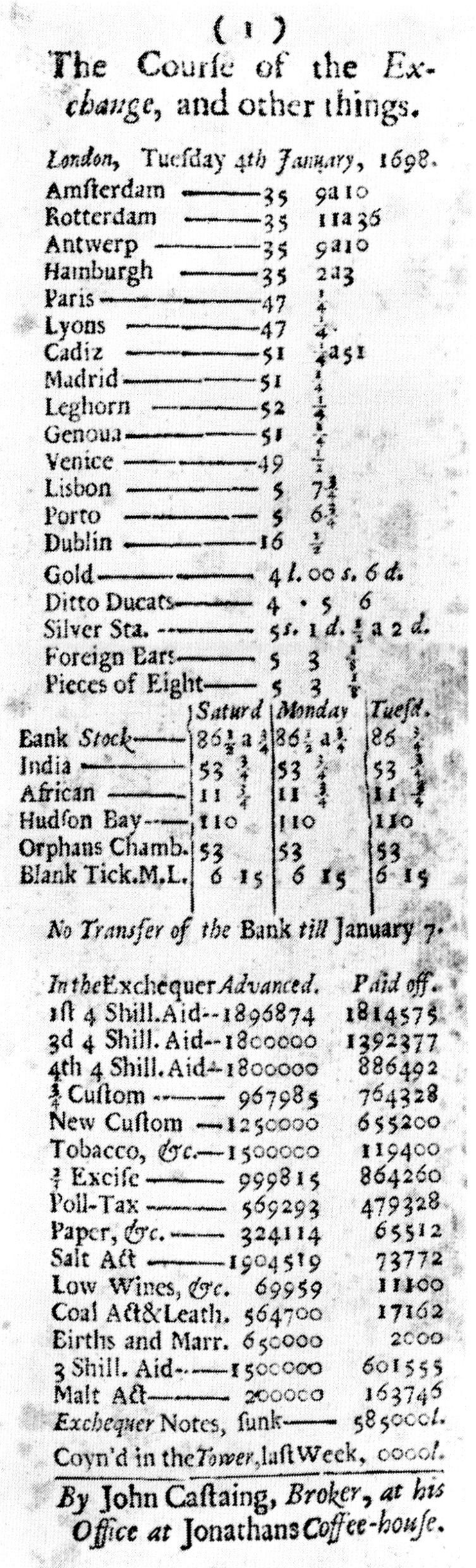
(1)

The Courſe of the *Exchange*, and other things.

London, Tueſday *4th January*, 1698.

Amſterdam	35	9 a 10
Rotterdam	35	11 a 36
Antwerp	35	9 a 10
Hamburgh	35	2 a 3
Paris	47	$\frac{1}{4}$
Lyons	47	$\frac{1}{4}$
Cadiz	51	$\frac{1}{4}$ a 51
Madrid	51	$\frac{1}{4}$
Leghorn	52	$\frac{1}{4}$
Genoua	51	$\frac{1}{4}$
Venice	49	$\frac{1}{2}$
Lisbon	5	$7\frac{3}{4}$
Porto	5	$6\frac{3}{4}$
Dublin	16	$\frac{1}{2}$
Gold	4 *l.* 00 *s.* 6 *d.*	
Ditto Ducats	4 . 5 6	
Silver Sta.	5 *s.* 1 *d.* $\frac{1}{2}$ a 2 *d.*	
Foreign Bars	5 3 $\frac{1}{8}$	
Pieces of Eight	5 3 $\frac{1}{8}$	

	Saturd	*Monday*	*Tueſd.*
Bank *Stock*	$86\frac{1}{2}$ a $\frac{3}{4}$	$86\frac{1}{2}$ a $\frac{3}{4}$	86 $\frac{3}{4}$
India	53 $\frac{3}{4}$	53 $\frac{3}{4}$	53 $\frac{3}{4}$
African	11 $\frac{3}{4}$	11 $\frac{3}{4}$	11 $\frac{3}{4}$
Hudſon Bay	110	110	110
Orphans Chamb.	53	53	53
Blank Tick.M.L.	6 15	6 15	6 15

No Transfer of the Bank *till* January 7.

In the Exchequer	*Advanced.*	*Paid off.*
1ſt 4 Shill. Aid	1896874	1814575
3d 4 Shill. Aid	1800000	1392377
4th 4 Shill. Aid	1800000	886492
$\frac{3}{4}$ Cuſtom	967985	764328
New Cuſtom	1250000	655200
Tobacco, &c.	1500000	119400
$\frac{2}{7}$ Exciſe	999815	864260
Poll-Tax	569293	479328
Paper, &c.	324114	65512
Salt Act	1904519	73772
Low Wines, &c.	69959	11100
Coal Act & Leath.	564700	17162
Births and Marr.	650000	2000
3 Shill. Aid	1500000	601555
Malt Act	200000	163746

Exchequer Notes, ſunk — 585000*l.*

Coyn'd in the *Tower*, laſt Week, 0000*l.*

By John Caſtaing, *Broker, at his Office at* Jonathans *Coffee-houſe.*

► *The Course of the Exchange, and other things. London, Tuesday 25th January 1698: the first price list issued by John Castaing, broker, 'at his office at Jonathan's Coffee-house'.*

Thus by the last decade of the seventeenth century there was a good deal of stock in the market, which was being regularly bought and sold in sufficient quantity to require the activities of specialised dealers and the publication of lists of current prices. A series of 'letters' or essays published in the summer of 1694 takes as its subject 'Joint-stocks and the various dealings therein, commonly known as Stock-Jobbing', and depicts a quite complex market which includes options and time bargains: 'The manner of managing the trade is this: the Monied Man goes among the Brokers (which are chiefly upon the Exchange and at Jonathan's Coffee House, sometimes at Garraway's and at some other Coffee Houses) and asks how Stocks go? And upon such information bids the Broker buy or sell so many shares of such and such Stocks if he can at such and such Prices: Then he tries what he can do among those that have Stock, or power to sell them; and if he can, he makes a bargain.' On another occasion the Monied Man is shown asking 'what they will have for Refuse of so many Shares: That is how many Guineas a Share he shall give for the liberty to Accept or Refuse such shares at such a price at any time within Six Months, or other time they shall agree for.' The 'means for Putting Stock' and bargains for time are also described, and specimen forms of contract given.

THE ROYAL EXCHANGE

The Exchange to which the writer refers was the second Royal Exchange, the first having been destroyed in the Great Fire of 1666. A year later Charles II laid the foundation stone of a new building which was opened by the Lord Mayor in 1669. Merchants and dealers in stock congregated there in a vast hall surrounded by an arcade and divided into distinct sections for the different merchandise, known as 'walks'. The dealers in stock had a walk near the central statue of Charles II wearing a Roman toga, surrounded by salters (who dealt in dry goods) and merchants from Italy and Hamburg. According to an eighteenth-century description of the scene the walls resounded with 'the din of new projects' and merchants from 'every civilised nation . . . might be seen in all the variety of national costume; and the flowing garb of the Turk, the fur-trimmed cloak of the Fleming, the long robe of the Venetian, the short cloak of the Englishman, were sufficiently striking to attract the eye of a painter to a scene so varied.'

The sober manner of the citizen 'formed a strong contrast to the courtier who came to refill his empty purse'; and a sad sight was provided by 'the broken-down merchant, pale, haggard and threadbare, haunting the scene of his former glory, passing his now valueless time among those who scarcely acknowledged his presence.'

At this date there was no formal distinction between the functions of the broker and the jobber. The words were used with a different connotation from today's usage – jobbing was applied to dealing in general and was a pejorative term for most of the eighteenth century, as in Dr Johnson's famous dictionary definition of a stock-jobber: 'A low wretch who makes money by buying and selling in the funds.' Brokers were less vilified; the term included, as it still does, agents dealing in commodities and shipping as well as stocks and shares. All brokers were

required to be licensed by the Lord Mayor and Aldermen. However, in busy times such as the joint-stock 'boom' of 1693–5 many unlicensed brokers were active. The majority of the newly promoted companies inevitably failed; complaints about unscrupulous company promotion were rife and a parliamentary commission was appointed in 1696 to 'look after the Trade of England'. This referred to 'the pernicious Art of Stock-jobbing' which had recently perverted companies and corporations to the point where no other use of them had been made than to enrich the 'First Procurers and Subscribers', who immediately sold their stock for far more than it was worth 'to ignorant Men, drawn in by the reputation, falsely raised and artfully spread, concerning the thriving state of their shares.'

There had already been one unsuccessful attempt to prevent stock-jobbing in 1693; a second one in 1696 also failed, but the following year an Act was passed 'To restrain the number and ill practice of brokers and stockjobbers.' The preamble to the Act stated that brokers and stockjobbers had lately set up and carried on 'most unjust practices in selling and discounting tallies, Bank stock, Bank bills, shares and interest on joint stock', and further accused them of illegally combining to raise or lower the value of such securities to their own advantage.

This was a direct result of the speculative mania of 1693–5 – the first such outbreak in Britain – and a particular incident involving a gamble on the price of guineas. The Act limited the number of stockbrokers to one hundred, and reaffirmed, with heavier penalties for infringement, the various provisions of earlier Acts. Brokers must be 'admitted, licensed, approved and allowed by the Lord Mayor and Court of Aldermen', swear an oath to 'truly and faithfully Execute and Perform the Office . . . between Party and Party', pay an admission fee, enter into a bond of £500 which would be forfeited in case of misconduct, and carry a silver medal as a token of admittance. Anyone acting as a broker without a licence was liable to a fine of £500 for each offence: the unlicensed stockbroker had in addition to spend an hour in the pillory on each of three days.

The limitation on numbers was much resented in the City and within a decade the Act was largely ignored although it was not finally repealed until 1867. The year after it was passed, in 1698, the stock dealers left the Royal Exchange, although the reason for their expulsion is not entirely clear. Certainly their numbers had risen sharply, and the building was becoming over-crowded: they were said to have been hounded out, accused of abusing the objects of the Royal Exchange, spreading false rumours of wars and political events, and luring innocent men to ruin by gambling. For whatever reason, they left the Exchange (although foreign stocks con-tinued to be dealt there for many years) and turned naturally to the warren of streets nearby, in particular Exchange or 'Change Alley, a twisting street (since straightened) running from Cornhill to Lombard Street which housed many coffee houses including Jonathan's and Garraway's. Secluded, yet with plenty of open space, conveniently near to the Bank of England, Change Alley (it gradually lost its apostrophe) became a name virtually synonymous with stock dealing and was referred to just as the Stock Exchange itself would be spoken of in future years. In 1700, and again in1703, the City authorities attempted to stop trading by 'Brokers, Stock-Jobbers and others . . . [who] do presume to meet and assemble in Exchange Alley', but deals continued to be done in the street for nearly two hundred years.

THE JOINT-STOCK COMPANIES

Most of the companies that had been floated in the mid 1690s soon disappeared, but several of the newcomers survived and flourished. A new East India Company was formed in 1698 and merged with the old one four years later to form the United East India Company. In 1711 the South Sea Company was established. British merchants had been supplying the Spanish colonies of South America with slaves acquired on the African coast, transported to Jamaica and sold there to Portuguese slavers; they had also been dealing in contraband goods with the mainland. After the fall from grace of the Duke of Marlborough, who had been prominent in leading the British forces in the War of the Spanish Succession, British traders, scenting the possibility of peace with Spain, set their hopes on direct access to the Spanish colonies, which might prove even more lucrative than trade with the East. A new joint-stock company had been formed in 1711 which converted (or 'ingrafted') over £9 million of unfunded debt arising from the expenses of the war into the shares of a new joint-stock company, 'the Governor and Company of Merchants of Great Britain trading to the South Seas and other parts of the Americas, and for encouraging the Fishery.' A sum of £568,000 annually was provided by

A BUBBLE BENEFACTOR

The north front of Guy's Hospital in Southwark, showing a patient being carried through the gates on a stretcher (c. 1800).

Although many fortunes made at the time of the South Sea Bubble vanished as it burst, some proved more enduring. Thomas Guy, a London bookseller, made a market in seamen's tickets. These were paid by the government in lieu of cash, and were not always readily convertible at the Treasury. Guy would buy them from seamen on shore leave, at a heavy discount (he was dubbed the meanest man in London), and exchanged them when the Treasury proved more amenable. He made a handsome fortune in this way, and also by prudent selling of South Sea stock, and when he died in 1724 left over half of his estate to found and endow Guy's Hospital.

Parliament to pay the Company 6% interest on the debt, and it was given a monopoly of the Spanish trade. Together these two new flotations, plus fresh capital raised by the Bank of England and the success of some of the smaller companies, brought the total share capital of the joint-stock companies to over £20 million by 1717. By this date there were three principal types of public debt, apart from what was already ingrafted into the stock of the major companies: 'long annuities' for periods of 89, 96 and 99 years and 'short' annuities for periods of 32 years. These debts could not be redeemed before their expiry dates without the consent of the annuitants and were consequently known as 'irredeemable.' Thirdly, there were redeemable stocks at 5% and 4%; the total sum involved was around £31 million. It was the proposal to allow holders of this debt to convert into South Sea stock, and the manipulation of the price of the stock, which set off the wave of speculative fever known as the South Sea Bubble. All share prices rose on the promise of easy money and nearly 200 new issues were made between September 1719 and August 1720, when the bubble burst, with a capital of over £220 million.

Some of these issues were for sensible enterprises such as various life, marine and fire insurances, one against losses incurred as a result of 'robberies on the highway' and another

◄ 'The Bubblers bubbl'd, or the Devil take the Hindmost': a satirical print of 1720 shows the interior of the Royal Exchange, with a stand bearing a scroll inscribed with a list of 'bubble' stocks

indemnifying employers against theft by 'any servant that is ticketed and registered with this society.' Many companies were floated for manufactures of different kinds, and many others for foreign trade. Objects included 'paving the streets of London', importing jackasses from Spain to breed with and improve British beasts of burden (this was the scheme of a clergyman who actually rented some marshland near Woolwich in which to carry out his experiments) and importing timber. Many were involved with the fishing industry, although this had been an unprofitable field for joint-stock companies for over a hundred years. Most were ill-conceived, some plainly fraudulent, but the fever to invest had gripped the nation. A popular broadsheet depicted the scene in Change Alley and its neighbourhood as the aristocracy and gentry thronged the streets:

> *Then stars and garters did appear*
> *Among the meaner rabble,*
> *To buy and sell, to see and hear*
> *The Jews and Gentiles squabble.*
> *The greatest ladies thither came*
> *And plied in chariots daily*
> *Or pawned their jewels for a sum*
> *To venture in the Alley.*

'There are few in London,' wrote the politician Edward Harley to his Aunt Abigail, 'that mind anything but the rising and falling of the stocks . . . so that unless I bring South Sea, African, Bank, cent per cent, par, etc. and such stuff into my letter I shall neither be fashionable nor fill it up.'

THE 'BUBBLE ACT'

The so-called Bubble Act (in fact a set of clauses added to an already existing statute), although purporting to protect the unwary investing public, was actually passed at the instigation of the

Company itself, which was becoming frightened by the number of rivals. It ruled that all companies formed without a charter, or under a charter originally granted for a different purpose, were illegal and all transactions in their shares were void. The promotion of such companies was declared a public nuisance and penalties for infringement of the Act could extend to imprisonment and forfeiture of all property, and any broker buying or selling shares in illegal companies was liable to a fine of £500 and prohibited from acting as a broker in the future. The Act came into force at the end of June 1720, initially causing only a temporary fall in prices as investors thought it would not apply to the more reputable companies – but by August the crash came. Proceedings were taken against several prominent companies, including the York Buildings Company, whose original charter for waterworks had been used as a cover for speculation in property, and the Royal Lustring Company, which had diverted from the manufacture of silk into insurance. Coming at a time when the market was already unstable because of a shortage of money and financial troubles in France, news of the prosecution of these companies was enough to precipitate a crash and the bursting of the bubble. The prices of South Sea shares during the year provide a vivid illustration of the mania: January, $128\frac{1}{2}$; March, 330; May, 550; June, 890; July, 1000; September, 175; and December, 124.

Almost all the companies floated during the boom years ultimately failed, but as few of them had actually got to the point of investing in land, equipment or property, their collapse did not involve the loss of much real as opposed to paper wealth. The South Sea Company itself continued to operate under new directors, never very successfully, ceasing to be a trading company in 1748 but continuing to deal in government securities; it became a sleepy backwater where one of the clerks in the 1790s was Charles Lamb, who portrayed its desultory atmosphere in his essays. The London and Royal Exchange insurance companies survived, as did the New River and Hudson's Bay companies.

The public, for a while, was cured of its mania for doubtful companies, but many rich people continued to invest. There was an increased distrust of brokers and jobbers, many of whom undoubtedly made a great deal of money. They already provided some of the stock characters of farce, the most famous example being by the playwright Susannah Centlivre in her 1718 comedy, *A Bold Stroke for a Wife*. The fourth act has a scene set in Jonathan's Coffee House in Exchange Alley, where stockjobbers and a 'Change Broker' are portrayed dealing briskly in stocks and shares and settling differences on previous accounts. Options, bulls and bears are mentioned:

> *'Are you a Bull or a Bear today, Abraham?'*
> *'A Bull, faith but I have a good Putt for next week.'*

By the end of the War of Austrian Succession in 1748, the market in securities, now firmly based in Jonathan's Coffee House, had increased considerably in sophistication and scale. A fire in 1748 had ravaged the Change Alley area, burning down Jonathan's, Garraway's, the Jerusalem and many other coffee houses and private offices and shops, but a public subscription was

◄ 'Jonathan's Coffee House, or an analysis of Change Alley, with a group of characters from the life' (1763). The Coffee House was established around 1680 by Jonathan Miles, and was swiftly adopted by merchants and brokers as their place of business. Note the devil at the right looking on with glee.

◄ The drawing of the state lottery in the Guildhall, 1739. Figures include two 'Blue Coat Boys' taking the tickets from the wheel, two men who call out the numbers of the tickets and whether they are prizes or blanks, and the Lottery Commissioners presiding at the table.

arranged to relieve the sufferers and most of the premises were swiftly rebuilt. The Seven Years War (1756–63) significantly increased government borrowing and the volume of securities traded at Jonathan's. Public lotteries reappeared, with a recurrence of the sale of shares in lottery tickets which had become very popular during the war of the Spanish Succession; tickets could also be hired and insured. A more important innovation was the introduction of quarterly settlement days, known as Rescounter Days from the Rescontre-Dagen observed on the Amsterdam Bourse, which were instituted in the 1740s, although intermediate settlement days were almost certainly observed as well, according to the dates of the opening and shutting of transfer books. Most of the bargains at the Rescounters appear to have been for transactions on margin – the brokers, on behalf of their clients, paid the difference between the price of the stock when ordered and its price on Rescounter Day. Settlement, continuation (not yet known as contango) and backwardation were all available by this period.

EVERY MAN HIS OWN BROKER

One of the most knowledgeable and persistent critics of brokers' trade in securities was Thomas Mortimer, whose book *Every Man His Own Broker* appeared in fourteen editions between 1761 and 1807 and was translated into German, Dutch, French and Italian. According to his own account, he wrote the book because of an unhappy experience in Jonathan's in 1756, and the work is certainly hostile to jobbers and speculators; like many of his contemporaries, he was deeply perturbed by what he saw as unnecessary trading in government Funds. However, his detailed advice to the public on how to buy and sell successfully gives one of the best pictures of stockbroking in the second half of the eighteenth century. He describes the difference between brokers and jobbers, the latter term usually being applied to those who speculated by subscribing to new government loans or buying and selling for time with no intention of taking up their stock or delivering it. This was contrary to the provisions of the 'Act to prevent the infamous practice of stock-jobbing' passed in 1734 – known as Barnard's Act after its promoter, Sir John Barnard – which was ineffective from the start. Mortimer divides jobbers into three classes: foreigners subscribing to the British Funds (he was particularly scathing about undesirable speculation by the Dutch in the National Debt); English gentlemen, merchants or traders also in the Funds; and stockbrokers jobbing on credit – 'jobbing brokers' – who carried out deals for clients or on their own behalf, and whom he blamed for the fluctuations of government stock prices. Two-thirds of brokers were unlicensed; according to Mortimer most of them acted as principals as well as agents and dealt only with each other.

As the number of investors and the volume of stock rose, the variations in the money market at home and overseas also encouraged buying and selling on behalf of domestic banks, insurance companies, bill brokers and foreign clients, and equally, rapid action to seize on any opportunity. Trust in and knowledge of those with whom you were dealing, so that you could be sure that payment would be made and stock delivered, became ever more important in the face of public opprobrium and hostile legislation. Because time bargains, under the provisions of the Barnard Act, were technically illegal and unenforceable as gambling debts, it became evident that the reputable market participants (even Mortimer allowed that there were some 'sensible, candid stock-brokers, men of unblemished reputations') would themselves have to enforce a code, or at least encourage a climate that would ensure the right conditions for trade. In 1761 the first moves in this direction were made by a group of 150 brokers and jobbers who formed what was essentially a club, based at Jonathan's Coffee House, to whose proprietors they offered to pay the quite large subscription of £8 a year per head in order to have the premises to themselves for a few hours each day to carry out share dealings.

THE MOVE TO SWEETING'S ALLEY

Unfortunately this arrangement did not last for long because those who were excluded objected; in 1762 a litigant named Reynous, who was not a subscriber, obtained a court ruling declaring that because Jonathan's 'had been a market (time out of mind) for buying and selling government securities' the brokers could not legally refuse permission to anyone who wished to do so. The next attempt to organise an exclusive club came a decade later. The opportunity arose out of the Bank of England's desire from 1765 to develop the front entrance to its building in Threadneedle Street. This involved various complicated transactions over adjacent properties, including the transfer to the Drapers' Company of five buildings in Sweeting's Alley which the Bank had purchased in the early 1760s. The negotiations hung fire for some years, during which it occurred to some of the habitués of Jonathan's that the site in Sweeting's Alley would be ideal for them to erect a building of their own, enabling them to leave Jonathan's which had become crowded and noisy.

After further complex negotiations the brokers were successful in obtaining a lease on all five buildings (which included three coffee houses, a perfume shop and a snuff shop). They arranged the termination of the tenants' leases, pulled down the houses and erected a three-storey building of their own which was opened in July 1773. It had a frontage of about thirty-five feet facing Threadneedle Street, with the dealing room on the ground floor and a coffee room on the first. Anyone could enter on payment of sixpence a day, a sum which would remunerate the owners for the cost of building and maintenance: it was known as New Jonathan's for a brief period, but before the end of the month the words 'The Stock Exchange' were, according to a contemporary account, 'wrote over the door.' Little is known about the constitution of this first exchange, other than that it had a Committee of Proprietors and a Committee for General Purposes representing the users – though how the latter was elected, without any formal body of membership, is not clear.

▶ *An historical, emblematical, patriotical and political print representing the English Balloon or National Debt in the year 1782.' The building is the Stock Exchange in Sweeting's Alley.*

STOCK EXCHANGE

THE STOCK EXCHANGE IN THE BANK OF ENGLAND

The Rotunda in the Bank of England, designed by Sir Robert Taylor.
This print of c.1785 shows some of the brokers who thronged it to deal in government securities, much to the annoyance of the Bank.

From the time it was first built in 1764 the Rotunda of the Bank of England was used as a marketplace for dealing in government securities. When it was rebuilt in 1795 by the architect John Soane, the Rotunda formed a circular space 57 feet in diameter and about the same in height, covered by a cupola and lit by a 'lantern' window supported by twelve caryatides, feminine figures representing the months of the year. Round the walls were recesses containing doors, desks, seats and fireplaces; branching out of the main hall were offices devoted each to a particular stock such as Bank Stock or Three per cent Consols.

A visitor to the Rotunda in the eighteenth century saw, between the hours of eleven and three, what a contemporary described as a scene 'truly ludicrous to the disinterested observer'. Jobbers crowded and jostled 'to catch a bargain . . . so loud and clamorous at times are the mingled voices of buyers and sellers that all distinction of sound is lost in general uproar'. This would be quelled by one of the Bank porters using a 'common watchman's rattle.'

It took an Act of Parliament to get rid of the jobbers; a clause inserted in the Bank Act of 1834 enabled the Governor of the day, Sir Timothy Curtis, to ban them unceremoniously. When Curtis was subsequently declared bankrupt, the news was greeted in the Exchange with three cheers.

The occupation of the new building was the earliest manifestation of a formalised, though not yet regulated, stock exchange. Stocks continued to be traded in other locations, of course; those of the major joint-stock companies were bought and sold in their own offices, and brokers and jobbers still congregated in the coffee houses and courts in and near Change Alley. By the end of the century the greater part of government stock was managed by the Bank of England which maintained the stock registers and recorded transfers. It is probable that the term 'the House' began to be used as a synonym for the Exchange when members in the Rotunda at the Bank of England would refer to colleagues being 'over at the House' in Threadneedle Street: it has also been suggested that it derives from the term coffee house.

London was by now becoming pre-eminent as the centre for trade in securities. The closure of the continental bourses was heralded by the French Revolution in 1789 which threw the financial system in Paris into disarray; bankers and other wealthy people fled to Amsterdam and London, and in 1793 the Paris stock exchange was closed. War and revolution followed in other countries, and when French troops occupied Amsterdam in 1795, there was a further exodus to London, which included brokers such as Raphael Raphael and Samuel de Zoete. Germany too was in turmoil, leading to a diaspora of Germans such as Johann Friedrich and Johann Heinrich Schröder, the sons of a Hamburg merchant; Emanuel Henry Brandt, also from Hamburg, the son of an insurance broker; Frederick Huth from Hanover; and, towering above the rest, Nathan Rothschild from the Jewish ghetto in Frankfurt.

THE GOVERNMENT BROKERS

*B*enjamin Cole was appointed Broker to the Commissioners for the Reduction of the National Debt at their first meeting at the house of the Chancellor of the Exchequer, William Pitt, on Tuesday 11 July 1786. Abraham Newland, Cashier at the Bank of England, was appointed as agent to the Commissioners, to accept the transfer of stock or annuities, and the two men were given very precise instructions as to what stocks to buy: Bank Three per cent Consolidated or reduced annuities, old or new South Sea annuities

Benjamin Cole, the first Government Broker: a portrait painted by Nathaniel Hone in 1776.

'according as it shall appear from the price of such respective annuities to be most advantageous.'

Cole's son, another Benjamin, succeeded him as Government Broker jointly with his partner, Peter Templeman, in 1801. The first Mullens, William Herbert, joined the partnership in March 1829, and the Mullens connection lasted, through various changes of name, until March 1986 when the function of the Government Broker moved into the Bank of England.

A 'Centrical Situation'
1798–1815

*I*N THE LAST YEARS OF THE EIGHTEENTH CENTURY the expenses of the war with France led to constant demands by Pitt's government for money from the Bank of England. At one point in 1797 specie payments were suspended and a financial panic ensued: prices of the Funds and of Bank stock were halved, although they recovered somewhat the following year. However the activities of the Stock Exchange continued to flourish and the size of, and turnover in, the National Debt increased rapidly. There was also a certain amount of movement in canal stocks, although 'canal mania' was mainly outside London.

In December 1798 the Committee for General Purposes, which represented the interests of the users of the Stock Exchange in Sweeting's Alley, was keen to extend its powers in order to exert discipline within the exchange and, especially, to be able to exclude defaulters unless they could show good reasons for their default. Committee members were constantly engaged in resolving disputes and sometimes investigating fraud, such as the celebrated case involving a broker named Martin. Martin was approached by a young and effeminate-looking gentleman, unknown to him, who requested him to sell £16,000 worth of scrip on his behalf. The broker was just explaining that he would usually expect some form of introduction, when a bystander, another broker called Lyons, was hailed by the stranger and readily recommended him to Martin. Some £10,000 worth of the scrip was sold, but the documents later proved to be forg-

OPENING of the BUDGET; — or — John Bull giving his Breeches to save his Bacon

eries, and it turned out that the 'stranger' was none other than Lyons' sister in disguise. The time taken up with this and other cases was probably one of the reasons that the Committee, weary of the consequent disruptions to their own business, decided to appoint a secretary, with a salary to be met by a payment of five shillings from each person who used the building.

THE STOCK SUBSCRIPTION ROOM

Not everybody was willing to pay this, leading to an impasse for which a solution was suggested by the Committee of Proprietors, who represented the owners of the building. On 7 January 1801 they proposed that the exchange should be converted into a Stock Subscription Room, with a minimum of 200 subscribers each paying ten guineas a year. The income from the subscriptions would be enough, they calculated, to give them a return on their capital investment and to pay the administration and costs of a new building. They invited the members

▲ *'Opening of the Budget; or John Bull giving his Breeches to save his Bacon: a 1796 cartoon by James Gillray, satirising Pitt's constant demands for money to finance the war against France.*

21

of the Committee for General Purposes to join them to form a United Committee which would draw up rules for the election of members.

A week later, on 12 January, the General Purposes Committee assented to the plan and members were informed that after 27 February 1801 the House would be 'finally shut as a Stock Exchange and opened as a Subscription Room on Tuesday 3 March at ten guineas per annum.' Anyone who wanted to become a subscriber was asked to write to the United Committee by the end of January: his request for admission would be the subject of a ballot, and this process would be repeated annually. As *The Times* reported, 'The object of the scrutiny is to keep out a number of very improper persons who have gained entrance to the Society, whose credit is extremely suspicious, and whose behaviour has been still worse . . .'

In mid-February the name of the building in Sweeting's Alley was formally changed to the Stock Subscription Room, and business was duly started on the new basis on 3 March 1801, on which date – though perhaps without any great recognition of the significance of the step among the brokers themselves – a regulated exchange first came into existence in London.

The changeover did not take place without a certain amount of discord. On the very day the new room opened there was a brawl – the proprietors had to send for a Constable to eject non-members, some of whom appealed to the Lord Mayor to decide 'whether the Subscription Room might be considered as a private property or a public market'; however, his Lordship 'would not take any cognizance of the affair.'

Victory went to the new proprietors, but there was a good deal more agitation, much of it at committee level. Just before the new room opened, the United Committee, anxious that the new organisation should 'acquire and preserve the most respectable character' and agreeing that 'it is indisputably necessary to prevent the practice of every disorderly action within the said room or below the bar thereof', resolved that such disorderly conduct should be the subject of a fine of two guineas, to be paid to the Secretary and allotted by the Committee to a charity. On 4 March the United Committee was dissolved and a new Committee for General Purposes was elected, consisting of twenty-one members of the former General Purposes Committee and nineteen new members. This new committee immediately passed a resolution that no proprietor of the Stock Exchange should have the right to vote for the election of new members, or any regulation affecting the Stock Subscription Room, unless he was elected to the committee by the subscribers 'at large.' The first rumblings of dissent began to be heard: a member named Hancock proposed the re-election of the old committee, a proposal strongly contested by the economist David Ricardo.

Shortly after this a committee member was himself given a fine for disorderly conduct but refused to pay it, claiming that the dissolution of the United Committee made its regulations void. Acrimonious discussion followed, centring on the proprietors' inability to make rules, and a number of the proprietors resigned, including the chairman, John Battye. Other upsets in the first years of the century included a complaint that four members of the committee had been unduly favoured in a lottery, apparently obtaining tickets at a discount; they resigned. Another mass resignation took place over a confused affair concerning plans for 'the relief of distressed members and their unprotected families' – over £400 was raised, but the House was 'suspicious', although about what is not clear.

Despite these problems and other wrangles, resignations and rejoinings, plans for a new building progressed rapidly under a new body of managing proprietors headed by William Hammond, who was a prime mover in the scheme. Their earliest recorded meeting took place on 4 March 1801 at the Antwerp Tavern; William Grey and Isaac Hensley reported that they had found suitable premises at the east end of Capel Court, off Bartholomew Lane, close to the Bank of England and the Royal Exchange. The new body formally approached the proprietors of the old Exchange, noting that the old building was too small for the 'Members who frequent it', and did not allow of 'all the conveniences which such a reputable society should have', and described the 'centrical situation' of the new site. They outlined the pro-

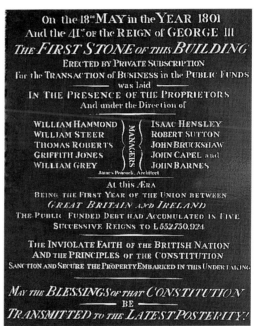

▼ *The foundation stone of the 1801 building, and a silhouette portrait of William Hammond,* ◄ *who laid the stone on 18 May 1801*

posed financial basis of the undertaking and offered the former proprietors one hundred £50 shares, equivalent to a third of the new concern.

This offer received a short and dusty answer, signed by Edward Wetenhall, secretary of the former proprietors: 'I am directed by the proprietors of the Stock Subscription Room to inform you they decline to accept your offer of 100 shares.'

The new proprietors agreed that this rebuff materially strengthened their own interests, and continued to meet frequently at the Antwerp Tavern, John's and the George and Vulture to further the building project. The plans became more ambitious, new plots on the site were acquired and it was decided to raise the capital to £20,000 by the creation of a further one hundred £50 shares. Several buildings were bought and pulled down, including a Debating Forum and Mendoza's Boxing Room. By 18 May the site had been cleared and the foundation stone – which was later lost during the comprehensive rebuilding in the 1850s, and then rediscovered during more building work in 1883 – was laid by William Hammond. It had a copper plate attached to it inscribed with both patriotism and optimism:

'On 18th May in the year 1801, and forty-one of George III, the first stone of this building, erected by private subscription for transaction of business in the public funds, was laid, in the presence of the proprietors, and under the direction of William Hammond, William Steer, Thomas Roberts, Griffith Jones, William Grey, Isaac Hensley, Robert Sutton, John Bruckshaw, John Capel and John Barnes, Managers; James Peacock, Architect. At this era, the first of the union between Great Britain and Ireland, the public funded debt had accumulated in five successive reigns to £552,730,924. The inviolate faith of the British nation, and the principles of the constitution, sanction and ensure the prosperity embarked in this undertaking! May the blessing of the constitution be secured to the latest posterity!'

After laying the stone at 4 p.m. Hammond made a short speech wishing prosperity to the members; the proprietors then gave a dinner to the managers and others at the London Tavern, at which, according to a newspaper report the next day, '300 gentlemen partook of an elegant entertainment and the day was spent in the utmost conviviality.' On 30 December a statue of Mercury, the Roman god of trade, was set over the front door (interpreted by 'a wag', as *The Times* reported, as the god of thieves), and the name The Stock Exchange was incised on the building's classical portico.

'A NEAT, PLAIN BUILDING' IN CAPEL COURT

The new building in Capel Court was opened in February 1802. It occupied an area of 4,000 square feet and was described as 'a neat, plain building, fronted with stone to the attic storey, which is of brick. In the interior, under the clock, at the southern end, is a tablet, exhibiting the names of such defaulters as have not been able, or willing, to make their payments good. On the east side, a recess is appropriated for the Commissioners for the Redemption of the National Debt, who make their purchases four times a week . . . there are three entrances, besides that in Capel Court.' One of these entrances was through the Hercules Tavern, whose landlady undoubtedly had an eye to future business when she gave permission for a passageway to be built at the back of her premises. A gallery ran round the main hall, equipped with desks, seats and bookcases – any member requiring a book would call up to a clerk to throw it down. The main hall was initially surrounded by piers and arches, forming recesses such as that allotted to the National Debt Commissioners, but these were later replaced by Ionic columns.

The hours of business were from ten until four (another issue which had caused dissent among the committee members) and holidays were frequent, including numerous royal family birthdays, and the anniversaries of the Fire of London and the martyrdom of King Charles I. All clerks had to be approved by the Committee and were given a ticket which had to be produced before they could enter the House.

The move itself was accompanied by the usual anxiety about documents and records, which were given into the safe-keeping of the Committee for General Purposes, and dual control was re-established under two committees, the other being the Committee of Trustees and

▲ *'New Stock Exchange': an interior view of the building in 1809, by Augustus Charles Pugin, from Ackerman's* Microcosm of London.

◄ *David Ricardo (1772–1823). The son of a Jewish broker who had emigrated from Amsterdam to London, the economist David Ricardo was much involved in the events surrounding the transition of the Exchange from an open market to a stock subscription room. He was a member of the Committee of Proprietors and later of the General Purposes Committee, and was one of the signatories to the original Deed of Settlement.*

Managers representing the proprietors. The General Purposes Committee appointed a secretary, John Hemming, at a salary of £50 a year. One of its earliest communications was received from the Deputy Governor of the Bank of England, stating that if any of the Clerks of the Bank were admitted as subscribers to the new institution, they would be 'immediately suspended from their respective situations.'

Three weeks after the move took place, on 27 March, a Deed of Settlement was signed, which, apart from its intrinsic interest, shows that while broking and jobbing were by now quite distinct, they were still frequently carried out by the same person. The deed stated that the new building was to be run by nine trustees and managers, in office for life, who would manage it on behalf of the proprietors, invest any reserve funds in government securities and 'fix the price at which subscribers shall be admitted to attend and transact business at the Stock Exchange, and such price of admission being paid by any subscriber, whether proprietor or not shall entitle him to attend and transact the business of a Broker and Stock Jobber, or either of them for the term of one year.' The deed also incorporated the provision for the capital of £20,000 in £50 shares, of which no one might hold more than four, and it stated that other matters, including the election of members, would be the preserve of the Committee for General Purposes. This body was to be thirty strong, elected annually by all the subscribers.

There were 551 members, besides clerks, at the time of the move (at least eight were excluded in the first ballot) and the reminiscences of one of them provide some colourful vignettes of City life. For some years there was a stall near the Capel Court entrance, where an old woman sold buns and other goods to the members, eventually retiring 'because the House was such a wicked place' – but not before she had saved a good sum of money. Mendoza's Boxing Room at 2 Capel Court was much missed by those members who had formerly patronised it and 'instead of knocking prices about, could go and knock somebody else about' or get knocked about themselves. They often brought their own chops and steaks for their lunch, taking them to a chop house to be grilled, paying a penny for the privilege and being provided with 'vegetables, bread and drink.' A glass of sherry was drunk over almost every bargain.

◄ *'The Alley': a print showing the bun-seller at the Capel Court entrance.*

SOME EARLY MEMBERS

Among the members of the new institution were a handful whose families, or firms, have survived until the present day or at least well into the second half of the twentieth century. Philip Antrobus was practising as a stockbroker at least as early as 1779, when he appears in the Bank of England ledgers in a purchase of Three per cent Consols, part of a new government loan, which he sold again a few days later; his second appearance in the ledgers shows him disposing of stock on behalf of Thomas Coutts, bankers to the Royal family. Antrobus served as a member of the General Purposes Committee of both the Stock Subscription Room and the new Stock Exchange, and his name and that of his partner John Wood are both included in the first list of members in 1801. James Capel, a cousin of the John Capel who was one of the original trustees, joined what had by then become Antrobus & Wood as a clerk in 1806, and in 1813 he became a member of the Stock Exchange and a partner in the firm, which was known as James Capel & Co. from the 1840s onwards.

▲ *Three early members: Philip Antrobus (1754–1816), James Capel (1789–1872) and Philip Cazenove (1798–1880).*

◀ *Brokers' medals, given to the hundred brokers licensed by the City of London. These belonged respectively to Richard Buller (licensed from c.1690–1714), Jos. Setcole (1714–27) and William Sharp (1801–30). Licences were finally abolished in 1886.*

Another firm whose business dates from the eighteenth century, although it was not among the original members of the Exchange, is Cazenove & Co. James de Cazenove, the descendant of a Huguenot émigré from France to Geneva, was living in London by 1775 and acted as both merchant and trader in partnership with his brother and two other Huguenots, dealing among other things with American stocks traded on the London market and occasionally in government Funds. James's fourth son, Philip Cazenove, one of the earliest partners of the stockbroking firm, was introduced to the Exchange as a clerk in 1819.

The *Course of the Exchange* had continued to be issued by various publishers, including the Edward Wetenhall who so haughtily rejected the advances of the new managers, and from 29 July 1803 became an official publication issued 'by the authority of the Stock Exchange Committee.' Edward and later James Wetenhall carried on its publication for many years; by January 1811 it was double the original size and quoted the British Funds, twenty other British securities, canals, docks, waterworks, insurance and the price of coal. Later that year the practice of giving dates of meetings, dividends and so on was resumed, and the list subsequently added bridges, roads, 'iron railways' (the first one to be mentioned was the Surrey Iron Railway), Irish Funds, mines, French Funds (from August 1816) and the securities of Prussia, Russia, Austria and Spain. Even at this date it was still appearing only twice a week.

What the press referred to as the 'schism' between the old and new proprietors of the Stock Exchange rumbled on for a while, and in July 1802 *The Times* reported that the Committee of Proprietors of the Stock Exchange 'erected in the year 1773' had 'resolved to open the House next Monday, as an open market for transacting business in the public funds. Each person is to pay 6d per day, as formerly.' This, if it happened at all, did not last, and in 1803 the lease of the old building was sold by the trustees, although it was known for a few more years as the Stock Exchange Coffee House.

The resentment felt by the brokers for the City of London authorities also continued to smoulder, and it burst into flames again in 1805. The brokers were still paying their annual tax of forty shillings to the City Corporation for their licence; in that year, after much discussion, a

THE TRAGIC BROTHERS

Abraham Goldsmid

The careers of the Goldsmid brothers, Abraham and Benjamin, provide a dramatic vignette of fluctuating fortunes in the early history of the stock market. Their first financial coup was successful competition with what had become a 'ring' of bankers as contractors for government loans; they were hailed as heroes and it was claimed that as a result of their success, the issue of the loans became much fairer and more open. Both brothers made substantial fortunes and gave largely to charity, but tragedy struck within a few years. Together with the Barings, the Goldsmids were contractors for the government loan of £14 million issued in 1810. Sir Francis Baring then died; the 'bears' mounted an aggressive attack, and the brothers' credit waned as the loan sank in value. After entertaining some of his friends to a 'sumptuous banquet' at his Surrey mansion, Abraham Goldsmid committed suicide, and his brother took the same action two years later.

large number of members decided to refuse to pay. The Corporation took out a raft of summonses against them, and decided to conduct one test case against a broker named Francis Bailey. He wrote a pamphlet, entitled *The Rights of Stock-Jobbers Defended*, which attempted to prove that stockbrokers were merely 'agents' and that there was no reason to classify them as brokers, but this did more harm than good to the brokers' cause. The Corporation prevailed, and the brokers were destined to chafe under the City yoke for many years more.

The Bank of England's Rotunda was still used as a market for buying and selling stocks, although after 1801 it was mostly used by people the Bank described as 'by no means of a reputable description, consisting in general of those who will not subscribe to the Stock Exchange or have been excluded, female jobbers and idle persons.' The dealers continued to make themselves thoroughly at home, going behind the counters of the Stock Transfer office to consult ledgers or even, on occasions, to enter transfers of stock themselves. In 1806 the exasperated Bank officials considered erecting a building in Tokenhouse Yard for use as a stock market, but were advised by their solicitor that they were 'under no obligation to do so', and the plan came to nothing. However, the demonstrable success of the new Exchange, and the fact that many would-be members were excluded either by ballot or by their unwillingness, or inability, to pay the annual subscription, provided fertile ground for agitation for either an open market or, failing that, the establishment of a rival exchange. The end of the first decade in Capel Court was marked by the attempt to form a National Fund Exchange for dealing in government securities, which should be open to everyone. A Bill was introduced into Parliament to this effect, but failed in the Lords.

Unhappily, John Hemming, the Secretary of the General Purposes Committee, was discovered to have supported the rival faction: he confessed to a parliamentary committee that he had 'communicated books and transactions' of his own committee to the solicitors of the

parties who were applying to set up the rival exchange, and was summarily dismissed from his post for 'treachery.' A new and efficient Secretary, Robert Watson Wade, was appointed in his stead. Subsequent investigation into Hemming's activities found serious deficiencies in the 'very loose and careless manner' in which he had kept the Committee's minutes: 'Not only are the transactions of the several meetings entered in the book in the most slovenly and disgraceful mode, with such frequent interlineations and erasures as to render the subject (intended to be recorded) extremely doubtful and confused but likewise many resolutions appear to have been passed by the Committee which have never been entered on the journals . . .'

In April 1811, there was a serious challenge to the authority of the Stock Exchange. James Pidding arraigned the Managers for 'exposing his name on the Blackboard . . . declaring him as defaulter.' The case was heard at the Old Bailey and the Exchange was found not guilty: the Managers declared robustly that 'we are inclined to believe that under no circumstances can we be found liable to any penalty for enforcing the Regulations of the Committee for General Purposes', and noted that it was indeed 'painful to our feelings to be exposed on trial in a court with common criminals.'

THE FIRST RULE BOOK

Perhaps because of this unhappy experience, a sub-committee of the same members who had investigated Hemming was commissioned later in 1811 to 'inspect the journals and papers of the Committee to make extracts of those rules and regulations they may think worthy of being preserved as the fundamental laws of this house.' After a painstaking examination of all existing records, including those of the old Threadneedle Street Exchange, they extracted and collected all the resolutions they could find, together with 'Decisions of Cases' which seemed relevant. Further sideswipes were made at the 'very loose and careless manner' in which the late Secretary had kept the minutes, but they managed to produce recommendations which were duly confirmed by the Committee for General Purposes in February 1812, and which became the basis for the first codified and printed rule book.

It is not a complex document. It confirmed that members were to be admitted annually by the Committee for General Purposes and pay a subscription at a rate fixed by the Committee

◀ *'Joint Stock Street': this cartoon of 1809 shows people looking at placards inviting subscriptions to unsound companies, pasted on the wall of a hospital for the victims of 'speculation mania'.*

of Trustees and Managers. Neither members nor their wives were to engage in any other business. New members must be recommended by two existing members and their names had to be posted in the House eight days before the ballot took place; clerks from the Bank of England, South Sea House, East India House and other 'public or private establishments' could only be admitted by express permission of their employers.

There were also quite detailed rules about settlement and default. The Committee would not become involved in any application to annul a bargain, or in disputes over bargains prior to the conclusion of a contract for a loan. These disputes were to be submitted to arbitration. The dealing activities of outsiders were to be limited by a ruling that no member should be obliged to accept a ticket payable by a non-member, or to pay a non-member for stock bought on the Exchange. Sellers who had not received a transfer ticket by 2 p.m. on delivery day were allowed to re-sell and claim any difference from the original purchaser; purchasers not receiving stock on delivery day could 'buy in' after 11 a.m. the following day. All buying in and selling out transactions had to be carried out via a broker. The rules recommended that the Secretary to the Exchange should be involved in these transactions, which differed from the practice in the previous century when the sellers usually prepared the transfer tickets.

The names of failures (or 'lame ducks') were to be publicly posted on the board under the clock, and their assets divided equitably among creditors; no defaulting member could make a private composition with his creditors, and no member might receive a larger share of his claims than others. A defaulter forfeited membership and could only be re-admitted if his creditors recommended it.

The way quotations were recorded was stipulated: prices were to be collected and published by 'a person authorized by the Committee' and the Secretary was to preserve the lists and make them available for inspection. The Committee 'earnestly recommended . . . those gentlemen of the Stock Exchange who transact business on commission for time to regulate the extent of such dealings (unless with sufficient security) as much as possible by their own ability to fulfil their engagements: being of opinion that every material deviation from this rule (unless for persons of well known property) is nearly as unwarrantable as if they had entered into such speculation on their own account.' And a heartfelt plea, not for the first time and certainly not for the last, was made for members to give up the 'rude and trifling practices which have too long disgraced the Stock Exchange in the past, and would not be tolerated in any other place.' These included letting off fireworks in the House and 'knocking off hats', both of which continued despite constant complaints.

A couple of years after the issue of the rule book there was a first, unsuccessful, attempt to introduce a minimum scale of charges. Competition between members was becoming fiercer, and it was already forbidden to poach clients from other members or to advertise by sending circulars to anybody other than one's own clients. A commission of $\frac{1}{8}$ per cent, with half commission available to bankers, was the norm, but there were no clear rules on the subject and when one member accused another, Luke Leake, of taking business away by undercutting, he was censured by the General Purposes Committee for poaching clients, rather than for any juggling with commission.

AN ORGANISED MARKET

By the end of the Napoleonic Wars in 1815, the Stock Exchange had become an accepted part of financial life displaying many features quite recognisable today. It was established on its modern site, with an official price list, most present-day dealing techniques in practice and regular settlement days. Firms tended to be small – usually just one or two men with a clerk, and dealing took place in very few stocks other than the public debt. Broking was by now a specialised business; the distinction between broker and jobber was clearly recognised, although it was still quite common for a member to combine both activities. The Exchange still chafed under restrictive legislation, the annoying necessity of licences from the City Corporation and the contracting system for government loans which gave rise to various speculative manoeuvres. Some of its enduring characteristics – a readiness to believe and respond to rumour, mercurial spirits, a canny grasp of current affairs, rather than any very profound understanding of the underlying economic realities – were clearly evident, as David Ricardo pointed out in 1814 when asked if he knew anyone in the stock market who could provide help on the question of circulation: 'The Stock Exchange is chiefly attended by persons who are unremittingly attentive to their business, and are well acquainted with its details, but there are very few in number who have much knowledge of political economy, and consequently they pay little attention to finance, as a subject of science. They consider more, the immediate effect of passing events, rather than their distant consequences.'

The Stock Exchange was still, and would remain, a frequent target for public criticism; but without the organised market which it provided to many thousands of investors, it would scarcely have been possible for the government to raise the vast amount of money needed for Britain to prosecute the wars against Napoleon.

THE NEWS OF WATERLOO

'Chelsea Pensioners reading the Waterloo Despatch',
painted in 1822 by Sir David Wilkie (1785–1841).

When news of the Battle of Waterloo finally arrived in London, the effect upon the Funds was much less dramatic than the price fluctuations which had accompanied some of the earlier rumours. Consols, which had stood at 66 in January 1815, failed to reach that figure again during the year, despite the victory. On 20 June they stood at 56.5, and by the end of the year had reached only 60.

It was a favourite City tradition that Nathan Rothschild had made several million pounds by having advance news of Waterloo. The ways in which this was supposed to have been received included a message being brought by a carrier pigeon (some stockbrokers used pigeons at this date, although they were only successful in good weather), and it was also rumoured that Rothschild had himself been present at the battle. However recent investigation has led to the conclusion that the news was first brought to London by an employee from the Rothschilds' Paris office. He beat by some hours the official bearer of the news, Major the Hon. Henry Percy, who delivered it to Lord Bathurst, Secretary of State for the War Department, at 11 p.m. on 21 June, three days after the battle. (Percy was so exhausted by his journey that he fell asleep while being questioned by the Chancellor of the Exchequer.) Rothschild certainly had the news before this, and did well out of it, though he could hardly have made millions of pounds: the market at the time was too small, and prices remained too steady.

A Two-way Traffic
1815–1840

URING THE PERIOD FROM THE BURSTING OF THE SOUTH SEA BUBBLE until the end of the Napoleonic wars, dealings on the Stock Exchange and in the various peripheral markets had been dominated by transactions in the Funds. The expansion of the Stock Exchange was a reflection of the growth of the public debt, which rose from £456.1 million, of which 95 per cent was funded, in 1801, to just under £745 million (92 per cent funded) in 1815. It peaked in 1819, but soon after that the picture changed radically. Government debt began a decline which was not halted until 1914; while it was not until just before the First World War that any considerable number of commercial and industrial firms became public limited companies. For nearly a century after the end of the wars with France the chief transactions on the Exchange were concerned either with the provision of domestic utilities – canals, railways, gas and water – or with overseas investment.

This last was a two-way traffic. New issues at home and abroad had both British and overseas subscribers; foreigners were able to deal in existing securities on the London market and British citizens could reciprocate. While a few foreign loans had been issued before Waterloo, it was only in peacetime that significant amounts of British capital began to flow overseas. Barings and Rothschilds took an immediate lead: Barings, which handled the financial arrangements for the occupying army as well as for reparations payments by France, was in a particularly strong position. A substantial loan was issued by the bank in 1815 and set the pattern for successive ones in a rising market with a method that was known as 'taking a loan firm.' In the first one, Barings accepted the French *rentes* at an agreed price and received a commission of $2\frac{1}{2}\%$, in addition to which they were entitled to any profits arising from selling the loan on to the public at a higher price. The contracting bank or other institution also acted as an underwriter, and so was at risk of losing money if the market fell. It was in this way that Barings laid the foundations of their subsequent fortune between 1815 and 1820. Rothschilds profited hugely too, by establishing themselves as bankers to the Holy Alliance, and in particular made substantial amounts of money from Russian and Prussian loans. It was at this time that Nathan Rothschild became one of the best known and most powerful figures in the City of London.

OPTION DEALINGS

In the home market there was a serious difference of opinion over option dealings in Capel Court. This practice had always been controversial: the Committee had condemned options when the Stock Exchange was opened, and when compiling the rule book missed a valuable opportunity to clarify the matter, perhaps deliberately, although admitting a couple of years later that it was well aware that gambling on the option system was increasing 'to a most

Pub⁴ by R⁴ Dighton. Oct⁴ 1817

A View from the Royal Exchange.

▲ *A View from the Royal Exchange: Nathan Rothschild, depicted in Dighton's* City Characters, *1817.*

serious and alarming extent' and was 'injurious to the regular business for which the House was established and by no means necessary thereto.' In 1819 a number of brokers suffered serious losses as their clients defaulted on time bargains, and the following year a group of members petitioned the Committee to ban options altogether. In July 1821, when the rule book was being revised, the Committee pronounced that time bargains for more than fourteen days would not be recognised as coming under Exchange rules, and would therefore be unenforceable, a timid compromise which satisfied hardly anyone. Two factions formed, with nearly 300 members in favour of a complete ban while an opposing group felt that options were essential and that any further restrictions on dealing practice 'would more resemble the severity of school discipline than those wise and liberal regulations proper for the Stock Exchange.'

The Committee was in a dilemma. It first decided that members would only be re-elected each March if they undertook not to deal in options, but this inflamed many others, and at the end of the year opinion began to swing in favour of the status quo. By this time a new threat to set up a rival stock market had arisen: considerable sums of money were raised and discussions about a new building took place.

Eventually, a compromise was reached. Options continued to be readily available and by 1832 puts and calls were widespread once more. Apart from this altercation, the early years of the 1820s were comparatively uneventful as far as the markets were concerned. In 1821 new members were first required to nominate sureties, who were bound to pay £250 should the prospective member be 'publicly declared' within two years.

BOOM AND BUST

By early 1824 the depressed state of trade in Britain was nearly over. A period of moderate prosperity was followed by a boom which was accompanied by strong speculation in stocks and shares and in commodities; commodity prices rose by a fifth between the beginning of 1824 and mid-1825 and some shares, such as mining, did spectacularly well. The growth and bursting of this bubble was carefully followed by a contemporary writer, Henry English, whose analysis showed that before 1824 there were 156 companies with authorised capital of just under £48 million of which £34 million was paid up, although not all of this was actively dealt on the Stock Exchange. The bulk comprised insurance, canal, dock, roadway, bridge and waterway companies. The National Debt, at £800 million, still played the most important role. However, during 1824 and 1825, 624 companies were formed or projected, with a nominal capital of over £372 million. Many of them came to nothing – 379 were stillborn and another 118 were abandoned within a few months of formation. Those which failed included the Bank of Great Britain, the London Genuine Snuff Company and the Economic Funeral Company, as well as one intended to 'combat the usury of pawnbrokers and pay dividends of 40 per cent.'

High Jinks

*F*rom the earliest days in Capel Court the floor of the House was the scene of innumerable games and practical jokes, as the volatile spirits of the brokers were vented in boisterous activities, whether to celebrate making money, to drown the sorrows of losing it or just to while away the hours of an uneventful day. Frequent notices from the Managers prohibited fireworks, footballs, 'butter slides' and other distractions; bags of sawdust or flour were burst over the heads of members gathered round the subscriptions lists. More dangerously, coat-tails and newspapers were surreptitiously set on fire. One especially scruffy broker, with 'a dirty neckerchief and untidy pigtail' and with his gilt buttons tarnished, was ceremoniously presented with a towel and a 'bar of primrose soap', and new and gullible clerks or members were traditionally despatched to find details of non-existent stocks such as Chinese Turnpikes or Sky and Deep Sea Junction.

The satirical press had an enjoyable time, advertising loans for the Lilliputians and Houyhnhnms and the prospectus of a Parliamentary Steam Company to energise the government in dealing with the avalanche of new issues they were required to authorise by Acts of Parliament. Rigs and corners abounded, especially in the new mining shares, and another contemporary, John Francis, who was an official of the Bank of England, later described the throngs outside the Stock Exchange, including stags 'with huge pocketbook containing worthless scrip . . . a group of boys eagerly buying and selling at a profit, which bore no comparison to the loss of honesty they each day experienced . . . In every corner and in every vacant space, might be seen men eagerly discussing the premium of a new company, the rate of a new loan, the rumoured profit of some lucky speculator, the rumoured failure of some great financier, or wrangling with savage eagerness over the fate of a shilling.'

The mania could not last. Coin and bullion at the Bank of England fell from £1,175 million sterling in October 1824 to £3.75 million by August the following year. At the beginning of December several banks failed, panic reigned and the Bank was almost drained of credit. It was saved at the eleventh hour by the discovery, in a vault, of a box of unissued and unnumbered pound notes printed with the date 1821. The printers were summoned to complete the dating and numbering process (and to print urgently some £5 and £10 notes) and the crisis passed, aided by Rothschilds and by the Bank of England's prudent discount policy. Nathan Rothschild personally stood aloof from the mania of 1825, his principal occupation during this period being found-ing the Alliance Life Office, but his firm played an invaluable role by buying stock at low but reasonable prices, which had it been thrown on to the market would have made disaster much worse. He also advised the government on how to cope with the crisis, an indication of the severity of which is that Three per cents had fallen nineteen points, from 94 at which they opened the disastrous year of 1825, to 75 by the end of it.

Henry English provided a trenchant analysis of the crisis. He pointed out that before the period of inflation, companies were formed which could not possibly be sustained by 'individual capital', whereas most of those formed during the boom 'were of a nature adapted only to individual enter-prise . . . The deceptive practices resorted to, to obtain a price far exceeding the real value of the property (in various Mining Companies), can only be explained by the guilty participation of the parties in the spoil . . . To acts of a similar nature is to be attributed the sacrifice of character which has been in too many instances of late the result of the proceedings of Joint Stock com-panies; when, by connection of honourable men with a class of designing projectors, the innocent have been implicated with the guilty.' He added a warning note: 'It is, how-ever, to be hoped that the lesson thus taught to the public, and, more particularly, men holding high stations in life, will be the means of preventing a recurrence of the events of 1824 and 1825.'

The stock market naturally profited from the surge of business which attended these events and from dealings in the 127 new com-panies (including forty-four mining companies) which did survive: after the crisis was past there were 283 companies in existence alto-gether. One result of the panic was that stockbroking had caught the

▲ *Share certificates for various annuities, including Consolidated £3 per cent – 'Consols'*

▶ *c. 1825 'Bubbles for 1825 – or – Fortunes made with Steam': promoters tout 'bubble companies', including the Poyais company, the Greenland Gudgeon Fishing Company and a Colombian Pearl Fishery.*

attention of the public as never before. The press had provided both description and comment, including an article published in 1825 which pointed out that the regulations requiring an annual election and a subscription of ten guineas had the salutary effect of segregating *bona fide* brokers from 'the jobbers in stock (or those who, though ostensibly buyers and sellers, are in reality illegal gamblers, and merely speculate upon the rise and fall of the Funds at fixed periods, without making any actual sale or purchase)' and who were largely confined to the Bank Rotunda. Some papers now began to publish daily financial articles. They had been publishing prices since quite early in the nineteenth century, but such lists were usually provided by a stockbroker who was allowed to put his name to them and thus in some measure evade the ruling against advertising. Another method of promotion was by the issue of medals or tokens, such as one produced by John Ashby of 3 Bartholomew Lane, Bank, who was a member of the Exchange from 1814 to 1834. The medal is engraved with

◄ John Ashby's medals, showing a bull and a bear, with the dates of 'Fixed Holidays' on the reverse.

pictures of a bull and a bear, each with the head of a man, and states that Ashby's office was open from 10 a.m. until 3 p.m. - except on thirty-two named holidays. (A list of dates on which the Bank of England was shut, published in August 1830, specified eighteen, including the 'Landing of King William III' on 4 November and the 'Papist Conspiracy' the following day.)

'THE CACIQUE OF POYAIS'

Foreign lending grew substantially in the 1820s. The infant republics in central and south America such as Brazil, Peru, Colombia and Chile were all keen to borrow, as, slightly later, was Greece; many of these loans turned sour for the borrowers who ultimately received little of the money. One of the most notorious, and most fraudulent, involved the tragi-comedy of Poyais. A Scottish mercenary soldier, Gregor McGregor, calling himself the 'Cacique of Poyais', began to sell land (to which he had no title) in a malarial swamp in the Gulf of Honduras, and raised a loan in London. His prospectus described Poyais as a sub-tropical paradise, where water ran over sands of gold, crops burst from the ground and tortoiseshell, diamonds and pearls abounded; an engraving of this wonderful place included both a church and a theatre. Unsurprisingly no interest was ever paid on the bonds, and most of the settlers, despite their possession of notes of the Bank of Poyais which they had exchanged for those of the Bank of Scotland, succumbed to poverty and disease.

THE FOREIGN MARKET

The Foreign Exchange, which was also known as the Foreign Market or the Foreign Funds Market, had its own rules: the most important distinction from the Stock Exchange was that merchants and traders were admitted. Originally, the Committee for General Purposes ruled that no member of the Stock Exchange might enter into

◄ Gregor McGregor (1786–1845). McGregor was born in Scotland, fought in the Peninsular campaign and became a general in Simon Bolivar's army before embarking on his fraudulent campaign to sell bonds for land in Poyais.

partnership with the members of the Foreign Exchange, or indeed deal in foreign stock at all, but this rule seems never to have been observed. Membership of the new exchange rose and fell quite significantly – at one time reaching a thousand – and another attempt at forming a completely separate institution was made in early 1825, when the Committee ruled firmly that anyone who 'became a subscriber to such New establishment or transacting business there will cease to be a member of the Stock Exchange'; this attempt fizzled out, presumably extinguished by the financial crisis later in the year.

During the period in which the Foreign Exchange existed as a separate entity, a significant legal decision was made. Its members were under the impression that time bargains in the stocks they dealt were illegal under the provisions of the Barnard Act; this did not stop them carrying out such transactions but it did mean that a dishonourable defaulter could claim that the whole bargain was a gamble and therefore beyond the law, and brokers usually did not feel it worth their while to pursue the matter. However, when one case did come

to trial, several judges ruled that the Barnard Act did not apply to foreign stocks – another instance of how its always ineffective provisions were being gradually eroded.

All foreign dealings were transacted at the Royal Exchange, as the foreign market had never moved from there. The rapid expansion of overseas business meant that this location became increasingly crowded and inconvenient, and in January 1822 a group of six members who traded there petitioned the Committee for General Purposes to 'sanction and allow' open market dealings in foreign securities within the House. Six months later another thirty members and firms, including what had by this date become Marjoribanks, Capel & Co., made the same request. The Committee was not sure whether it was able, under the Deed of Settlement, to comply, but its doubts were set at rest by taking counsel's opinion and the quotation of foreign stocks was authorised on 4 October. The Managers

▶ *Foreign Funds – A list dated 1828, issued by Menet & Cazenove.*

FOREIGN FUNDS.

London, January 1 , 1828.

	Price.	Exchange.
AUSTRIAN Metallic 5 per Cent. Bonds in Florins, Dividends payable 1st May and 1st Nov	91	10 Florins per £ Sterl.
BRAZILIAN 5 per Cent. Bonds, in £ Sterling, Dividends payable 1st April and 1st October........	59 7/8	
BUENOS AYRES 6 per Cent. Bonds, in £ Sterling, Dividends payable 12th January and 12th July ..	45	
CHILE 6 per Cent. Bonds in £ Sterling, Dividends payable 31st March and 30th September		
COLUMBIAN 6 per Cent. Bonds in £ Sterling, Dividends payable 1st May and 1st November		
Ditto ditto, Divs. payable 15th January and 15th July.	26 1/2	
DANISH 3 per Cent. Bonds, Div. payable 31st March and 30th September............................	59 1/2	
FRENCH 5 per Cents. or Rentes, Dividends payable 22d March and 22d September................. ƒ.	107 1/4 . 1 ƒ. 25. 2.	
Ditto 3 per Cents. Divs. payable 22d June & 22d Dec. ƒ.	67 1/2 7 ƒ. 11	
GREEK 5 per Cent. Bonds in £ Sterling, Dividends payable 1st January, and 1st July		
Ditto, 1825.............................	16 1/2	
GUATEMALA 6 per Cent. Bonds, in £ Sterling, Dividends payable 1st February and 1st August ..		
MEXICAN 5 per Cent. Bonds, in £ Sterling, Divs. payable 1st Jan. 1st April, 1st July, 1st October		
Ditto 6 per Cent. Bonds, Dividend ditto ditto	25 1/4.	
NEAPOLITAN 5 per Cent. Bonds in Ducats, Dividends payable 1st January and 1st July..........		Fcs. 4: 40 per Ducat. Do.25: 65 per £Sterl.
Ditto 5 per Cent. Bonds, in £ Sterling, Dividends payable 1st February and 1st August............		
PERUVIAN 6 per Cent. Bonds in £ Sterling, Dividends payable 15th April and 15th October	25.	
PORTUGUESE 5 per Ct. Bds. Dividends payable 1st June and 1st December.....................	71 1/2 . 2 .	
PRUSSIAN 5 per Cent. Bonds in £ Sterling, Dividends payable 1st April and 1st October..........	100	
PRUSSIAN .. Ditto .. new, of 1822, Dividends payable 1st January and 1st July	99	2 - 0 : .
RUSSIAN 6 per Cent. Paper Ruble, Dividends payable 1st January and 1st July................	82	13 . per Ruble.
Ditto 5 per Cent. Metallic or Silver Ruble, Dividends payable 1st March and 1st September............	88.	3s. 1d. Ditto.
RUSSIAN 5 ⅌ Ct. Certs of £111; £148; £518, & £1096 in £ Sterl. Divs. payable 1st March and 1st Sept. ..	91 . 90 3/4	
SPANISH Bonds of 1821, Dividends payable from 1st Nov. 1823	10 3/4.	
Do. of 1823, Dividends payable from 1st Nov. 1823 ..		

Prices of French Funds, in Paris, the 29 Decr.

	Exchange on London,
5 per Cent. Rentes..................ƒ. 104. 60.	1 Month .. ƒ. 25/5
3 per Cent. Rentes..................ƒ. 67. 30.	

JOHN F. MENET & P. CAZENOVE,
No. 7, Broad Street, and Stock Exchange.

[Turn over.

THE END OF THE LOTTERY

ALL LOTTERIES WILL END FOR EVER. 18th JULY 1826.

'All lotteries will end for ever, 18th July 1826': at the top of Robert Cruikshank's etching, the figure of Time and the lottery contractors watch Blue Coat boys holding up winning numbers; below, promoters advertise the last lottery.

The first public state lottery in Britain was started by Elizabeth I in 1566 to raise money to improve the country's harbours; over 400,000 tickets were sold and the draw for prizes – of money and silver plate – took four months. Lotteries were officially banned for a brief period from 1699 to 1709, but Queen Anne was strongly in favour of raising money by this method and they became an established way for the government to do so, although frequently criticised for 'encouraging the spirit of gambling among the poor'. Brokers dealt in state lottery tickets, banks accepted them as securities, and the government and licensed promoters used lotteries to finance all

or part of such undertakings as the building of the British Museum, the repair of bridges and many projects in the American colonies.

However, lotteries provided a fertile soil in which swindlers and charlatans flourished, and by the end of the eighteenth century tickets – often all blanks – were used as lures to buy anything from clothes or meat pies at a market stall to a bottle of medicine from a quack. In 1826 they were banned – much lamented by brokers for whom ticket dealing had provided a considerable part of their income – and became a 'statutory public nuisance' under English law until the launch of the National Lottery in 1994.

provided a room next to and connected with the original building, and a Foreign Funds Market was established in it.

However, the collapse of the market for joint-stock company shares after 1825 was accompanied by a similar slump in foreign government bonds. What little foreign business there was in this period was unprofitable, and the separate existence of the Foreign Funds Market began to look precarious. Many members left the market altogether, and the ninety that remained now began to believe that their only salvation lay in joining the main Stock Exchange. They petitioned the General Purposes Committee to agree to a merger.

After much discusion it was decided in early 1828 to offer to admit to the Stock Exchange members of the Foreign Funds Market of over five years' standing, on the nomination of two Managers and two Committee members. In return, the Foreign Funds Committee agreed to 'surrender the whole management of the Foreign Stock Market to the Committee for General Purposes of the Stock Exchange.' This was agreed, but some members of the Foreign Exchange were of course inadmissible for various reasons; a separate Foreign Room continued to exist for some years, and its committee retained some executive powers. In 1831 the rules covering both markets were amalgamated, and the Foreign Funds Committee was wound up, although the Foreign Room continued to be used for deals in any business outside the National Debt. The same year a letter signed by sixteen members noted sadly that 'the Foreign market is now and for a considerable time past has been without business, on which account they hope that such relief as is practicable will be afforded in granting them access to the English market.'

Eventually, in February 1835, the Committee relented, probably as much because of lack of space in the original building as for any other reason, and the Foreign Room was finally abolished. The remaining members were allowed full membership of the Stock Exchange and the Committee exercised discretion in favour of those who were technically ineligible because they also practised some other business.

One member who got into serious financial difficulties in the Foreign Market was James Wetenhall, who had been publishing the price list since 1807. In 1829 he was obliged to 'take the benefit of the Insolvent Debtors Act' (thus being automatically disqualified from membership of the Exchange). Six members petitioned the Committee for General Purposes to waive the regulation which prohibited insolvent members from re-admission until two years after their discharge. Wetenhall, they said, was 'a very honest man, though a very unfortunate one', who had lost money in the Foreign Market and incurred considerable expense through family illness, but had never been a defaulter. The Committee voted unanimously in his favour and allowed his reinstatement.

The early 1830s were a time of considerable agitation in Britain. George IV's death in 1830 'on Saturday 27th June at $\frac{1}{4}$ past three o'clock AM' is noted carefully in the minutes of the Committee for General Purposes, in a small box drawn in the middle of the page. There was uneasiness at home during that year because of the unrest in France, with rick burning

in the south and workmen drilling in the industrial north preparing for class war. Political demonstrations accompanied the passing of the Reform Bill in 1832. However foreign government securities then began to revive, followed by renewed interest in joint-stock companies and joint-stock banks. Railway shares were becoming more important; by early 1835 there were active dealings in the Blackwall Railway Company and three years later there were large transactions in London and Brighton railway stock.

AMERICAN ISSUES

The 'Spanish panic' took place in 1835, and then in 1837 there was another panic, this time largely attributable to the American market. Most of the South American loans were rapidly in default, few of the mining companies lasted, and although after the 1825 panic there had been comparatively few foreign issues in London, a good deal of capital had found its way abroad by other means, much of it to America. The eastern seaboard states were beginning to build up canal and railway systems, financed by state governments by the issue of bonds or by forming land banks whose liabilities they guaranteed. Most of these bonds arrived in Britain. There were a few public issues, such as that made by Barings in 1829 for the state of Louisiana, but the most prevalent method was for shares to be distributed by merchants or by banks with American connections. The promoters of new issues naturally wanted an active market, sought immediate quotation and, if necessary, artificially (or fraudulently) stimulated dealing. The American states

◀ *'Joseph Stearns Jnr., Stock Ex, 20th August 1828'. Joseph Stearns (1804–68) was a member of the Stock Exchange from 1827 until his death in 1868. Together with other members of the Exchange at the time, he had his silhouette cut by the famous French silhouettist, August Edouart, in August 1828. One set of the portraits was originally lodged with the Exchange; a copy of Joseph Stearns' portrait was rescued from the wreck of a ship in which Edouart was returning to France from North America, and given by the artist to the Stearns family.*

proved almost as unreliable as the South American ones – three of them, Louisiana, Mississippi and Michigan, all repudiated their debts, and five others ceased paying dividends, at least temporarily. The American panic was short but unpleasant, bringing ruin to several members of the Stock Exchange.

Regional exchanges

It was not only in London that the effects of the boom were felt – the pace of company promotion had picked up all over the country from 1834 onwards. In his speech on the budget in 1836 Poullet Thomson, the President of the Board of Trade, felt obliged to warn of unsound companies started up 'for objects either of the most absurd kind, or for objects such as private individuals are perfectly able to accomplish . . . In 1825, London was the great centre of speculation, but I am afraid that these companies now have their origin in other parts of the country . . .' The boom was especially strong in Manchester and Liverpool, enhancing the attractions of stockbroking as a profession, and leading to the formation in 1836 of the Manchester Stock Exchange and the Liverpool Sharebrokers' Association, forerunner of the Liverpool Stock Exchange which moved into a permanent building in 1844. Dublin had had a Stock Exchange since 1799. These, and the other provincial exchanges which were to be established during the 1840s, represented a significant expansion of the British securities market, in both the range of securities and number of investors.

The Spanish panic

Early in 1835 events in Europe took a turn which roused the Stock Exchange from a period of stagnation. News of the expulsion of the rebels Don Carlos from Spain and Dom Miguel from Portugal was greeted with sympathy in the City: both countries were in default on their bonds and urgently needed to borrow more money. Further bonds were successfully issued and foreign loans became wildly popular. By May, however, it had become clear that the market was loaded with worthless foreign stocks, and on 21 May panic hit the Stock Exchange. Spanish stock fell by 10 per cent at one time and Portuguese securities fared even worse, falling by between 20 and 30 per cent within a week.

A contemporary account of the 'Spanish panic' sets the scene: 'Frantic confusion marked the alleys and the neighbourhood of Capel Court . . . almost every third man was a defaulter . . . all foreign securities were without price . . . with a desperation which will never be forgotten the jobbers closed their books and refused to transact any business, and awaited the result in almost abject despair . . . the blackboard was found inadequate to contain the names [of defaulters]. Additional time was granted to settle the accounts, and the holders of foreign securities formed themselves into a society 'to purchase all stock below forty. Many of the members were ruined, but a whip-round in the City did mitigate things to some extent.

The Wheel of Fortune
1840–1865

T HE PROVINCIAL STOCK EXCHANGES PLAYED AN IMPORTANT PART in financing Britain's increasing railway mileage, and there were major groups of investors in Lancashire, Yorkshire, Birmingham, Bristol and on the north-east coast. *A Circular to Bankers* written in 1835 went as far as to assert that: 'It is a remarkable fact that the railway system advanced and became established in the public confidence without the assistance of the Stock Exchange. The support accorded to it was almost exclusively from capitalists, and men of thrift and opulence, in the mining and manufacturing districts of the north of England . . .' While the author was obviously thinking of men such as George Hudson of York, the so-called railway king, this is exaggerated – shares in the Liverpool & Manchester Railway (incorporated in 1825), for example, were actively traded on the London Stock Exchange from the beginning, although only about four or five London brokers, and a correspondingly small number of jobbers, specialised in rail shares. In most cases the names of London brokers appeared on the prospectus, although a subscription list containing the names of prominent local people was more likely to receive the necessary Act of Parliament giving permission to the new company to lay down the lines.

Forming a new railway company was done in much the same way as canal companies had been established. Applications for shares were usually invited by advertisement, and when these were received, allotment letters were sent out and the recipients were required to pay a deposit and (until 1858) to sign a subscription document. They then received 'scrip' – part-paid stock or shares. The signatory to the subscription document was liable for further calls, even if he had sold the shares, and even if the new owner defaulted.

At times of speculation such as the first 'mini' railway boom in 1835, companies were flooded with applications, but by the end of the 1830s the public had lost so much money that confidence in railway shares was at a low ebb; it was also felt that parliament had given the companies too much power. By 1840, railway building was almost at a standstill and share prices were low. Just as a decade earlier, trade and industry were in a generally low state and civil riots took place in some districts. (The first use of trains to carry troops to places of unrest, to put down riots, was at this period.) Gradually, however, the pendulum swung back; passenger revenues, at first disappointing, picked up as the convenience and speed of rail travel became more appreciated, and by the end of 1843 nearly 3,000 miles of track had been authorised by parliament, of which over two-thirds was complete and in use. The year 1844 saw something of a trade boom in which rail shares participated, and the stage was now set for the 'railway mania' of the following year.

RAILWAY MANIA

'The whole country was speedily seized with an irresistible craving to take a solid and serious part in the great movement,' wrote Edward Callow, then a stockbroker's clerk, in his

◀ An 1823 share certificate of the Stockton & Darlington Railway Company, the world's first passenger railway.

▲ *'Travelling on the Liverpool and Manchester Railway': a coloured aquatint of 1833 by I. Shaw. The upper train is drawn by 'Jupiter' and the lower by 'North Star' (an improved version of the 'Rocket').*

reminiscences of the boom of 1845, published at the end of the century. 'Never since [the time of the South Sea Bubble] has the spirit of speculation been so rife in the whole land, and throughout almost all classes, as when the great railway mania set in, and Great Britain, from John o' Groats to the Land's end, was mapped out with projected railways. A Solicitor or two, a civil engineer, a parliamentary agent, possibly a contractor, a map of England, a pair of compasses, a pencil, and a ruler, were all that was requisite to commence the formation of a railway in these halcyon days – at any rate so far as drawing up the prospectus was concerned. Then that document had to be embellished with the names of a few noble and gentle country landowners and well-to-do manufacturers, if the district contained any, as provisional directors. These were all the ingredients for forming a railway company. Many, indeed, were started in the market

with no more ingredients, and the shares in them were extensively dealt in, even in some instances before the company was provisionally registered.'

The frenzy for letters of allotment brought a new class of Stock Exchange hanger-on into existence – the Alley men or Little-go men, as they were known. Because no deposit money was required with a letter of application, virtually anyone who could write a legible hand was welcome to fill in the application form and ask for an allotment. Thousands did so, in both London and the provinces, who had no intention or indeed any possibility of paying the deposit to the banker which would be required if shares were allotted to them. This was one of the earliest manifestations of widespread 'stagging' – a word which gained currency at the time – and Capel Court was dubbed 'Stag Alley.'

Shares were more likely to be allotted to someone applying from a 'good' address, and there were many tales of servants, writing from their employers' houses in Mayfair or Belgravia, who made a quick fortune which enabled them to retire. This was the initial luck of William Thackeray's footman C. Jeames de la Pluche Esq. whose story is told in *The*

THE RAILWAY KING

*I*t was the Reverend Sydney Smith, the Victorian wit, who first called George Hudson 'the railway king', and certainly Hudson more than any other man epitomises the years of railway mania in the mid-1840s. He quickly grasped the potential of steam, prophesying years before it happened that he would live to see the mail carried from London to Newcastle by steam power, and he was destined to play a major role in the great Victorian drama that changed the face of British landscape, and the country's commerce, for ever.

Hudson started his business life as a linen-draper in York, but in 1827 a legacy from a great-uncle enabled him to begin his career as a railway promoter, and by 1844 there were more than a thousand miles of completed line in his domain. He worked indefatigably to promote new lines – at first in the north of England and then throughout the country – and to buy up rival railway companies or obstruct, sometimes by dubious means, those of which he could not gain control. He had an unerring eye for publicity and the type of dramatic gesture that enthralled the owners of shares in his companies: the opening of the Newcastle and Darlington Junction line in 1844 was marked by the arrival of a 'flying train' which steamed into the Gateshead terminus with copies of that morning's London newspapers, having covered the distance of over 300 miles at an average speed of thirty-seven miles an hour – a considerable feat at that date.

As the boom took hold Hudson became ever richer and more famous. Three times mayor of his native city of York, he later bought what was then London's largest private house, in Albert Gate at the entrance to Hyde Park. He was elected Tory MP for Sunderland, became the confidant of the Duke of Wellington, successfully fought off a

'Off the rail' – a Punch *cartoon of 1849 showing George Hudson, the railway king, dethroned by bankruptcy.*

parliamentary plan to nationalise the railway network, and was notable for his lavish hospitality.

In the aftermath of the boom his life began to turn sour: railway shares depreciated sharply in 1847, he got deeply into debt and was accused of fraud. For twenty years he was embroiled in a Chancery suit with the North Midland Railway Company. After 1849 he spent much of his time overseas, and on his return to England he was briefly imprisoned in the county gaol in York Castle for contempt of the Court of Exchequer for non-payment of a debt. The last years of the railway king were funded by an annuity raised for him by friends and well-wishers, and he died, poor and discredited, in 1871.

"STAG" STALKING IN CAPEL COURT.

◀ *'"Stag" Stalking in Capel Court': a* Punch *cartoon in 1845 at the height of the railway mania.*

Yellowplush Papers. Jeames, who started life as plain James Plush (a reference to the plush trousers worn by footmen), told his employer that 'he had been speculating in railroads, and stated his winnings to have been thirty thousand pounds . . . he had dated his letters from the house in Berkeley Square, and humbly begged pardon of his master for not having instructed the railway secretaries who answered his application to apply at the area bell.' However poor Jeames, after taking an apartment in Albany, becoming a director in thirty-three railroads and proposing to stand for Parliament at the next general election 'on decidedly Conservative principles', eventually came to grief, lost all his money and ended up as the landlord of the Wheel of Fortune public house.

Punch had great sport with the railway mania, publishing satirical 'money market reports' on schoolchildren buying railway scrip from the old woman who went round with sweetmeats in a basket, and poems such as 'Verses on a Young Lady Stag', Little Kitty Lorimer, who tripped in muff and tippet to buy scrip in Capel Court. *The Economist* noted that 'Everybody is in the stocks now. Needy clerks, poor tradesmen's apprentices, discarded serving men and bankrupts – all have entered the ranks of the great monied interest.' Such was the excitement that trading continued in the coffee houses and alleyways of the City long after the four o'clock closure of the Stock Exchange, and within the Exchange itself the brokers were almost swamped with business, so that the accounts, which normally took only one or at the most two days to settle, 'nearly exhausted the week' before differences could be paid, transfers made and the books adjusted. There was a big influx of new members, too, some of them of doubtful financial standing, and their older colleagues had 'the mortification to see persons who formerly had been of little reputation on the Exchange, and in many instances even their own clerks, carrying on an extensive and profitable business in shares.'

The Alley men rapidly became the pawns of the more unscrupulous members of the Stock Exchange, who bought allotment letters from them and paid them a small sum for signing the deed (the major responsibility in these transactions). Having enabled the Alley men to pay the deposit they then took the scrip receipts as their own at an agreed price, thus escaping the risk of calls as original subscribers. However the Alley men sometimes turned

Queen's evidence, becoming known as 'stag hunters' – often at the same time as acting on their own account.

Of course it was too good to last. In August the Board of Trade doubled the deposit required of promoters of railway bills from 5 per cent to 10 per cent of the capital proposed. On 16 October 1845, when Bank Rate was raised from $2\frac{1}{2}$ to 3 per cent, panic set in. All shares suffered, railway shares most sharply, and it was estimated that fewer than half of the 1,263 railway companies were able to provide the deposits required by the government. Calls on capital to the full amount were swiftly becoming payable, and Edward Callow recalled that those who a week before looked upon their bundles of railway scrip as representing undoubted wealth, were now madly anxious to get rid of them at any price obtainable, heedless of the real and intrinsic value of many of them and 'not thinking for a moment of separating the wheat from the chaff – the sound lines that had already obtained their parliamentary powers from the speculative and opposing schemes.'

The bolder spirits in the Stock Exchange who 'went in for bearing everything' made more money during the first few weeks of the panic than they had during all the preceding months, but every day, as orders to sell poured in from all over the country, the markets fell and failures both outside and inside the Exchange became all too frequent – within the House 'the sound of the hammer declaring defaulters was heard with disastrous frequency day after day' until what Callow calls 'an entire stoppage of all speculation' took place for a while.

The aftermath of the railway boom, although it was a factor, was not the main cause of the major commercial and financial crisis of 1847; the aggressive discounting policy of the Bank of England after the passing of the Bank Charter Act, together with the failures of the English and European corn harvests and the consequent imports of expensive wheat, caused a heavy drain of gold. The crisis deepened during the year and was eventually brought to an end by the agreement of the Bank to exceed the fiduciary issue of notes, as it was authorised to do by the government. It did not actually have to do so – just the knowledge of the government's letter of authority was enough to turn the tide.

Special settlements

The crisis year of 1847 also saw a new Stock Exchange rule about special settlements. A special settlement had been instituted at least as early as 1824, and probably before, to meet the case of various foreign loans which turned sour in 1824–5. During the 'railway mania' there were so many disputes and points of argument that the Special Settlement Rule was recommended by a special sub-committee and finally passed by the Stock Exchange Committee in 1847. It laid down what constituted the coming-out of scrip, and stopped partial settlement in which preferential payments were made – something which went against the whole ethos of the Exchange. It also enforced the completion of contracts by rules regarding buying-in

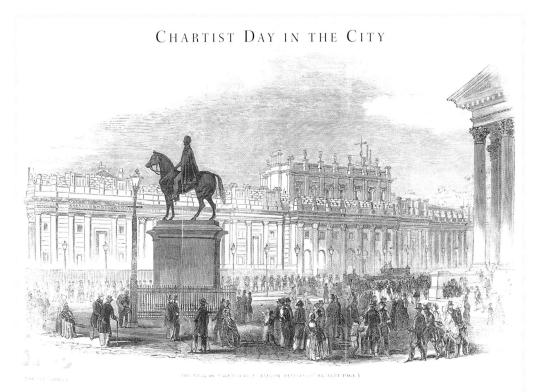

CHARTIST DAY IN THE CITY

B y the mid-1840s extremists had taken control of the Chartists, a group of political reformers formed in 1838 as a result of disappointment with Grey's reforms and the failure to enfranchise the workers. It was decided to hold a mass meeting on Kennington Common on 10 April 1848; the government tried to ban it, and Wellington posted troops to guard London. Most of the City institutions, including the Bank of England and the Royal Exchange, were defended with armed guards and sandbags.

Although the main route of the march did not go through the centre of the City, an outlying group, some 12,000 strong, assembled in Finsbury Square and marched towards London Bridge via Bishopsgate and Gracechurch Street. The Committee of the Stock Exchange – minus the chairman and his deputy, both of whom were acting as special constables at the Royal Exchange

'Chartist Riots: the Bank of England in a state of defence'. Fortifications, sandbags and loopholes were constructed by the Bank above its windowless wall facing Threadneedle Street. Illustrated London News, 15 April 1818.

– met to discuss the possibility of closing the House, noting that the Lombard Street bankers had already sent their securities for safekeeping to the Bank of England, but 'Mr Mullens suggested that such a Step might occasion serious and unnecessary alarm, not only throughout the country, but all over Europe'. Members waited nervously until 2 p.m. when news arrived that the procession had been abandoned and the Chartists were leaving Kennington Common. In Capel Court the national anthem was sung 'in the most enthusiastic style' (hats, commonly worn indoors at this date, having previously been removed) and 'Consols immediately went up.'

► *Samuel Gurney Sheppard, c. 1886.*

and selling-out, and attempted to rectify the serious delays which had frequently occurred in the issuing of scrip certificates.

A more important result of the railway boom, however, was the creation of a large market quite independent of government credit. Small investors were for the first time able to find a home for their savings in private enterprise, as the fixed income securities of the successful 'Home Rails' such as the Great Western or the Lancashire & Yorkshire ultimately became almost as solid and respectable as Consols; by 1853 they accounted for almost 16 per cent of the value of all securities quoted on the London Stock Exchange (British Funds accounted for 70 per cent, foreign loans for nearly 6 per cent).

In 1852 the Stock Exchange celebrated the successful completion of the first fifty years in Capel Court. It was by now the largest and most important stock exchange in the world, with paid-up capital of securities estimated at £1.2 billion: 'the Stock Exchange is the channel through which all the money business of London flows', Robert Hichens, 'broker to the London Joint Stock Board and to several Lombard bankers', had commented a few years earlier. Its success was reflected in the value of its shares, on which £50 was originally paid up in 1802; unlimited in amount but with calls restricted to £50 per share in any one year, they remained at £50 paid until 1853, when another £25 was called for rebuilding purposes. Large and increasing profits had been made for the proprietors throughout the whole half century, and the dividend had reached £15 per share by 1850. The *Official List* had grown in size and amount of information, reflecting the growth of the Exchange; although until 1843 it was still only published twice a week. In 1844 a daily Railway list was instituted to accompany it, and eventually, in 1857, the two were combined into one large general list, published daily.

Firms were still mostly small, many of them consisting of one member and his clerk; Cazenove's and Capels, with five partners each by the mid-1840s, were among the largest, their size reflecting the substantial amount of business they carried out on behalf of banking clients. Good business could still be done by less substantial firms. The first ledger of Sheppard and Sons (eventually to become Sheppard & Chase) covers the year 1850–1 and shows details of transactions on behalf of some 140 clients carried out by James Sheppard and his sons Robert Sheppard and Samuel Gurney Sheppard, generally known as SGS and an important Stock Exchange figure in later years. These transactions range from small sums of under a hundred pounds, to accounts worth tens of thousands such as that for John Masterson Jr (a brother-in-law of Isaac Braithwaite, a partner in Foster & Braithwaite), whose firm specialised in railway finance and later became Agra and Masterman's Bank. His transactions in a month often ran to £50,000 or more.

Commissions in the 1850s

A list of brokers' commissions published in mid century shows the commission chargeable on transactions in English stock as 2s 6d per cent. On shares, the rates were 1s 3d under £5; 2s 6d when the shares were worth £5 and under £20; 5s between £20 and £50 and 10s on shares amounting in value to £50 or more. The majority of business was still in the Funds. The National Debt amounted to £830 million, and the current theory that it must be reduced, and might even be repudiated, encouraged gambling. This was recognised by the Bankruptcy Act of 1849, which stated that a certificate was to be refused to a bankrupt if he had lost £200 in the year preceding the filing of the petition by any time bargain in Government or other stock; it also provided that the certificate should be withheld if he had lost £20 in any one day by wagering or gambling, although a subsequent legal decision established that the loss of £20 in a day by paying Stock Exchange differences was not gaming or wagering.

The rule book had by this date expanded significantly from the 1812 version, and now contained 150 rules altogether. The Exchange was to be closed on Good Friday and Christmas Day, plus every day appointed by Royal Proclamation as a day of 'fasting or thanksgiving', but on no other day unless by order of the Committee. The Committee met at one o'clock on the day preceding any Bank Holiday to determine whether the Exchange should be closed the following day or not. Hours were now from half past ten until three o'clock, except on Mondays 'when business shall not commence before eleven o'clock', and Saturdays, when it closed at two o'clock, 'and the Committee will recognise such bargains only as are done within these hours.' The Committee also stipulated that they did not 'feel themselves called upon to entertain any question submitted to them by anyone not a Member of the Stock Exchange against any Member, unless such Member shall have been employed by the complainant in the capacity of a Broker.'

There were several rules about quotation of prices, including one that gave rise to many objections which stated that 'No smaller number of scrip shares than five shall be permitted to mark in the price list; nor shall any number of shares or stock requiring a transfer be permitted to mark that shall be sold at less than the market price owing to the stamp rendering a sacrifice necessary.' There were limits to the amount of stock which could be quoted in the Official List, and other rules covered ex-dividend quotations and fulfilment of bargains – transfer receipts had to be delivered by four o'clock, while 'English omnium or scrip not paid in full must be delivered on or before two o'clock' on the due date. The rule dealing with buying-in and selling-out was emphasised by large type: in all cases the purchase or sale had to be made publicly and the Committee recommended that the Secretary should be employed as Broker on such occasions. Default was also dealt with in detail: every member who had had dealings with anyone who had acted dishonestly towards him 'should insert the name and address of such individual in a book, which is kept by the Clerk of the House, and open to the Members of the stock exchange'; the Committee reserved the right to affix the name of defaulters whose conduct was considered dishonourable 'on the blackboard.'

By now there were just over 900 members, still paying a subscription of £10 a year. Edward Callow describes their normal business dress: top boots, breeches, blue coat with gilt buttons, spotless white 'neckerchief and ruffles' and hair tied neatly back in a pigtail. On days when business was flat (for example during the weeks when the Funds were closed for preparing the dividends and no investment transfers could be made) members would frequently take the day off and go with their families on outings to places such as Hornsey Wood House, Ranelagh or Hampton Court. When they were in the City, the custom for the older members was to go to Birch's at about midday for a 'basin of soup and a glass of Madeira'; the Auction Mart Coffee Room was also popular for a glass of sherry. The younger men frequented an inn called the Gun. Members all had to have City premises in order to become freemen, without which they could not become sworn brokers: the Plasterer's Company was popular, as it was relatively cheap, and the payment of £80 secured livery plus broker's licence. Another contemporary account of stockbrokers notes that they spend their money freely, 'affect a stylish appearance' and, if married, have 'a nice villa at Norwood or Clapham.' Some of the free-spending aroused suspicion, if not outright hostility, and defaulters in particular were often heavily criticised – in 1854 the Committee received complaints about the lifestyle of one Thomas Trulock, a re-admitted defaulter who still owed a large sum, and who had 'a house in the Regents Park and another at Crawley. He keeps six hunters, two carriage horses, a close carriage and several open ones, three grooms, coachman and footman and is constantly out with the hounds.'

'FOR DIFFERENCES ONLY'

In 1852 the case of Grizewood v. Blane had important repercussions for the stock market. Grizewood was a jobber, and Blane the principal of the broker with whom he had been dealing: Grizewood sued Blane for differences in the price of some railway shares, and the case came before a jury, who had to decide whether either the jobber or the speculator really meant to purchase or sell the shares. The judge, Chief Justice Jervis, told the jury that if they decided that the transaction was for 'differences only' then it was, in his opinion, a gambling transaction and as such not legally enforceable. The jury did so decide and, much to the

▶ *The Currency Question; or, the Stock Exchange out for the day.*
Jones: 'I say, Brown, things are deuced bad in the City.'
Brown: 'Then I'm deuced glad I'm at Epsom.'

dismay of members, the ruling of the Chief Justice was subsequently upheld in the Court of Common Pleas. In this particular case, the member was the plaintiff, but a flood of actions ensued almost immediately on the part of unscrupulous principals who saw an easy way out of unprofitable bargains. Some consolation was obtained in 1854, when it was ruled that even if a contract was void as between the jobber and the broker or his principal, the broker was able to sue his principal for work done and money paid in carrying out the contract.

REBUILDING THE HOUSE

The House was again becoming uncomfortably crowded with members and their clerks, despite a fair amount of extension which had taken place to the original building. It had first been extended westward, then east and north, with new frontages acquired in Shorter's Court and in Throgmorton Street. Now the Committee decided that it was time for a complete rebuilding, which began in June 1853. The Managers spent £6,000 on further enlarging the Capel Court site, and the plans of an architect named Thomas Allason were adopted. W. Cubitt & Co. was given the building contract, at an original estimate of £10,400, although the final cost was nearer to £20,000, and before the rebuilding began, the Hall of Commerce in Threadneedle Street was rented to provide temporary premises for the Stock Exchange. This was a massive and lavishly appointed building on the site of a French Protestant church which had been burnt down in the fire which destroyed the second Royal Exchange building in 1838. The Hall of Commerce was reputed to have cost its proprietor, Edward Moxhay, who had made his fortune in biscuits, some £70,000; it was used as a sort of combination club and exchange, and a certain amount of mining speculation took place there, but it had never been very successful, particularly after the rebuilding of the Royal Exchange. However, it provided a useful temporary home for Stock Exchange members during the rebuilding period.

The new Stock Exchange building opened in March 1854. It was designed in a style influenced by that of the halls housing the Great Exhibition of 1851, and was constructed of brick, with a wooden roof, ironwork in the piers and beams and elaborate plasterwork (later replaced by marble) inside. It provided twice the floor-space of the previous building. Mabey's restaurant was situated in the basement, and there was also a small luncheon bar run by an elderly woman who claimed to have lost money because most of her customers were Jews, who promised to pay her 'on Saturday', on which day of course they did not come to work. The various markets – English for stocks and exchequer bills, Foreign for stocks, Railways, Mining and Miscellaneous – had their own distinct areas. Porters guarded each entrance, but the public, if minded to peer inside, could do so through the glass folding

▶ *Interior view of the Hall of Commerce, Threadneedle Street,*
the temporary home of the Stock Exchange during rebuilding in 1853–54.

doors in Hercules Passage, where according to a contemporary report they would be rewarded by the sight of 'a great number of well-dressed, sharp looking gentlemen talking very energetically and apparently doing a great deal of business.'

The Exchange remained a target for righteous indignation on the part of some writers – one, in the year the new building was opened, described time bargains as 'gambling more ruinous, . . . [and] demoralisation more extensive, than all the hells ever could produce.' In their defence, it must be said that members were not especially keen on time bargains, but would participate in them if desired to do so by their clients.

War was declared against Russia in 1854, and lasted until 1856, adding a further £16 million to the National Debt. The following year, 1857, was marked by the Indian Mutiny, and by a panic in America where railroads were overburdened with debts and several banks went under. In Britain, the Bank Charter Act of 1844 was temporarily repealed to allow the Bank of England to exceed its limits on the note issue, although, as had been the case ten years before, knowledge of the repeal proved adequate in itself to stem the panic and the provisions of the Act were not actually infringed. It was a disastrous episode for the Stock Exchange, where, despite the fact that the price of Consols fluctuated less than in the past, over seventy members failed. The Committee took the unusual step of granting time to pay to all members who could manage ten shillings in the pound, and declaring no defaulters after the first few days of the panic – many defaulters did return to the Exchange and subsequently flourished.

The Corporation's yoke

Early in 1858 Sir George Grey presented a petition from the Exchange to the House of Commons, asking for relief from the 'yoke' of the City of London which stockbrokers still bore and still resented. A Bill was followed by a Royal Commission, which recommended that the 'statutory exactments' should be repealed as they did not appear to be 'productive of any benefit'; shortly afterwards, the Secretary to the Treasury announced that Sir John Barnard's Act, being obsolete, would be repealed. This prospect stirred up considerable controversy, in particular a violent diatribe in a pamphlet which attacked the veracity of the evidence given to the Royal Commission by the stockbrokers and also made an impassioned appeal for an open market. (Among other things, it claimed quite untruthfully that the new building was 'unfit for a public market, having neither light nor the means of access.') The net result was that Barnard's Act, which had been flawed from the first and was indeed by now quite obsolete, was finally repealed, but the submission to the City, despite another surge of objection and agitation in 1864, was destined to remain in force until 1886.

The next major preoccupation was the vexed subject of commissions – to fix or not to fix? Brokers' charges were the subject of much discussion in the press, one correspondent claiming that many brokers charged 2s 6d per share on all shares of the value of £5 and above

– so that on a purchase of 200 shares for £1,000 he had to pay commission of £25. A further grievance was that although most railway shares had been converted to stock, brokers continued to charge commission of so much per share. The agitation for reform grew to such a pitch that a meeting of members was called at the end of October 1860, and it was agreed that a committee should be established to look into the whole question of commissions and to decide if it were practicable to set a scale and how to enforce it. Despite the misgivings of many of the members, a twelve-strong committee was set up and duly reported; at a further meeting in May the following year, a minimum scale was actually agreed. However, although it was decided to communicate the details to the Stock Exchange Committee with a view either to procuring the authority of the Committee to enforce its adoption, or to having it incorporated into the rules, nothing further happened officially. In fact the unofficial scale was widely adopted, although the Committee adamantly refused to intervene in disputes on the subject – when James Foster of Foster & Braithwaite complained that a fellow broker was undercutting him, the Committee frostily declined to interfere or decide in any way, what the scale should be.

CAVEAT EMPTOR

The Companies Acts of the early 1860s were also of considerable interest to members. The old stagging stratagems had been restricted: applicants were now required to deposit with the bankers of a new company one or two pounds per share, and, in order to achieve this, promoters of new companies not only had to provide an impressive list of directors and a promising prospectus, but were frequently tempted to create an artificial premium for the shares in the market. So questionable had the methods of achieving this become that in 1864 the Committee determined not to allow any dealings in new undertakings until after allotment had actually taken place. This was a recurrent and thorny question in the history of the Exchange, in this particular instance focusing on a 'corner' in the shares of the Australian and Eastern Navigation Company Limited. The Committee carried out a lengthy examination into what had happened and refused to grant a settlement: the company folded amidst great bitterness on the part of the directors, who claimed that some of the Committee members had been personally involved because they sold the shares. However, the Committee stood by its decision and a few months later amplified the existing rule against dealing before allotment, although the taboo lasted barely a year. In 1865 the restriction crumbled in the face of the numbers of the public who demanded such transactions; many of the members who had supported the ban the previous year now required the Committee to rescind it, which it finally did, tacitly acknowledging the impossibility of enforcing such a ban however desirable it might be. *Caveat emptor* was indeed one of the prevailing watchwords of the nineteenth-century City.

The Stock Exchange Investigated 1866–1890

ᴬLTHOUGH PUNCTUATED AT EITHER END BY TWO OF THE Cɪᴛʏ'ꜱ most notorious nineteenth century crashes – Overend Gurney in 1866, Barings twenty-four years later – the years between 1866 and 1890 were a time of growth and prosperity for the Stock Exchange. It is also the period of which we have perhaps the clearest and most detailed picture of the workings of the Exchange, from the immense bulk of evidence given to two investigations, the 1875 Select Committee on Foreign Loans and the 1877–78 Royal Commission on the Stock Exchange.

In the late 1850s the famous old discount house of Overend & Gurney had come under the control of 'young and imprudent partners', who diversified into grain trading, shipowning, railway finance and many other businesses of a highly speculative nature. The discount business continued and was highly profitable, but much of its capital was locked up, and in July 1865 Overend, Gurney & Co. was launched, described by the *Bankers' Magazine* as 'the

THE ILLUSTRATED LONDON NEWS.

SATURDAY, MAY 19, 1866.

VL.—VOL. XLVIII. WITH A SUPPLEMENT, FIVEPENCE

◀ *'Black Friday, 11 May 1866: the doors of Overend Gurney are shut.'* Illustrated London News, *19 May 1866.*

THE MONETARY PANIC.

not soon forget Friday, May 11, 1866—" Black a been designated with great propriety. On that ary unsettledness of some weeks past, which the d risen to a gale, culminated in a tornado, the of which was far beyond all precedent within

memory of the living, and which, if it had continued four-and-twenty hours longer, seemed likely to involve in disaster and wreck all the money establishments of the country. Happily, and, let us add, owing in great measure to the moral courage and promptitude of the Government, the fury of the commotion was as shortlived as it was violent, and before Saturday was

gone the panic may be said to have subsided ; and credit, whic had been suddenly prostrated by the irresistible force of th hurricane, albeit trembling and bewildered, stood erect onc more.

From time to time, for two or three months past, there hav appeared phenomena in the money market which were inter

triumph of limited liability.' On 10 May the following year it failed with assets of only £11 million against liabilities of nearly £19 million. The next day, 'Black Friday', Walter Bagehot noted the 'complete collapse of credit in Lombard Street and a greater amount of anxiety than I have ever seen'; but by the evening the worst of the crisis was over, helped by the steadiness of nerve of the Bank of England and of Rothschilds.

The events of 1866 and the two or three years before that led to the passing of the 1867 Leeman's Act, which was intended to stop speculation in the shares of banks (one of the causes of the Overend collapse), and to prevent sales of shares by those who did not possess them. Although the Committee paid lip service to the provisions of the Act it was almost entirely ignored by the members. Business was depressed in the wake of the Overend crisis, which had shed a lurid light on the true meaning of limited liability, previously only imperfectly understood. During the trial in 1869 of six Overend directors for conspiracy to defraud, it became clear that limited liability on shares which were only partly paid up was in fact almost unlimited liability, and the vast expense of winding up companies was also exposed. Although the directors were acquitted, the very fact that, despite their reputation and experience, they had become involved in criminal proceedings was another hard lesson, and investment in companies fell into disfavour. Domestic business on the Exchange was almost at a standstill, and the only excitement was a mild panic caused by false rumours of the death of Louis Napoleon. The Franco-German war which broke out in 1870 brought the transfer of a good deal of business in international stocks from the Paris Bourse to the Stock Exchange in London, but the immediate effects of the war were disastrous, one financial writer computing that 'the total depreciation on the Stock Exchange represented a sum sufficient to cover the cost of a general European war of a couple of years' duration.'

HUMPHREY'S CLEARING HOUSE

By the early 1870s the mechanics of clearing had become a serious inconvenience. A scheme for clearing stocks and shares on the same principle as that by which bankers cleared cheques had been proposed by one Henry Abbey over twenty years earlier, but had come to nothing. In 1872, a Settling Room was organised in the basement, where clerks could meet to arrange payment and delivery – previously carried out on the floor of the House – but even this proved inadequate. In December 1873 there was a private meeting of members to consider a clearing scheme suggested by Benjamin Humphrey, which was subsequently approved by a special sub-committee.

Humphrey's Clearing House was set up in a basement in Drapers' Gardens: it operated independently, but was granted 'certain concessions' by the Exchange. At first fewer than fifty members made use of it, but numbers increased account by account until, in 1877, 523 firms, representing about a thousand members, were using its services. Humphrey collected from his patrons a proportion of the total clearing clerks' charges, calculated at so much per hour, paying the men slightly less and retaining the surplus. Many of his clerks were 'broken down members drawing pensions from the Stock Exchange Benevolent Fund' who were paid a guinea a night plus refreshments, with dinner at 10 p.m.

This rather unorthodox system worked well enough for a few years until the failure of one of its members, and the return of his cheque, in 1890. The creditors could not decide how to get payment, and after some weeks of chaos, a Stock Exchange member called W.B. Bellars put forward a new clearing scheme. The Committee agreed to inaugurate a Settlement Department, managed by Bellars and under the control of the Exchange (something which it had previously refused), with the stated object 'to assist the settlement in accordance with the rules and regulations of the House.'

THE PROBLEMS OF FOREIGN LOANS

Foreign loans, meanwhile, had become a serious cause of disquiet. Contracts for loans with Honduras, Santo Domingo, Costa Rica and Paraguay were particular problems. Loans from all four countries were repudiated, some of them for quite hare-brained schemes: Honduras had ambitions to build an inter-oceanic railway for which it came three times to the London market, the last project, in 1872, being for hydraulic lifts to carry ocean-going ships across the Isthmus and drop them back into the sea on the far side. About 150 doubtful foreign loans, involving sums amounting on paper to £720 million, had been launched in the past fifteen years. Questions were asked in Parliament, and in February 1875 a Select Committee was appointed to look into 'the circumstances attending the making of Contracts for Loans with certain Foreign States, and also the causes which have led to the non-payment of the principal moneys and interest due in respect of such Loans.'

Several members of the Stock Exchange gave evidence, including the chairman of the General Purposes Committee, Samuel Herman de Zoete, the senior partner of the broking firm de Zoete & Gorton. He was questioned closely as to just how much enquiry the Exchange made into the likelihood of the borrowing State actually repaying the loan, the reasonableness or otherwise of the amount, and the *bona fides* of the allotment; if the Exchange were to make such searching examination, de Zoete replied, 'I am afraid we should never get through the business.' It was plain from his evidence and that of others that the conduct of the Exchange in permitting settlement of bargains and authorising inclusion on the official price list gave minimal protection to the purchasers of the shares, and the Select Committee's report, issued in 1875, was suitably scathing.

The majority of it was taken up with a rehearsal of the circumstances of the loans and the malpractices of the promoters, but it also provided advice and recommendations. It was felt that the people introducing the loans had ignored the financial resources of the borrowing states: an enquiry would have shown them to be quite inadequate for the repayment of the liabilities. The prospectuses had been exaggerated and the means by which the public had been induced to lend money on insufficient security were flagrantly deceptive. Dealings in the stock by the loan contractors before allotment to the public were singled out for particular censure, and after detailing the methods by which a 'fictitious market' had been frequently created, the report hinted that in some of the more serious cases criminal prosecution might be in order.

The report noted that everything went 'on under a cloak of secrecy.' The Select Committee had been informed that if a law was passed which made the actions of promoters and underwriters public, all transactions in public loans would be driven overseas – if the terms described were the only terms on which profits from such loans could be retained in England, said the report, then they were too dearly earned at such a price. Among the things held up for disapproval were pre-allotment dealings and artificial driving up of prices, 'puffs' appearing in the press which gave a spurious attraction to the loans, and bear raids, but the question of how, and by whom, fitness for official quotation could best be decided was ducked altogether. 'The business of the Stock Exchange is to buy and sell, not good securities only, but all securities that are dealt in, and it is hardly fair and hardly wise to entrust to it the power of suppressing those questionable proposals by which it alone, of all the public, is certain to benefit.' As long as it possessed the power to expel members, it should remain self-governing. The report ended by expressing the hope that the history of the foreign loans which it contained 'will tend to enlighten the public and to make it more difficult for unscrupulous persons to carry out schemes such as those which . . . have ended in so much discredit and disaster.'

Despite the scandals of the South American loans, those from North America were flourishing. Yankee rails became some of the stars of the market during the 1870s, having been quoted in the *Official List* since 1830 and enjoying a chequered career in the intervening decades, virtually disappearing altogether in the American panic of 1837. At the end of the Civil War, however, they returned with much éclat, and the American Department was one of the most active in the whole Exchange.

British capital was also going into many companies operating railways, water supplies, gasworks and other utilities overseas. There was nearly always one broker associated with the issuing house concerned (usually the smaller merchant banks, investment companies and some of the London joint-stock banks). A few of them advertised without using an issuing house at all, asking for subscriptions to be paid directly to them or through a broker, and this became a common practice, especially in overseas rail stocks: the firms of Mullens, Castello, Capel and Scrimgeour all acted as brokers to railway companies in the 1860s and 1870s.

After a lull in the second half of the 1870s, there was further substantial flow of capital overseas, and the growing use of the telephone and telegraph played a major role in the expansion of business between London and continental Europe, New York and Johannesburg. Some of the domestic transactions at this period were very large, and were carried through with great speed. One became almost legendary – a broker received an order to sell some

THE ERIE KING

Tom Nickalls,
the 'Erie King'.

American railroad shares constituted one of the roughest markets in the 1860s, and the Erie Railroad was the subject of a long and bitter struggle between the New York and London Exchanges to control the stock, which became a virtual gambling counter. Tom Nickalls, a jobber in London's American market, was at the centre of the excitement as efforts to dislodge the millionaire financier Jay Gould involved the purchase of tens of thousands of shares, which were shipped over to the United States to be voted on. A contemporary account paints a vivid picture of Nickalls 'half buried in bundles of stock', his tiny office piled high with Eries on tables and on the floor.

Nickalls, who was dubbed the Erie King, was born in England in 1828 and spent most of his childhood in Chicago; after his return to England in 1845 he married into a well-known Stock Exchange family and worked there for fifty years. His booming voice as he entered the market with the cry 'I buy Eries' was the signal for the other jobbers to gather round 'and the price . . . was pulled up and down' as he dictated. His reputation was enhanced when the railroad tycoon Cornelius Vanderbilt died and most of the other jobbers were selling: Nickalls continued to buy, and profited handsomely from his strong, instinctive feel for the market.

£150,000 of Consols on behalf of a banker who wanted the money the same day. The broker entered the market at 12.40 p.m.; by one o'clock the transaction was completed and the money paid.

THE 1876 DEED OF SETTLEMENT

At the beginning of 1876 a new Deed of Settlement for the Stock Exchange came into force. The old one, dating back to 1802, was by now outdated and unsuited to the enormously expanded Exchange, and the Managers, who felt that it limited their powers unwarrantably, had for some time been anxious to amend it. The principles of the old deed were enshrined in the new one, but each original share was split into ten new shares, making a total of 4,000. No proprietor could hold more than ten shares, and any new proprietor must be a member of the Exchange: if a 'stranger', or non-member, inherited shares he or she had to sell them within a year.

THE ROYAL COMMISSION

The mealy-mouthed report of the Select Committee had not quelled increasing public dissatisfaction with the Exchange, and within a couple of years questions were again being asked in Parliament, where the Exchange was heavily criticised on the familiar grounds of encouraging gambling (in the words of a Tory MP, J.R. Yorke, this state of affairs was promoted because the Exchange admitted 'a low class of member with small security'), failing to act on its

TELEGRAPH, TICKER-TAPE AND TELEPHONE

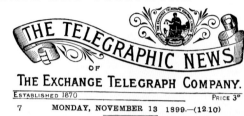

THE TELEGRAPHIC NEWS

OF

THE EXCHANGE TELEGRAPH COMPANY.

ESTABLISHED 1870 — PRICE 3ᴰ

7   MONDAY, NOVEMBER 13   1899.—(12.10)

The War in South Africa.

The Exchange Telegraph Company states that the following telegram has been received at the War Office:—

"From the Officer Commanding in South Africa. Cape Town, 12th November, 8.45 p.m. Following message received from Nicholson, Buluwayo,

News of the war in South Africa from the Exchange Telegraph Company, Limited

The invention of the telegraph in 1837 revolutionised the work of the Exchange. During the 1840s London was linked by it to all the major cities in Britain. The submarine cable to France was established in 1851 and to New York fifteen years later, so that the sixteen-day-old American prices that the stockbroking firm of Satterthwaite was using in the mid-1850s were replaced by prices that had arrived on the floor of the New York Exchange only twenty minutes earlier.

The next development, the ticker-tape machine, was invented in the United States and had been in use on Wall Street for some time before the Exchange Telegraph Company, Limited (it was very insistent on the comma) approached the Managers in 1872 with a request, supported by 655 members, for room in the House. A trial period of one month, subsequently renewed, was granted; the company was allowed to collect information on prices in the House and transmit it to nearby offices.

It had premises in Cornhill, a Stock Exchange reporter at a salary of £600 a year (out of which he had to obtain and pay two assistants in collecting financial news) and a telegraph operator in the Settling Room, whose machine transmitted at the rate of six words a minute. Relations with the Managers were polite but strained at first – they tried to get the Extel reporter to leave the House at 4 p.m., and did not wish him to have both his clerks there at the same time. The first subscribers were almost all members, but outside brokers also joined and were the targets of fierce opposition within Capel Court. Complaints to the Committee about information 'leaking' to outsiders were investigated by several sub-committees in the 1880s, and Extel was finally obliged to undertake to reject any new applications from outside brokers, dealers and 'open stock-exchanges', and to do its best to

eliminate those who already subscribed to its services.

Another innovation of which the Managers were initially suspicious was the telephone, first appearing in 1878. They were apprehensive that business would be diverted away from the Exchange if buying and selling prices quoted on the floor could be instantaneously matched against those obtainable elsewhere, and that an inter-office market, trading on Stock Exchange prices, might be established between non-members. It was not until 1880 that a telephone was installed; three years later a telephone room was in use. Members still found the service inadequate (few of them being as cautious as one firm which famously had the instrument installed in the partners' lavatory to discourage its use), and in 1888 the General Purposes Committee issued an ultimatum to the Managers, warning them that business 'would flow into other channels' if they continued to refuse to improve telephone facilities. The proprietors backed down and the telephone soon became an indispensable stockbroking tool.

▼ *Thursday morning in the City – any change in the Bank rate?' – an engraving of 1870.*

rules and having been involved in the recent spate of unsuccessful foreign loans. In March 1877 Lord Beaconsfield's Conservative government decided to appoint a Royal Commission, although this move was strongly criticised by both *The Economist* and *The Times*, the latter remarking tartly that it was not the 'machinery' which needed re-adjusting, rather that 'the remedy for fraudulent ventures is the punishment of those who concoct them.'

The Commission's remit was 'to inquire into the origin, objects, present constitution, customs and usages of the London Stock Exchange, and the mode of transacting business in, and in connection with, that institution, and whether such existing rules, customs and mode of conducting business were in accordance with the law and with the requirements of public policy, and if not, to advise in what respect they might be beneficially altered.' The chairman was Lord Penzance, and there were eleven members including three members of Parliament (one of whom was J.R. Yorke), and several prominent City figures including Sir Nathan Meyer Rothschild, Benjamin Buck Greene, a former Governor of the Bank of England, and Septimus R. Scott, the chairman of the Stock Exchange Committee, who took a major part in examination and cross-examination in the ten-month hearings, which began

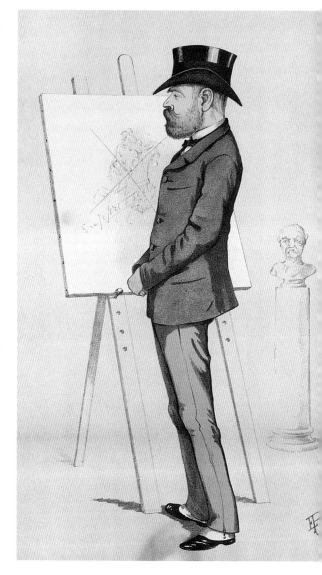

► *'Our special artist': a drawing of the Stock Exchange member and noted caricaturist F. Carruthers Gould.*

on 9 June. These usually took place on Saturday afternoons, after the House was closed for business for the weekend, and in the course of the sittings over fifty witnesses were called.

Between them they answered nearly 9,000 questions and the minutes of evidence ran to nearly 750,000 words. Certainly a harsh, sometimes glaring light now illuminated many of the corners of Capel Court which had previously been obscure, at least to the general public. 'Secrecy permeates every branch, pervades all the acts, and shrouds the arcana of that mighty body – secrecy is the inherent and palpable cause of all its misdoings in the past, and the blot which, if not removed, must ever attend it, with its demon-like influence, in the future ...' fulminated J. Smith Latham – identified frostily in the list of witnesses as 'Not a Member of the Stock Exchange', a major speculator who wanted to voice his grievances over what he claimed had been a conspiracy between his broker and other members to defraud him of around £9,000.

First to be examined was Francis Levien, Secretary to the Committee for General Purposes, who had prepared and duly read to the Commissioners a short and admirably succinct statement of 'the origin and objects of the institution known as the Stock Exchange'; its objects, he stated, were:

1st. To provide a ready market.

2nd. To make such regulations as would ensure the prompt and ready adjustment of all contracts.

Levien was closely questioned about the necessary qualifications for becoming a member – there were none, but he stoutly refused to concede that any previous apprenticeship,

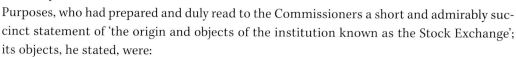

before attaining membership, was in any way necessary: 'credit and personal character are more desirable than anything else,' he asserted, and in any case most members had previously been clerks. The public perception of stockbrokers was rather snidely voiced by one of the Commissioners, Coleridge Kennard, who suggested that further restrictions on entry (beyond the recent rise of sureties and entrance fees) would be desirable to curb 'the easy admission of young gentlemen who go and play at lawn tennis, and tell their friends "I can put you on to a good thing"; . . . if you could restrict those sort of people from joining you, you would do a great deal to allay the excitement, and would do away with a great deal of the immorality into which this commission is appointed to enquire.' However, the Secretary would have none of it: a monetary restriction would not suffice and 'the best restriction is to take all the means in one's power to see that the applicant is a person of good character and credit.' He did admit, however, that those with previous experience as clerks were less likely to fail, as had been shown by a recent investigation into defaulters.

The questioning soon became much more technical, and Levien and succeeding witnesses were pressed hard, if politely, on the exact methods of buying and selling, brokers' commissions, speculative business, clearing, new companies and foreign loans and so on. The Government Broker, John Henry Daniell, who told the Commissioners that he had been a member of the Stock Exchange for thirty-one years, gave a summary of the different markets, which included at that date the English market (Consols, exchequer bills, India bonds and India government securities); Indian guaranteed railway securities; the foreign market for all the various foreign bonds, the joint-stock bank market, the colonial bond market, the foreign obligations market, foreign railway shares, the 'heavy' railway market (dealing in the stocks of five major lines), markets in other railways, the mining market, the American market ('which is a very large one') and the tramway market. Questioned on the difference between a broker and a jobber – a topic to which much time was devoted – Daniell told the Commissioners that 'I look upon a broker and a jobber as totally distinct.' This was certainly true in the Consols market, but there were many cases where the two activities overlapped, with the 'jobbing broker' especially active in American securities. Until 1847, there had been no formal ban on 'dual capacity', or acting as both principal (jobber) and agent (broker); in that year the Stock Exchange Committee had recognised the potential conflict of interest if one party or firm acted as both in the same transaction, and partnerships between the two were banned as 'highly inexpedient and improper.' The ban was restated in 1876, but, like so many Stock Exchange rules, this one had never been rigidly enforced.

'A MOUSE OF A REPORT'

Not everything that was said in evidence by the members found favour with their fellows, and a drawing done at the time by F. Carruthers Gould, a member who was also a noted caricaturist, portrays three witnesses as birds of prey, with a distinct suggestion that they had fouled their nest. One member in particular, Roger Eykyn, had demanded wholesale changes in the constitution of the Exchange and in the way the Committee for General Purposes was run. However, there was no cause for alarm. 'Predictably', in the words of City historian David Kynaston, 'the elephantine scale of evidence produced a mouse of a report.' This, published in 1878, evinced various points of discord – only eight members signed the whole document, while the other four, including Scott, expressed reservations in separate reports appended to the main text (Scott's minority report amounted, in fact, to a spirited defence of the *status quo*).

The Committee for General Purposes was commended for the way it administered its own rules 'uprightly, honestly and with a desire to do justice', which could only benefit the public 'in a market of such enormous magnitude.' The fact that the absence of any written contract 'had in practice no evil results' was also admired, and the Commissioners noted approvingly that 'out of the millions of contracts made on the Stock Exchange, such a thing was hardly known as a dispute as to the existence of a contract or as to its terms.' The system of dual control, whereby the Exchange was governed by the two distinct committees of Trustees and Managers on the one hand and the General Purposes Committee on the other, was considered less admirable, and the Commission recommended that the two bodies should amalgamate.

The jobbing system was approved: 'The dealers constitute a class which is a distinctive feature of the London Stock Exchange; it has no parallel on the foreign Bourses or on any of the provincial Stock Exchanges, but we have no hesitation in affirming that it is one of extreme value to the public . . . The buyer or seller can make his bargain at once without seeking out someone else who wants to buy what he has to sell, or wants to part with what he wants to buy. So great is the accommodation provided by the system that purchases required on the provincial Exchanges or the foreign Bourses are constantly sent to London to be made on the Stock Exchange there.'

Considerable discussion had taken place during the hearings on the topic of speculation (did the Stock Exchange encourage gambling?) and on the protection of the public against fraudulent or questionable ventures such as those cited in the case histories. The Commission felt that the Exchange could hardly be held responsible for gambling on the part of the public, although stiffer penalties should be exacted on members who indulged in 'extravagant speculation' among themselves. More interesting was the attitude revealed by the report to whether the Committee could do more in its vetting of quoted companies. It was criticised not for doing too little, but for on occasion doing too much. The very fact that a company was quoted was liable to give it 'a sort of spurious stamp of genuineness or soundness', and sometimes the Exchange gave investors the impression that listing and recommendation were one and the same. One suggestion was that enquiries might 'be undertaken by some public functionary and enforced by law', although one Commission

▲ 'Birds of Paradise':
a caricature by
Carruthers Gould

member objected to this.

More revolutionary was the Commission's suggestion that the Stock Exchange should be incorporated either by Royal Charter or by Act of Parliament, with by-laws only alterable by the Board of Trade or 'some other public authority' – a method of state regulation to which three of the four dissenters objected. As far as brokers' commissions were concerned, the Report agreed that it was unnecessary to fix them. A Committee on the Official List should be set up, to 'dissipate unjust suspicions' and to preserve the confidence of clients in their brokers; bargain-marking should be made compulsory; and, perhaps most radical of all, it was suggested that the public might be able to visit the House, to see for itself that all was fair and above board. Outside brokers and their 'bucket-shops' (a term that perhaps surprisingly was already in use at this date) should be licensed.

The net effect of all this effort was almost non-existent. None of the four major suggestions put forward by a majority of the Commissioners (legislation against pre-allotment dealings; an independent body to arbitrate on settlement and official quotation; incorporation; and admittance of the general public) was adopted. A few minor cosmetic changes were made, but the spirit of *laissez-faire* and the fear of offending powerful City interests which had certainly lain behind the 'mouse of a report' meant that business could, and did, continue much as usual.

FREEDOM FROM THE CORPORATION'S YOKE

One indirect result of the Royal Commission which was unanimously welcomed by members, was the sloughing off of the hated submission to the Corporation of the City of London. Some alleviation had been achieved by the Brokers' Relief Act of 1870, but, although this abolished the bonds and sureties which brokers had to guarantee to the City authorities, various other irksome conditions still obtained and had attracted the disapproval of the Royal Commission. In 1884 the Exchange told the Corporation that it intended to bring in a Bill to abolish the Brokers' Rent (which brought in an income of around £9,000 a year); the City authorities capitulated and the final Brokers' Relief Act of 1884 passed unopposed and came into force in September 1886. The centuries-old yoke was finally removed.

GORGONZOLA HALL

The major event of the 1880s, however, was yet another extension of the Stock Exchange. There had already been several enlargements since the rebuilding in the middle of the century; from 1880 onwards the Managers had been acquiring, piecemeal, various buildings fronting on to Throgmorton Street and Old Broad Street. Mr J.J. Cole was retained as architect, and he designed a large building adjacent to the old Exchange. This was the New House, its predecessor being known as the Old House, and was opened on 9 January 1885. It contained the Foreign Market, the offices for the Managers, an entrance and offices for tenants in Old Broad Street, and, most notable of all, a huge dome seventy feet in diameter and 100 feet high.

The style of the New House was described as 'Italian, almost Roman', with massive pillars, entrance lobbies and staircase all of Pavonazza marble – the walls of the old House were also covered with marble at the same time – its curious veining immediately attracting the nickname of Gorgonzola Hall. The New House created an additional 8,000 square feet of space, and was originally floored in oak two inches thick: but the boots of members quickly wore it away, and it was replaced with teak. The basement contained a much extended Settling Room, lined with oak panelling and glazed tiles. The Committee's offices were next door, originally approached by a handsome marble staircase which was later demolished to make more room; the Committee Room itself, forty feet long, had plaster panels and wallpaper of an Italian design by the artist Walter Crane, a friend and associate of William Morris in the Arts and Crafts Society. The Managers' Room was less imposing but still over twenty feet long, and the floors above these offices were occupied by the Settling

74

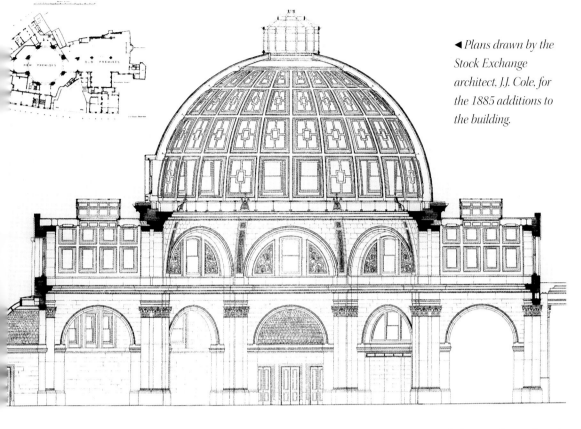

◀ *Plans drawn by the Stock Exchange architect, J.J. Cole, for the 1885 additions to the building.*

Department 'where the work of adjusting the accounts is carried on while members sleep.'

Gorgonzola Hall was not immediately popular; the Managers' meetings – usually concerned with staff problems, arguments about the price, quantity and quality of coal and the preponderance of undesirable people (including 'beggars of the roughest and dirtiest kind') hanging round the entrance – were preoccupied during the winter and spring of 1885 with complaints about the inadequate 'warm air system' of heating the new building. Members frequently had to wear their overcoats during working hours, and much illness was ascribed to the draughts and chill.

THE FIRST BARINGS CRISIS

A chill of a different kind ran through the City at the end of the decade. The merchant banks were all at this date handling foreign government loans and trying to extend their businesses in other ways: Barings, the foremost City house, promoted banking, railway and water companies in Argentina and Uruguay. When credit became tight in 1890 it was trapped with depleted assets and temporarily unsaleable shares, and on 8 November was forced to call on the help of the Bank of England.

The firm's failure would have brought ruin not only to many members of the Exchange,

▲ *'Same Old Game': a* **Punch** *cartoon of the Barings crisis, November 1890.*

▲ *An early photograph of 'Gorgonzola Hall'.*

but to banks, discount houses and the whole financial system, and the Bank of England's Governor Lidderdale acted promptly by raising a guarantee fund, on the strength of which the Bank lent Barings the money it needed. While not directly involved in the negotiations, the House shared in the general relief that the crisis had been averted, and on 30 December the Chairman, Deputy Chairman and Secretary of the Exchange called on Lidderdale and presented him with an address of thanks for 'the firm and decisive manner in which your great influence as Governor was so wisely and courageously exercised.'

Barings was subsequently reorganised as a limited company and after several years managed to pay off all its debts without recourse to the guarantors.

High Noon 1890–1914

THE FIRST SOUTH AFRICAN GOLD MINING COMPANY floated in London was the evocatively named Limpopo Mining Co. in 1846: there was a certain amount of speculation in this company and others which followed it, although this never reached anything like boom proportions. During the 1880s gold was discovered in the Rand by the Struben brothers, leading to the foundation of Johannesburg (and the establishment of that city's Stock Exchange) on what had previously been farming land, but it was not until 1894 that 'Kaffirs', as the South African mining shares were known, became a really popular market.

THE KAFFIR MARKET

The depression following the Barings crisis was lifting, the Yankee market was flourishing, and towards the end of 1894 an American mining engineer, John Hays Hammond, set about canvassing the jobbers and brokers specialising in African mining shares, providing charts and diagrams of deep-level mines to be hung in their offices, embellished with alluring estimates of likely profits. The *Financial Times*, founded six years earlier, profited enormously by publishing the prospectuses of the new companies, and by the middle of November a full-scale boom was under way. However, it brought problems in its wake. The Committee did not officially 'recognise' the South African securities, ostensibly because they were not issued publicly in the approved manner – although this was equally true of many foreign government securities and most American railway shares, both of which were accorded a quotation in the *Official List* and cleared in the Stock Exchange Clearing House. These privileges were denied to the Kaffir market, most of whose dealings took place in the nearby streets where many of the dealers in mining shares had their offices, amidst scenes of hubbub and excitement which proved alluring enough to attract some jobbers away from their regular markets.

Two of the more prominent jobbers who made the switch from the American market, accompanied by much good-natured ragging from their colleagues, were Tom Nickalls, the Erie King, and the extrovert Harry Paxton, who had won a celebrated walking match from London to Croydon against a fellow member in 1891. He covered the distance within one minute and eighteen seconds of his allotted 'time allowance', despite the facts that his opponent was a well-known athlete and that Paxton himself weighed nearly nineteen stone. A good deal of members' money was riding on the result, although it is doubtful if any wager equalled the £7,000 that Paxton had lost to Nickalls the year before on the outcome of the Oxford and Cambridge boat race.

Paris played a major role in the Kaffir market, as arbitrage was done between there and London, whose role as a financial centre was strengthened by its provision of a ready market in the shares, and the fact that it allowed speculators to carry over accounts from one fortnight to the next. The London money market lent large amounts of short-term money to the principal jobbers and brokers who were involved with Kaffirs, and many syndicates and investment groups were set up specifically to exploit the boom. Their usual method of operation was to buy large blocks of shares on a rising market, hoping to be able to offload them again before the price began to fall. Other factors contributing to the boom were that many mines were controlled from London, by firms of mining engineers based in the City, and London was by now well established as the leading bullion market.

'In clubs and trains, in drawing rooms and boudoirs, people are discussing "Rands" and "Modders"; even tradesmen and old ladies have taken to studying the *Mining Manual*, the rules of the Stock Exchange, the highways and byways of stockbroking,' noted a financial journalist, concluding that 'in short, we are in one of those eras of feverish speculative activity.' Purchase of Rand shares during the boom was estimated at some £40 million. One of the many brokers who made handsome sums of money out of mining was Ronald Herbert Savory, a partner of Foster & Braithwaite, who bought himself two estates on the proceeds, one in Chertsey and the other, Kelling Hall, in Norfolk.

Of more lasting consequence was a change that older members noted with disapproval. An influx of new members, unschooled in the *mores* of the Exchange, disrupted the previously fairly even tenor of the market, where each broker traditionally dealt with a particular firm of jobbers in each market - even to the point that if a broker came into the market and found 'his' jobber absent, the other jobbers would endeavour to find their missing colleague. During the Kaffir boom, such niceties were discarded, and this change in market manners proved permanent.

On Christmas Eve 1894 the market was still booming, with crowds of brokers blocking Throgmorton Street long after the House had closed, bidding for shares in the new account; a staff of forty worked on the settlement throughout Christmas Day. The mid-January settlement proved equally chaotic and exhausting. The Committee, in the face of mounting criticism, took no action – a state of affairs ascribed by one financial paper to the fact that most of them were elderly, had 'in the vernacular, "made their pile", and who had notions that anything outside securities of a high and dry character ought rather to be impeded than assisted.' Eventually the Clearing House did allow in some of the major South African securities such as Buffelsdoorn and Consolidated Investment, but the after-hours scramble in the street went on.

Other shares were also on the rise during the Kaffir boom, notably Westralians, following the discovery of gold in Coolgardie and Kalgoorlie in Western Australia at the beginning of the decade. However, Kaffirs, boosted by orders from overseas and especially Paris, were still supreme – French investors took nearly £100,000 worth of mining shares during 1895, and on one day in April the scene in Throgmorton Street was likened by the press to Babel, with the excitement being such 'that it was difficult for two parties interested in the same stock to get together.' By the time the Tories returned to power in the middle of that year, a political editor noted that 'speculation had seized the public mind to an unprecedented degree' and that 'the riches of the rand had created a feverish excitement in the public mind that penetrated every part of the country.' After reaching its apogee in August, however, the boom began to falter; massive selling in Paris the next month sent prices plummeting. It was the beginning of a downward slide which even the intervention of Barney Barnato, rumoured to have laid out £3 million in support of shares in which he had a particular interest, could not halt.

Gloom prevailed, darkening after the Jameson Raid on 31 December. Two troopers who had taken part in the raid were later

▲ *A caricature of the financier Barney Barnato, as the ringmaster of the 'Kaffir Circus' in rehearsal for the Stock Exchange's Christmas pantomime.*

allowed to walk through the House 'unmolested' and indeed were loudly cheered, although the Committee took a dim of view of their visit and suspended the jobber responsible, Tom Nickalls' brother William, for two weeks. The boom was fizzling out, and many of the companies floated at the height of the excitement proved of no value and disappeared, justifying the old description of a mine as 'a hole in the ground owned by a liar.'

SETTLEMENT PROBLEMS

The chaos surrounding the arrangements for mining settlement remained a source of resentment for many members, and the Committee came under sporadic attack for its apparent indifference to the problem. At the elections of March 1896 eleven new members stood for election to the Committee, on a platform calling for reforms including changes to the process of buying-in and selling-out and 'the improvement of the Settlement Department.' All thirty existing members also stood for re-election, and 2,588 members turned out to vote instead of the usual few hundred (in 1889, only eleven had bothered to do so). Seven of the 'old guard' were defeated, and the Committee of Reform, as it was dubbed, carried out a series of adjustments including setting up a new Buying-in and Selling-out Department, appointed by the Committee, to be responsible for tracing the transaction in question to whoever was responsible, and claiming the difference.

SHARE AND LOAN

Another department, the Share and Loan, was the subject of unwelcome attention when its Secretary, Sir Henry Charles Burdett, resigned after seventeen years' service. He was a self-made man who had combined his post at the Stock Exchange with much philanthropic work on behalf of hospital charities, and he was greatly put out, on resignation, to be given a

cheque for one thousand guineas – with the suggestion that he should buy himself 'a service of plate' – but no pension. When he enquired about this he was rather brusquely informed by the Managers that the circumstances of his retirement (he was only fifty years old) did not justify a pension, and that 'they were sure that members of the Stock Exchange would be opposed to any such grant.' Sir Henry riposted with claims that he had added nearly £4,000 a year to the resources of the Stamp Department by reorganising it, and had invested a capital sum of £30,000 in *Burdett's Official Intelligence.*

The Managers remained adamant and no pension was forthcoming, whereupon he sent back the cheque in a huff and appealed directly to the members. They too were unmoved, apparently feeling that the heavy amount of outside work he had carried on,

◀ *A caricature by 'Quiz' of Sir Henry Charles Burdett, KCB, Secretary of the Stock Exchange Share and Loan department.*

The Battle of Throg. Street

The outdoor dealing in mining shares led to the episode known as the 'Battle of Throg. Street', which rapidly became the stuff of Stock Exchange legend. Members had been allowed a virtual monopoly of the streets in the neighbourhood for after-hours trading, but on the evening of 19 March 1895, it was evident that the City police, after several warnings, intended to bring a test case. There were more police about than usual, and some 'experimental hustling' took place; a member named Macbrair was arrested for obstruction, struggled, and was led ignominiously away by three policemen. A bold but misguided attempt at rescue resulted in three more arrests, and the unlucky members were hauled through the streets accompanied by a throng of their colleagues plus various passers-by. 'Are there any witnesses?' asked the inspector at the police station. 'The whole crowd says they're witnesses,' was the lugubrious reply of one of the constables. The offenders were bailed, and greeted with stupendous cheering on their return to the House.

The following day they appeared at the Guildhall in front of Alderman Faudel Phillips, all four charged with obstruction and one member additionally with assaulting the police. There was so much noise, laughter and general badinage among the spectators that the court was several times threatened with closure. The Alderman upheld the right of the police to keep the thoroughfare clear, two defendants were fined £10 and £5 respectively and the other two cases were dismissed, although they were all told that there would be 'disagreeable consequences' if their actions were repeated. That evening Throgmorton Street was more crowded than ever – 'I want to pass along, but there are so many policemen in the way that I can't,' one member remarked plaintively. A chain of empty cabs drove up and down the street; one was commandeered by the irrepressible Harry Paxton, who was loudly cheered as he rode along bowing to either side. 'Who pays for these cabs?' he shouted

'The Block of Throgmorton Street', showing 'the Leviathan', Harry Paxton, being arraigned by an inspector and marched off by the police.

when another procession took place, obviously arranged by the police. He in turn was arrested and taken to court, but his case was dismissed – although the presiding Alderman noted that the street had been turned into a bear-garden and must be open for all, and not just for members. Maybe the Stock Exchange could provide extra accommodation, he suggested, perhaps in the Royal Exchange?

Two months later, when a third incident took place, Alderman Bell remarked that he could not understand why 'members of the Stock Exchange which took heavy fees could not provide a place of sufficient size where they could transact their business.' The Committee's rather feeble response was to caution members against 'countenancing by their presence the scandalous disturbances which take place in Throgmorton Street after the closing of the House.'

plus the lucrative directorships he had taken on immediately on leaving the Exchange, did not justify a pension. His successor received a considerably smaller salary – £1,500 a year instead of Sir Henry's £4,500, which had included commutation of profits from the *Official Intelligence* – and it was stipulated that he was to be in his office each morning by 10.30 a.m. The following year 'this monument of research and statistical perfection – this encyclopaedia of Stock Exchange securities' as a contemporary called it, appeared for the first time as *The Stock Exchange Official Intelligence*. However, it continued to be known as 'Burdett' for many decades to come.

CELEBRATIONS

The House was able to forget the disagreeable events surrounding Sir Henry's departure in a series of patriotic celebrations as the end of the century approached. The first was Queen Victoria's Diamond Jubilee on 21 June 1897. 'Nowhere throughout the British Empire – and this is saying a very great deal – was the completion of the sixty years of the reign celebrated with more enthusiasm or in a more remarkable manner than in the Stock Exchange,' remarked a contemporary observer. An official programme was produced, and a message

◄◄*The American Market taking place in Shorter's Court after the Exchange closed at 3.30pm.*

◄ *Charlie Clarke leading the House in singing the national anthem, on the day of the outbreak of the 'Transvaal War', 11 October 1899.*

sent to Windsor Castle: 'The Members of the Stock Exchange respectfully send their loyal and heartfelt congratulations to Her Most Gracious Majesty. They have just with the greatest enthusiasm sung the National Anthem.' Members and, exceptionally, some ladies, assembled in the Great Eastern Railway Market for cheering and patriotic songs, conducted by Charlie Clarke, 'the wag of the House'; the noise and songs 'eventually died away, but not until some days afterwards', while bunting and illuminations remained in place for three weeks.

The next excitement to stir the fervour of the Exchange was the arrival of Lord Kitchener, who, 'with the laurels of his Soudan victory fresh upon his brow' came to the City in December 1898 to raise funds for Gordon College, which he was establishing in Khartoum. After visiting the Mansion House he came to Capel Court, and was greeted by an immense ovation which all but drowned the attempts to sing 'See the Conquering Hero Comes.' 'I have not come here for nothing, gentlemen,' said Kitchener as some of the Committee escorted him round the Exchange, 'I want £100,000, and I expect to get it.' More than a thousand pounds was subscribed on the spot.

The loyalty of the Exchange was noisily demonstrated on the occasion of the Queen's eightieth birthday on 24 May 1899. The slump in Trunks and Kaffirs was forgotten as Charlie Clarke climbed on to the Grand Trunk bench, holding a copy of the National Anthem in one hand and a walking-stick baton in the other. 'As the clock struck eleven the jarring markets subdued their clamour, and, amidst a general shout of "Hats off!" a pair of trumpeters stole timidly to the side of the conductor and blared the first notes of the National Anthem', followed by further patriotic singing and the despatch of yet another loyal address.

THE BOER WAR

On the day of the outbreak of the Boer War (or the Transvaal War as it was usually known at the time), 11 October 1899, Charlie Clarke made his most dramatic gesture. After leading the House in singing the National Anthem, he announced that President Kruger had 'failed to comply with his bargains.' To immense cheering Kruger was then symbolically 'hammered' and hanged and burned in effigy, and around a thousand members marched to the Guildhall to declare their support for government policy.

The war was 'peculiarly connected with the Stock Exchange,' noted a financial writer of the day; 'it has been undertaken on behalf of the Uitlanders, practically without exception engaged in the mining industry; its effects, it is trusted, will be to bring more prosperity to the Rand mining companies.' The National Debt was considerably enlarged, and the Kaffir market was 'in a state of nervous anxiety.' Even so members contributed generously to various charities, providing over £20,000 within the first month of the war to funds such as the Lord Mayor's fund for Transvaal refugees, and donating nearly £3,000 in cash plus thirty-eight of their own horses to a horse fund. Charlie Clarke – who else? – brought a pony on to the floor of the House with a collecting box on its back for money to buy tobacco for the Royal Dublin Fusiliers.

As the war dragged on, false rumours of the relief of Ladysmith circulated, much as rumours of the end of the Napoleonic wars had done years earlier, the relief when it actually occurred in March 1900 being celebrated by the wearing of red-white-and-blue favours and scarves, and cheers for Generals Buller and White. On the news of the relief of Mafeking in May, the City, in the words of the *Financial Times*, went 'almost crazy'; the Exchange was open, but no work was done. A stereoscopic photograph of the crowded floor of the House was taken (copies being sold in aid of war charities), and the Exchange 'then degenerated into a somewhat riotous condition, members marching about in cheering columns, waving flags and blowing trumpets, while the noise of the inevitable coaching horn was heard over all.'

A HUNDRED YEARS IN CAPEL COURT

The new century was a reminder that the centenary of the move to Capel Court would occur in 1901, and in July 1900 a two-man sub-committee was appointed by the Managers to decide on an appropriate form of celebration. It was agreed that a banquet should take place

▲ *The Stock Exchange celebrating the Relief of Mafeking, 18 May 1900.*

on Saturday, 12 May 1901, the anniversary of the laying of the foundation stone, and a guest list, headed by the Prince of Wales, was drawn up. The dinner would take place in the Stock Exchange itself 'if that could be arranged': if not, in one of the halls of the City Livery companies such as the Goldsmiths or the Fishmongers. The Prince had to decline, on the grounds that he had already accepted too many engagements for the following summer, and all the plans were halted by the death of Victoria on 22 January 1901; in the end the banquet was cancelled, the centenary merely being marked, at the request of the Managers, by closing the Exchange on the Saturday in question.

'The House, emotional to excess in other directions, never weeps', but dealing virtually ceased at the news of Victoria's death and the sound of the ticker-tape was almost the only one to be heard. Consols barely moved – from $96\frac{1}{4}$ the night before she died, to $96\frac{1}{2}$ the day after. 'This was taken as incontrovertible evidence of national stability.' Reflection, like

SOME NOTABLE FRAUDSTERS

Ernest Terah Hooley (1859–1947)
Hooley was an enormously successful company
promoter whose greatest coup was the Dunlop rubber
flotation in 1896, from which he made some £2 million.
However, he was three times imprisoned for fraud and
died bankrupt.

Horatio Bottomley (1860–1933)
The Stock Exchange would have nothing to do with the
company promoter Horatio Bottomley after an unsavoury
incident concerning Westralian shares. His colourful
career included involvement with the early days of the
Financial Times, *the establishment of the super-patriotic*
magazine John Bull, *a spell as a bankrupt and as the*
Independent MP for South Hackney, imprisonment for
fraudulent conversion from 1922–27, and death in poverty
and obscurity.

weeping, was something the House was not given to, but maybe some of the more thought-ful members spared a few moments to look back over the past century.

Business was flat as Edward VII came to the throne – the House was concerned with the aftermath of the crash of the London & Globe Finance Corporation in December 1900, a company floated by the infamous financier Whitaker Wright, the collapse of which caused the failure of thirteen stockbroking firms and twenty-nine members, one of whom had been on the Exchange for fifty years: 'the very hand of Barker, the waiter, shook like an aspen leaf as, amid death-like silence, he announced failure after failure.'

However, a brief survey of the first hundred years in Capel Court told a tale of almost unbroken expansion and prosperity. By now, over 3,000 commercial, financial, industrial,

Barney Barnato (1852–97)
Known as the 'Ringmaster of the Kaffir Circus', Barney
Barnato had an almost magical flair for the stock market,
although he was never a member of the Exchange. During
the Kaffir boom he operated from a club in Throgmorton
Street known as the Thieves' Kitchen. On a voyage home
from South Africa in June 1897, he suddenly leapt
overboard, was rescued, but died without regaining
consciousness.

Whitaker Wright (1845–1904)
Whitaker Wright was the architect of the London &
Globe Finance Corporation, whose crash caused havoc
on the Stock Exchange at the turn of the century. He
was eventually charged with fraud, found guilty and
sentenced to seven years' penal servitude, but
committed suicide with a cyanide pill before he could
begin the sentence.

land and investment companies, and over 1,000 mining companies were quoted. There were 1,052 proprietors, 4,227 members and 2,771 clerks; and apart from the overall growth in numbers, the character of the House had changed considerably in the last twenty years. Victorian literature contains several memorable portrayals of stockbrokers, such as Trollope's weak, vulgar Sexty Parker or Thackeray's Jos Sedley in *Vanity Fair* who, in his prosperous days, maintained a 'famous' cellar of port and drove around town in 'a large family coach with two fat horses in blazing harness, driven by a fat coachman in a three-cornered hat and wig' and a black servant sitting beside him. Most of these fictional characters have something undeniably raffish about them; but by the end of the century the social standing of the Stock Exchange had risen, and the financial prospects it offered had begun to attract members of the aristocracy and the upper classes. As early as 1875 Lord Walter Campbell, brother-in-law of Victoria's daughter Princess Louise, had caused a stir by becoming a member, and by 1900 there were three members of the House of Lords, nearly thirty sons of peers and ten members of the House of Commons. One titled young gentleman, however, became notorious when he was over-heard telling a friend that in the House he felt 'like an orchid in a turnip field,' and 'an orchid' was swiftly adopted as a nickname for any member with a title. In the early 1900s C.T. 'Pubbles' Barclay, a Cambridge rowing blue, became the first old Etonian jobber when he joined the firm of Hensley & Aston in the Railway market; however his health was not good and he subsequently decided to become a broker with Sheppards, Pelly, Price & Pott, as broking enabled him to sit down rather than spend most of the day on his feet.

There was a large number of members of foreign birth, espccially Germans and Swiss but also including Canadians, South Africans and Australians. Many British partnerships recruited for-eigners to strengthen their overseas connections, such as William Koch, a Belgian, who was hired by Panmure Gordon in 1877 and who later became head of the firm, and several Germans who became partners in Helbert Wagg and Raphael. An effort in 1891 to restrict the entry into the market of non-British members, who were at that date accused of starting a round of cuts in commission rates in their struggle for business, had little effect. In 1876 there were an esti-mated sixty to seventy foreign members, comprising something over 3 per cent of the total; by 1914 there were 214, or 4.5 per cent of the total.

THE RUBBER BOOM

A brief but fierce rubber boom took place in 1910, fuelled by the enormous increase in the demand for rubber in the UK by the elec-tricity and infant motor industries. Dealing became so hectic that one member was rumoured to have been discovered in a faint at the end of a day's trading, having collapsed earlier but remained upright because of the crush around him. Certainly the rubber market was comparable with a rugger scrum, with members and their clerks fighting to get into it and, having done so, taking some time to fight their way out again.

THE STOCK EXCHANGE MURDER

Sir Marcus Samuel became Lord Mayor of London in 1902 and the first case he heard on the Bench at the Mansion House was a murder – 'a rare thing fortunately in the City', as he himself noted.

The victim was Reggie Baker, a jobber in the Westralian market, who had been summoned outside by a note delivered by a telegraph messenger working at Lombard Street Post Office. In the street he was stabbed to death with a clasp knife produced from the muff of the young woman who had sent in the note, a milliner's assistant known as 'Kitty' (her real name was Emma) Byron. When brought in front of the Lord Mayor in the Coroner's court she declared 'I killed him willingly, and he deserved it, and the sooner I am killed, the better.' The Coroner showed the knife – 'a very formidable weapon, with a blade fully four inches long' – and the inquiry was then adjourned. When it reassembled a few days later, several witnesses testified against Kitty Byron, including a cutler from Oxford Street who had sold her the knife.

The pitiful story quickly unfolded. Kitty and Reggie were lovers, living in lodgings in Duke Street while he awaited a divorce; she had bought the knife and killed him after learning from a maid in the house that he intended to 'discard her' after his divorce came through. Their landlady, to whom Reggie owed rent, told the court that she had asked Kitty, 'If you are not his wife, why do you stay with him?' to which the pathetic reply was 'I love him so, and another thing, I cannot get a character for another place.'

She was found guilty of manslaughter, to the charitable satisfaction of the Stock Exchange who had hoped that the 'hapless creature', obviously dragged down by association with 'a man of loose habits', would not be convicted of murder. The Lord Mayor, however, described the verdict of the Coroner's jury as 'on the evidence, impossible to understand.' At the Old Bailey shortly afterwards the new jury found her guilty of 'wilful murder' but made 'the strongest possible recommendation to mercy'. Kitty was sentenced to death. Numerous petitions were got up in her favour, including one by Stock Exchange members and one by clerks from the House, and on Christmas Eve it was learned that the Home Secretary had advised the King to commute the death sentence to one of penal servitude for life, which was duly done.

ARREST OF KITTY

Drawings from the **Illustrated Police News** *of scenes from 'The Sensational Tragedy in the City', 22 November 1902.*

DOMESTIC MATTERS

Various administrative matters occupied the early years of the century. Subscriptions were raised from thirty to forty guineas and on Lady Day (25 March) 1900 it was decided that clerks should also pay this sum after four years' apprenticeship – their entrance fee went up to 250 guineas, and that for members who had not been clerks was set at 500 guineas. The question of dual control resurfaced. H.H. Paine, a member who was trying to alter the terms of the Deed of Settlement in 1901, urged its abolition and wanted every member to become a shareholder in a new Stock Exchange company with a tenfold increase in capital; an annuity scheme would 'induce members no longer actively engaged in business to retire.' (One of the jobbers in the railway market, William Baines, had been a member since 1836, and he was able to recall another elderly man who had been in the French army during Napoleon's retreat from Moscow.)

Even if all the old and inactive members had retired, however, the problems of overcrowding would not have been solved. Managers and Committee were all too aware of this, and when over 3,000 members petitioned for a sub-committee to investigate the whole question of restricted membership, they had to act. In 1904 the nomination system – which lasted for over sixty years – was brought in: would-be new members had to buy a nomination from a retiring member or from the estate of one who had died. There was no sum fixed for a nomination, which became, as one commentator put it, 'not so much an auction, more a ransom.' Clerks with more than four years' service were allowed to put their names on a waiting list for election without nomination. They also had to buy one share in the Exchange, while others were required to buy three. These changes must have pleased the reformer Paine – all members were now or would eventually become proprietors, and the new regulation spelt the ultimate death of dual control: one day in the future, Managers and Committee would merge. Joining the Exchange was still comparatively cheap; a clerk wishing to be elected would need about £450 (worth perhaps twenty times as much today) plus a share, then worth approximately £175; yet only a few years later an American financial writer noted the cost of joining the New York or French exchanges as the dollar and franc equivalents of £16,000 and a massive £92,000 respectively.

THE END OF DUAL CAPACITY

The end of dual capacity – acting as both jobber and broker – was brought about in 1909 as a result of the Committee's ruling that the two functions must henceforth be completely distinct. If a jobber wanted to become a broker, or *vice versa*, permission must be sought from the Committee. Brokers could deal with non-members if this gave them genuinely better terms, but jobbers were not allowed to do so, with the exception of those who practised arbitrage – that is, transacting business with foreign brokers, usually in Wall Street or Paris.

▲ *'During a City Crisis:*
a member is 'hammered'
as markets plunge in
1907.

Another running sore, that of commissions, was attended to the following year, probably because of the separation of capacity. The
Committee held a meeting with the Council of Associated Stock
Exchanges in the provinces, which was considering the introduction
of fixed minimum commissions, and discovered that the Glasgow
Stock Exchange had already done so. The Committee in Capel Court,
true to form, took no immediate action, but in 1911 it was again in
communication with the Associated Stock Exchanges, this time
pointing out that one of the problems was the impossibility of
enforcing the rule restraining a dealer from dealing with a non-
member 'if he is able to employ a broker at a nominal remuneration
to pass his bargains through.'

However, the Committee was by now of the opinion that a minimum scale was essential, and one was drawn up and submitted to
a vote by the whole House. It was defeated. After some amendment
it was re-submitted and passed by a small majority of 1,670 votes to
1,551; in March 1912 a scale was adopted. The charge was 2s 6d per

► *The Liveliest Place of Business in the World' – Ragging scene in the Stock Exchange, 1908.*

cent on stock, which had been fairly standard for some time, and varying commissions from $\frac{1}{2}$d for those of five shillings to fifteen shillings, to 2s 6d per share on those of £20 to £25. For shares of higher value the charge was $\frac{1}{2}$%.

These changes to capacity and commission rates were to have very far-reaching consequences for the Stock Exchange. In both cases the bigger, more progressive firms were against the measures, which were voted through by the large number of members operating on their own or in small partnerships. They were in essence restrictive practices – the direct, if unstated, result of the fact that things had never picked up again after the end of the Boer War, and there was simply not enough business to go round a House which had received so many new members as a result of the Kaffir boom. The open communication which had been in place between London dealers and provincial brokers was limited because transactions now had to go through London brokers and bear commission charges, reversing the trends towards external contacts which had been fostered by improved communications. The new 'ring fences' can be said to have artificially delayed the deregulation of the market, which finally took place in the Big Bang, by nearly three-quarters of a century.

LIMITED LIABILITY

Gilt-edged securities were now declining in volume, and formed only about 10 per cent of all quoted stocks, of which half went to fund the National Debt. The major success story of the last years of the nineteenth and first years of the twentieth centuries was that of commercial companies. These had been growing in number since the passage of the Joint Stock Companies Act and the Limited Liabilities Acts in the 1850s and 60s. Coal, iron and steel companies were among the first to take advantage of limited liability, including Cammell and Co. and John Brown & Co.; and there was a Channel Tunnel company as early as 1872. Cunard became a limited company in 1878 (offering its shares to the public two years later), but even in 1882 there were still only £64 million of Stock Exchange securities in British industry out of a total quoted of £5,800 million.

The popularity of industrial shares increased sharply during the boom of the late 1880s and the cheap money of the 1890s. (Bank Rate was unchanged at 2% from February 1894 to September 1896, and the yield on Consols averaged only 2.475 for three years.) Nearly all the big flotations carried out in London were offers to the public of shares in established businesses. By the outbreak of war quoted joint-stock companies controlled virtually all the banks and nearly all the larger breweries, and dominated the cement, wallpaper, soap and tobacco industries, as well as most large units in coal, iron and steel and heavy engineering.

THE OUTBREAK OF WAR

Business was still slack in Capel Court during the spring and early summer of 1914, although the jobber Hubert Meredith doubted 'if one person in a thousand anticipated what was to be the climax.' Meredith reported a conversation he had in July 1914, after the news of the assassination at Sarajevo, with Le Blanc Smith, a member of the Stock Exchange Committee: 'I suppose,' I said, 'if anything in the nature of a European war were to break out, you would close the Stock Exchange?' He ridiculed the suggestion. 'If you ever see,' he said, ' that business on the London Stock Exchange has been stopped, you can rest assured that the end of the world has come.'

It was not until Austria-Hungary's ultimatum to Serbia on 23 July that the financial markets began to reflect the turn of events. Between 27 and 29 July the exchanges of Paris,

THE BANK RATE DOUBLED
The Globe
CITY SPECIAL

MARTIAL LAW THROUGHOUT GERMANY
WESTMINSTER
LATE EXTRA.

Evening News
STOCK EXCHANGE CLOSED
12 O'CLOCK EDITION

▲ *'Newsboys' in the City before the First World War.*

Brussels, Toronto, Madrid, Vienna and Amsterdam were closed, and time bargains were suspended on the German and Italian exchanges. On 30 July St Petersburg and Montreal closed. The Committee for General Purposes met late into the night: on arrival in the City the following morning, members found a notice stating that the Stock Exchange was closed and that the mid-August settlement would be deferred to 27 August. Germany declared a state of war the same day. Le Blanc Smith's prediction had been confounded, and the world of Capel Court, if not at an end, would never be the same again.

THE HOUSE AT PLAY

*S*ports and games of almost every description had keen and often extremely successful practitioners among members of the Stock Exchange. Some of them, such as cricket, shooting, racing and stalking, naturally provided the all-important social contacts which could lead to profitable business. A book in two volumes, *The House on Sport*, published at the beginning of the twentieth century, contained chapters written by members proficient in sixty sports including pigeon shooting, boxing, swimming, figure skating and rowing, as well as some which seem unlikely to have provided new business prospects, such as tricycle racing and shooting wild sheep in the Sahara.

Sporting wagers were naturally frequent, and one made in the Kaffir market about walking the fifty-two and a quarter miles from London to Brighton – 'I'll bet you won't do it in fifteen hours!' – resulted in the famous Stock Exchange Walking Race on 1 May 1903. Cups, money, medals and trophies were presented to the prize fund, and those taking advertising space in the race programme included special boot makers, 'knitters of bone', a chiropodist and manufacturers of foot lotions and mutton extract. A doctor provided his services, free of charge, 'although luckily no mishap occurred to render them necessary on the road.'

The weather for the walk was 'more befitting a November hunting morning' than May Day, but sightseers crowded the route, few participants fell out, and none were disqualified. The winner, with a

A member arriving at Brighton at the end of the London to Brighton Walking Race on 1 May 1903.

time of nine and a half hours, was E.F. Broad, a 22-year-old clerk in the broking firm of Percy Marsden & Co., who had been in Margate with two professional trainers for the previous fortnight. Public interest was intense: 'The wiring of the results and full particulars for the press' took about a thousand telegrams, and the race was said to have 'set all England walking.'

War and Peace
1914–1929

THE CRISIS WHICH HIT THE CITY ON THE OUTBREAK OF WAR was probably felt more strongly in the Stock Exchange than anywhere else. It was the largest and most important securities market in the world, and the closure in the last days of July of the continental bourses, as well as the turbulence of the foreign exchange markets, meant that brokers who had bought stock for foreign clients were unable to receive payment - seven firms were hammered on 29 July for that reason. Prices fell sharply after England went to war with Germany on 4 August, which put at risk the many firms who were holding securities on borrowed money, and if overseas banks had insisted on calling in their loans the whole market might have collapsed.

The Committee's decision to close the Exchange until further notice and postpone settlements until the end of August provided a breathing space. The government announced a two-day extension of the August Bank Holiday, and Parliament hurried through a Postponement of Payments Act on 3 August. This put off almost all commercial payments, including those due on Stock Exchange transactions, for a month – subsequently extended for a further two months. During this period some of the foreign bourses re-opened and the foreign exchange markets settled down. The Act did not however relieve the problems of stockbroking firms holding securities on borrowed money; the Committee circulated members to get the true position and discovered that £81 million was borrowed, just under half of this from joint-stock banks and the bulk of the rest from overseas banks with offices in London. Enquiries in the provincial exchanges revealed a further £11 million outstanding.

The government was actively concerned and by the end of October (after various arrangements had been made to help the discount market and accepting houses) a scheme was announced under which the joint-stock banks, with a guarantee from the Bank of England, agreed not to press for further repayments of Stock Exchange loans, while the Committee undertook to ensure that the benefits of the scheme were passed by the money brokers to the ultimate borrowers. Meanwhile the Exchange itself remained closed, but this did not mean that deals were not taking place. A certain amount of business was done in the street, and rather more under what was known as the 'challenge system.' This had been available since 1911, and now became much more popular. It involved a broker who wanted to

FINANCING THE WAR

A poster by Frank Brangwyn, RA, advertising War Bonds.

The government financed the war with a series of loans on an unprecedented scale. The first was in November 1914, £350 million of 3½ % at 95, repayable in 1925/28. This was very successful, aided by the offer of the Bank of England to lend subscribers the issue price, on the security of the stock itself, at 1 per cent below Bank Rate. The following June there was a second War Loan, 4½ % 1925/45 issued at par, this time with the incentive that the public could buy it at Post Offices in small amounts – £25 bonds or even five-shilling vouchers. This was another success, raising a sum only a few millions less than the whole of the 1914 National Debt. The third, the 5% War Loan of 1917, was issued at 95 and repayable 1929/47 – another smash hit which raised over £2,000 million as the public heeded the urgings of the Chancellor, Bonar Law, to borrow from their banks and invest in it. The City was urged to supply 'all the silver bullets it can turn out' by the *Financial Times*, while the *Financial News* proclaimed that 'every Cheque is a She££ Fired at the German Trenches.'

deal in a particular stock advertising the fact, plus his telephone number, on the Exchange Telegraph Co.'s tape. In the middle of August the company offered to publish details of the challenges on their tape free of charge during the closure of the House, and the Committee gratefully accepted the offer.

Share auctions were also held by firms such as Knight Frank & Rutley, which were used by solicitors anxious to settle the estates of deceased clients, and the *Daily Mail* published prices at which readers wished to buy or sell shares. Predictably these various arrangements were the subject of complaints to the Committee, mostly on the grounds that they depressed prices. Jobbers in the Consols, Colonial stocks and Canadian railway markets came to an unofficial agreement 'in the interests of the banks and also to strengthen the hand of the Committee, in dealing with any scheme for the re-opening of the House', not to deal at prices below those obtaining on 30 August; however they complained that this effort at maintaining minimum prices was being frustrated by the various unofficial systems which had sprung up, and by the fact that jobbers in other markets were infringing on theirs. After considering these and other complaints, in mid-September the Committee issued a list of recommended minimum prices for all Trustee stocks, which were to be transacted for cash only with no options allowed.

Re-opening the Exchange

As the war news became slightly better towards the end of the year prices recovered and plans for re-opening the Exchange got under way, stimulated by the fact that some of the provincial exchanges had begun to allow informal sessions. The Committee had several priorities: it was necessary to take precautions against any sudden drop in prices which might occur if the war took a turn for the worse, and also to make sure that no enemies could gain access to the market. It was essential to prevent gold being dispersed by the sale of securities in London by neutrals, and government loans had to be protected from competition. The Committee sent its scheme for re-opening to the Chancellor of the Exchequer, and took part in negotiations with the Treasury, the Bank of England and the clearing banks. They agreed a set of temporary regulations and on Christmas Eve it was announced that the Exchange would re-open on 4 January 1915.

The restrictions under which dealing would, after an absence of five months, once more be allowed in the House were much more onerous than anything previously experienced. Minimum prices were to be maintained until the end of January at the earliest, and they could be amended or extended at the discretion of the Committee. All bargains were to be for cash only; no options were allowed (except in connection with old contracts). Any dealings in new issues made after 4 January 1915 needed the approval of both the Committee and the Treasury, and all securities dealt must have been in the physical possession of a UK resident since 30 September 1914; brokers had to obtain a written declaration from clients that they

The Stock Exchange War Memorial.

were not dealing either directly or indirectly on behalf of enemy aliens. No deals were allowed before 11 a.m and after 3 p.m. (or 1 p.m. on Saturdays).

A notice from the Committee and signed by its Secretary Edward Satterthwaite acknowledged that members would find these new rules irksome, but 'as they have been imposed by the Treasury and are recognised by the Committee as being "absolutely in the national interest" at the present time, the Committee are sure that they can rely upon the loyal acceptance of them by the Members of the Stock Exchange.'

As soon as the House had re-opened, members began to work hard to regain the business they had lost to alternative systems, most of which dwindled or disappeared altogether in the next few months, although the large provincial exchanges, primarily Liverpool and Manchester, managed to maintain the market in Consols which they had established during the five months the House had been closed. The system of minimum prices had never been popular in Capel Court, especially since the *Daily Mail* and those banks which in the words of disgruntled members 'touted for stockbroking business' were free of any such restriction. The Committee – whose hands were in any case tied by the Treasury – felt that they were necessary to protect both members and the public from any sharp falls which might follow bad war news, but by November 1915 British Funds, Indian and Colonial Corporation stocks and foreign stocks were removed from the list. Others followed and by July 1916 prices of all stocks were completely free.

Controls over new issues

New issues were another area giving rise to considerable problems, and control over capital issues got progressively tighter as the war progressed. At the end of January 1915 a committee under the chairmanship of Lord St Aldwyn, a former Chancellor of the Exchequer, was set up to advise the Treasury on the subject, and it was announced that foreign issues would not be allowed and that any for the Empire would only be permitted in cases of 'urgent necessity and special circumstance'; domestic issues would have to satisfy the Committee that they were in the national interest. There was an immediate flood of applications, some for wildly optimistic ventures such as re-building towns in Belgium after the war, others, which were mostly approved, for producing films (although building cinemas did not meet with success). *The Economist* estimated that around 1,400 applications were made in a three-week period, but as the government's own calls on the market increased it became more and more difficult to secure approval, and by early 1916 hardly any new issues were coming to market at all.

The previously lucrative American market dried up almost completely. As the British government was financing the purchase of war supplies in the USA for both the UK and the Allies, every possible source of dollars had to be tapped, and regulations progressively brought in culminated, in January 1917, in the government's acquisition of the power to requisition securities, which meant that many dollar stocks were taken over in this way. Home markets were also affected, partly because of further government requisition of such things as railway branch lines, which were torn up and sent over to the battlefields in France and Flanders. Many different estimates of the amount of securities that disappeared from the House have been made: the final figure was probably of the order of £1,000 million, as cited by the Chancellor, Austen Chamberlain, in his budget speech in 1919, where he was presumably referring to the total of private and official sales. This figure represented about a quarter of British holdings of overseas securities, but the loss to the Stock Exchange was exacerbated by the fact that what were sold were all high-quality stocks which had been the subject of wide and active dealings.

'Enemies' in the House

The loss of business was felt throughout the House, but those with significant amounts of foreign business were naturally most affected. Some members quit stockbroking altogether, going into commodity trading or becoming private bankers. However the group that suffered the most was the large contingent of members of German or Austrian birth or extraction. These, especially the German Jews, had presumably already become inured to a certain amount of fun being poked at their accents – before the war more German than English was reportedly spoken in some parts of the House, notably the copper and American markets. Remarks both anti-German and anti-Semitic were certainly far more overt than would be acceptable today, and often contained quite bitter jibes about undercutting prices, something of which foreign-born brokers were continually accused. Once war had broken out the position of this group, even though many of them were naturalised British citizens, became increasingly difficult. Their presence in the House caused considerable resentment, and after the sinking of the SS *Lusitania* by a German torpedo in May 1915, some ugly incidents took place. German and Austrian members who showed their faces on the floor were 'hustled' out, and eventually the Committee was pressurised into advising them to stay away from the market. Rather touchingly over a hundred of them posted in Capel Court public declarations of loyalty to the British cause, but in November the super-patriotic Charlie Clarke (he of the community singing) headed a large group which urged the Committee not to re-elect naturalised German and Austrian members, although with some exceptions.

The Committee took no direct action at this stage, although it was unsympathetic towards complaints of rough behaviour. However, a Stock Exchange Anti-German Union was formed and finally pushed the Committee into agreeing, in March 1917, not to re-elect some fifty of the 142 members of 'enemy birth' identified by the Union. A member called Edward Cuthbertson circulated his colleagues with a letter protesting at the Committee's action as 'a flagrant violation of the principles of justice and freedom.' He received one reply of almost unparalleled vindictiveness, referring to his 'beastly impudence' in daring to write it and expressing the wish that when 'your wife, daughters and female relations have been raped to death by the Hun, when your sons have been slaughtered by them, your house burned and your disgusting person driven into the ignominious slavery you so richly deserve, I hope you will see no occasion to change your views.' The writer went on to regret that there was 'no immediate prospect of your being put to the test by the sons, nephews and male relations of those friends on whose behalf you have indited such a nauseating and pusillanimous letter.'

In March 1918 the Committee ruled that no 'former subject of a foreign power' was eligible for membership unless he had been resident in a British dominion for ten years and naturalised for five; German, Austrian, Turkish and Bulgarian subjects were totally inadmissible except by permission of the Committee in 'special circumstances.' Two members who failed to gain re-election because of their German birth actually sued the Stock Exchange, but the Court of Chancery ruled that the Committee had the absolute power to elect or re-elect whom it chose. The ban on non-British members would last until 1971.

Whatever their origins, most firms which survived the war suffered not only personal tragedies but severely dented finances. Of those large firms whose accounts survive,

Cazenove, for example, made a hefty profit in the year ending March 1913 of £24,430 (worth about forty times as much today) and nearly £19,000 the following year, but during the war its profits averaged less than £4,000 a year. Foster & Braithwaite's total income fell and the minutes of a partners' meeting in 1916 expressed the position all too plainly: 'the War has caused a serious shrinkage in the value of securities necessitating a drastic writing down by reason of which and the contraction of business caused by the War there are no profits available for distribution . . .'

THE PEACETIME MARKET

When peace was finally declared in November 1918, Charlie Clarke was ill, but the tradition of community singing was upheld by Arthur Wrightson who conducted the National Anthem with a gold baton subscribed to by fellow members. Yet the general mood of the Stock Exchange was subdued. It was clear that the whole market had been permanently and radically altered over the past four years. Foreign investment, flourishing in the pre-war years, had come to a standstill; the American market had all but disappeared; the role of the Exchange within domestic money and capital markets had been severely curtailed by the restrictions on account trading, options and arbitrage. Meanwhile rival stock exchanges such as New York had flourished and offered newly strengthened competition, and at home banks and other non-members had gained valuable experience in selling securities.

There was also the question of relationships with provincial exchanges in Britain, which had been badly affected by prolonged wrangling over rates of commission and the failure to agree a national minimum. In 1916 some provincial brokers had formed the British Shareholder Trust Ltd, which, exasperated by what it described as the 'high-handed and overbearing attitude' of the London Stock Exchange, aimed to enable country brokers to investigate the soundness of new issues, provide a source for them to obtain 'sound issues at fair prices', and ensure that British capital should be used for the development of British industries and not 'for the purpose of German economic penetration.' It did not get very far – the London Committee ruled in January 1918 that no share of commission was to be given to any of its members, and many of them quit.

The size and composition of Stock Exchange membership had changed significantly. Jobbers still slightly outnumbered brokers, as they had done before the war, but recruitment to the profession had naturally dwindled during the war years, and although women had been successfully employed in some offices as typists and 'filists', most of them had to give up their jobs to men returning from the Forces. Overall membership fell from 4,855 in 1914 to 3,994 four years later, and there was considerable support among the members for keeping the numbers at or below 4,000. The Proprietors and Managers, whose income from subscriptions had fallen while expenses rose, were of course keen to expand numbers; a plan by the members to buy out the shareholders and run the institution themselves came to nothing and

NOTICE.

RULE 17.

COMMITTEE ROOM,
THE STOCK EXCHANGE.

THE THROWING OF PAPER BALLS & OTHER MISSILES IS STRICTLY PROHIBITED.

By Order,
EDWARD SATTERTHWAITE,
Secretary, C.G.P.

◄ *One of the many notices posted in the House.*

other schemes also foundered. Eventually, in the early 1920s, an unofficial ceiling of 4,000 was accepted by all parties, while subscriptions had to be put up.

Many of the wartime restrictions on the operations of the Exchange remained in force for some time. Control over domestic capital issues was ended in March 1919, and arbitrage business was officially permitted in April, although the Committee, to members' considerable annoyance, did not allow it until September. There were still problems as far as the American exchange was concerned and arbitrage dealings with New York did not resume until the end of 1920. Dealing for the fortnightly account, too, remained in abeyance despite approaches made by the Committee to the Treasury and the Bank of England: the Deputy Governor of the Bank, Montagu Norman, said in February 1920 that in his opinion the only circumstances in which the government would agree would be if 'they were assured that the whole pre-war debt in London and all the provincial exchanges had been liquidated.' By the middle of the following year this had largely been achieved, and the government agreed that account dealing could be resumed, but this prompted an immediate outcry from some of the smaller member firms, both brokers and jobbers, who were anxious about the risk involved.

Somewhat disingenuously they argued that the 'genuine and clean', non-contango business done by the Stock Exchange since the war had wiped out its pre-war reputation as 'little more than a "Gambling Institution" ' – its current position, playing 'a very important part in the public life', should be maintained by continuing the delivery of all purchases paid

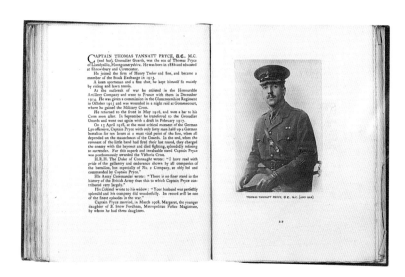

*Captain Thomas
Tannant Pryce, VC,
Grenadier Guards.*

for and all securities sold at the end of each account. The Committee, however, decided to allow the re-introduction of contango dealing from September 1921 onwards, realising that many firms would not be able to survive without it.

BOOM IN INDUSTRIAL SHARES

A short and frenzied post-war boom was not accompanied by any marked rise in prices, partly because of the restrictions on dealing. It was a boom in industrial shares, with financial mergers, flotations and recapitalisations surging to fill the vacuum created by the war. Some £400 million worth of new issues came on the market in 1919 and 1920, including coal mines, textile manufacturers, and manufacturers of cars and car accessories such as non-splintering glass for windscreens.

Boom was, once again, followed by slump, and international business, which had been dealt such a devastating blow by the war, was slow to recover. However, by the autumn of 1922 the last of the wartime controls had been lifted, and various gifts of plate were made to the Committee in appreciation of the 'great services' they had rendered during the war. The Trustees and Managers gave a Georgian silver salver, and Governor Norman presented 'a handsome silver-gilt dish' (later valued for insurance purposes at £5,000) on behalf of the Bank of England. Of more sombre and lasting significance was the Stock Exchange War Memorial, sited on the western wall of the House, unveiled by the Earl of Balfour on 27 October 1922 at a short service during which the hymn 'The Supreme Sacrifice' was sung, and the Last Post and Reveille sounded on a trumpet. A total of 127 members and 255 clerks had been killed during the war; their number included one holder of the Victoria Cross. This was Captain Thomas Tannant Pryce of the Grenadier Guards, who had joined the broking firm of Henry Tudor & Co. in 1913, and who gained a posthumous VC for his feat of holding up a German battalion with only forty men during the Lys offensive, finally charging with bayonets when their last rounds of ammunition had been fired.

A steam-engined lorry and trailer crowded with City workers at Bank, London, during the General Strike in May 1926.

❛ The Stock Exchange will shortly be on the dole. In none of the markets is there any semblance of activity . . .' noted Autolycus (Walter Landells) in the *Financial Times* on 10 February 1926; a few days later he reported that the 'lusty roar of the bull [in the rubber market] has died away to a timid bleat.' The 'labour position' hung over the market like a blanket', and by mid April, when the coal dispute was raging, things looked still blacker. However, by 29 April the mercurial disposition of the House was taking it for granted 'that the coal dispute is settled', and when those hopes were proved false, and a General Strike became inevitable, it was announced that the Exchange would certainly not be closed because of the crisis and Autolycus pronounced that 'the very idea of a closing the House is scouted as a sign of weakness, which, if adopted, would be construed as a concession to the forces of disorder.'

The strike began on 3 May; on the 6th the Exchange Committee Rooms were opened for recruits between the ages of twenty-four and forty-five, to be enrolled as Special Constables. They paraded that evening after the close of business, and a crowd gathered to cheer the arrival of cars 'laden with truncheons and whistles, and other articles of police equipment.' One of the Exchange's 'Specials' succeeded in rescuing a woman he saw 'floating in the water' near Blackfriars Bridge at 1 a.m. by diving into the Thames; others, less spectacularly, drove omnibuses and even trains.

The news of the end of the strike, on 12 May, was announced in the House at lunchtime by one of the waiters, galvanising those members who were present into frenetic excitement. 'Cheers rolled round all the markets of the House . . . lines of men started off, at the double, to the telegraph offices and the telephone boxes.' On the floor, the volume of sound rose to a single note 'strident and triumphant, above all the uproar caused by the rushing feet, the staccato snap of the pneumatic telegraph tubes, the shouting of the waiters, the electrified enthusiasm in the air and the intense relief felt at the proof that the General Strike weapon, as a national menace, no longer existed, and that the attempted coercion had failed in the face of voluntary effort.' Share prices in due course recovered and in the oil market 'they bid for Shell as though nothing short of securing the shares would have saved their lives.'

►*The motoring boom – the shop floor of the Morris Motor factory at Cowley, Oxford, in 1930.*

By the end of 1922 the perennial subject of commissions had re-surfaced once again. For the last decade these had been regulated by a minimum scale, and now nine of the largest broking firms mounted a campaign for a lower scale of commissions and a modification of the rules as far as major lines of stock, such as Government and Colonial securities, were concerned. The influential group consisted of Cazenove & Akroyd, Cohen Laming Hoare, Grieveson Grant, Heseltine Powell, Mullens, R. Nivison, Rowe & Pitman, J. & A. Scrimgeour and J. Sebag, but the campaign fizzled out the following year in the face of opposition from the large numbers of smaller firms, together with improving market conditions.

Advertising was another controversial topic. The war had created hundreds of thousands of new domestic investors, mostly to the various war loans, but the majority of them were unsophisticated in the ways of the City and unfamiliar with traditional broking methods. They represented much potential business for any brokers who could contact them, and advertising was practised by outside brokers who were not members of the Stock Exchange, and by the various bucket-shops. A report by the Departmental Committee on Share Pushing estimated that there were between 600 and 800 such firms altogether. Advertising was allowed by the New York Stock Exchange, but the Committee held firm and refused to allow individual members to advertise, although from 1922 onwards the Trustees and Managers paid for advertisements in the local and national press offering to supply enquirers with a list of brokers who would deal without a personal introduction. Predictably, as the list contained names of London member firms only, this nettled provincial brokers and eventually the advertisements appeared in London papers only.

Because of the heavy government borrowing during the war, the stock market at this period was loaded with 'British Funds', which comprised during the 1920s and 30s about a third of the total quoted value of all securities, compared with under 9 per cent before 1914. The importance of foreign loans had diminished considerably – many had been wiped out during the war, and the Americans were now providing strong competition. The industrial share boom of 1927–9, which was an echo of the boom taking place in the US, reflected the growing popularity of motor cars, radios and gramophones, and domestic aids such as washing machines and refrigerators. Flotations at this period included not only the Decca record company but also many of much poorer quality and more fleeting existence, such as the Anti-Sag Parent Company, proprietors of the Anti-Sag Mattress Support, and another which promised to extract 'essential fats' from the contents of hotel dustbins.

THE HATRY SCANDAL

Unfortunately such a boom provided considerable scope for fraud, of which one of the most spectacular exponents was the financier Hatry, whose crash in 1929 had a profound effect on the City. Clarence Charles Hatry was born in 1888 and had early experience of financial dealings when the family silk merchant business, which he had taken over at the age of eighteen on his father's death, went into liquidation leaving him with personal liabilities of £8,000, almost all of which he managed to clear within a couple of years. He became an insurance broker, and in 1914 acquired control of the City Equitable Fire Insurance Co. Ltd, which he subsequently sold to another famously crooked entrepreneur, Gerard Lee Bevan, for £250,000. Hatry's dealings became extensive – and extensively tangled – during the 1920s, and despite further liquidations he set up a series of investment trusts, notably Austin Friars Investment Trust (later re-named Austin Friars Trust and floated on the stock market in 1927), the Oak Investment Trust and the Dundee Trust. He used these as the basis for a complex mesh of promotions and Stock Exchange deals, some of which were perfectly sound. His Drapery and General Investment Trust, for example, was set up in 1927 in order to run department stores and was later sold to Debenhams, while Allied Ironfounders, established in 1929, lasted until it became part of Glynwed in 1969. Other issues were less straightforward. The Photomaton Group, which obtained rights for automatic machines for taking photographic portraits (the ancestor of today's 'photobooths'), was at the centre of a web of companies whose shares were manipulated by Hatry in a series of ingenious Stock Exchange dealings.

It was Hatry's most ambitious scheme, to gain control of some 60 per cent of the British steel industry by merger and consolidation, that ultimately brought his downfall. From the start it was viewed with suspicion by Governor Norman on both managerial and industrial grounds. After buying two US steel companies in early 1929, Hatry set up Steel Industries of Great Britain Ltd just as money was becoming dear in London and share prices began to slide. By June he was desperately short of cash and making increasingly frenzied efforts to borrow from the banks on the security of duplicated certificates in shares of his own companies and in the stock of Wakefield, Swindon and Gloucester corporations, three of the many local authorities to whom he had lent funds. Finally and belatedly, warning bells rang in the City; the banks grew uneasy and on 19 September Sir Gilbert Garnsey, a partner of the accountancy firm Price Waterhouse, was asked by Lloyds Bank to investigate the affairs of the Hatry Group.

Hatry and three of his associates immediately confessed that they and a fifth man (John Gialdini, who fled to Italy) were 'guilty of criminal action' connected with the various companies. Hatry stated that at least fifty or sixty brokers, both in London and in the country, would be seriously embarrassed, that his companies had sold securities which they did not possess and borrowed money on contracts, while some of the lenders held 'fictitious securities' as a cover for advances.

He further claimed that 'the crash would be the biggest the City would ever see, involving, say, £20 million', although Garnsey, who went immediately to Norman, told the Governor that Hatry was 'incoherent' and that too much reliance should not be placed on his words before a full examination of his affairs had taken place. Norman in turn informed the Chairman of the Stock Exchange, Archibald Campbell, who called an emergency meeting of the Committee the following day, 20 September. As an immediate measure, permission to deal in seven of Hatry's securities was suspended. On the same day Hatry made a statement to the City police and was charged with obtaining £209,000 from the Porchester Trust on fraudulent security of the City of Wakefield. The Governor told the banks that he wished them to co-operate with the Stock Exchange; privately he expressed the opinion that the affair had 'smirched us all, especially in the eyes of foreigners, which we can ill afford, and I cannot but think that all who have been dealing with the [Hatry] group have knowingly been running an unnecessary risk.'

Settlement was due on 26 September, but it was not effected until 13 February the following year. The intervening months were spent in feverish work on the part of a specially appointed Stock Exchange sub-committee to find a way out under which, in Norman's words, 'the general public should suffer no loss from a delivery of bad securities and to make a pool for professional loans.'

The four-man sub-committee questioned thirty-two firms of brokers and four of jobbers, concluding that although Stock Exchange rules had been breached, the size and nature of some of the deals should have alerted members that irregularities were being made. It was calculated that a sum of £1 million was needed for the pool – £800,000 of this was put up by the brokers and jobbers concerned and the balance ostensibly contributed by other Stock Exchange firms, although a considerable proportion of it was in fact provided by the banks. The fund was vested in the Royal Exchange Assurance, which acquired all shares sold and, in dealing with the genuine investing public, paid for them in full. The final scheme for

GERARD LEE BEVAN AND CITY EQUITABLE

MR. BEVAN'S WILD SPECULATIONS.

—◆—

BALANCE SHEET WHICH DID NOT DISCLOSE THE TRUE POSITION.

——

RECEIVER'S STATEMENT.

——

Gerard Lee Bevan, the son of Barclays Bank chairman Francis Augustus Bevan, was born in 1869. After Eton, Cambridge and two years with Barclays, he became a partner of the stockbroking firm Ellis & Co. (which had been formed in 1778) in 1893 and senior partner nineteen years later. The firm prospered and its turnover was at one time estimated as £12 million per annum. However, once Bevan was in charge his four junior partners had little say in how it was run.

During the First World War Bevan involved Ellis & Co. in heavy speculation in industrial shares, and in 1916 the firm purchased from Clarence Hatry a large shareholding in the City Equitable Fire Insurance Co., which was enjoying a 'war boom' like other insurance companies. Bevan, described by his biographer as 'arrogant, vain and irresponsible', became its chairman, dominating the board as he dominated his stockbroking partners. After the war, Ellis & Co. got into serious difficulties and Bevan started to make unsecured loans to the brokers from the insurance company, and to falsify City Equitable's accounts, making an almost impenetrable tangle of financial deals. His reckless plunges into industrial shares finally brought Ellis & Co. to bankruptcy. It was 'hammered' in the House in February 1922, eight days after Bevan had fled to France, although because of the ban on contango dealing at this period, its downfall had little effect on the Stock Exchange.

The case attracted intense publicity, however, as it coincided with the downfall of the fraudulent company promoter Horatio Bottomley. Bevan was hunted across Europe, arrested and briefly imprisoned in Vienna. He then served six years in prison in England after being found guilty at the Old Bailey on sixteen counts, mostly concerning the publication of false balance sheets and fraudulent conversion. He eventually emigrated to Cuba, where he became manager of a distillery, dying of sleeping sickness in April 1936.

settlement, simple in outline, was intricate in detail: buyers who paid in full received from the trustees of the fund good-delivery shares, or if this was not possible, had the shortage made good in cash. Buyers who could not pay in full were saved from failure through the fund; bad-delivery shares were destroyed. The scheme did not protect from loss those who had bought Hatry shares at an excessive price, but it did protect them from the further consequence of having bought forged shares. The settlement passed off without a hitch, ending what the *Daily Telegraph* described as 'the nightmare hanging over the Stock Exchange' for the previous five months.

There had been nothing like it before; the Stock Exchange's famous, or notorious, belief in *caveat emptor* had meant that it had rarely been activated by any consideration other than the interests of its own members. Those of the investing public had been of little or no concern, and the Committee had almost entirely ignored the

▼*An* Evening Standard *newspaper seller during the Hatry crisis in 1929. In the background is the Charing Cross Hotel, where Hatry and three of his associates had confessed their fraud to the Marquess of Winchester, chairman of some of Hatry's tangled financial enterprises.*

suggestions on this topic made by the investigating commissions half a century earlier. Why the sudden change of heart? The general admission that wartime regulations had successfully curbed some of the worst excesses of pre-war markets certainly played its part, and a further factor is likely to have been the appointment, in October 1929, of the Macmillan Committee on Finance and Industry, which caused considerable apprehension in the City (it did not report until 1931). Now, basking in the approval of the Governor of the Bank, the City and the press – even *The Times*, which had been very critical of the delays in settlement, applauded the final scheme – the Committee further tightened up its rules on quotation and, internally, set up a new Records Department to keep track of major financial operations and who was performing them.

Hatry and three associates were sent to prison in 1930 for what Mr Justice Avory called 'the most appalling frauds that have ever disfigured the commercial reputation of this country'; the case, tried at the Old Bailey, was a sensational one and tickets for the public gallery were hotly contested. Hatry was sentenced to fourteen years' penal servitude, but was released in 1939: he then engaged in many other business ventures, including running Hatchards bookshop in Piccadilly for a short period, and continued some minor wheeler-dealing until a few weeks before his death in 1965.

◀ *In 1923 the Trustees and Managers arranged for the Stock Exchange to receive its own coat of arms, with the motto* Dictum Meum Pactum *(My Word is My Bond).*

Dark Days
1929–1945

THE EXPOSURE IN SEPTEMBER 1929 OF HATRY'S FRAUD coincided neatly with the end of the bull market in the United States, which had been running with particular strength since the beginning of 1928 and which culminated in the Wall Street crash – so neatly indeed that several commentators have seen a connection between the two events. But as John Galbraith showed conclusively in his classic account *The Great Crash 1929*, there had been small but telling indications of the coming crash for some months.

The trend of the American market was downwards during September and October but there were still good days among the bad, and turnover on the New York Exchange was almost always above $4 million a day and sometimes over $5 million. New issues were frequent and commanded a good premium over the offer price. It was not until Black Thursday, 24 October, that a wave of panic selling set in: nearly 13 million shares changed hands, many at rock-bottom prices, and were often unloaded with great difficulty, but even on that day the market picked up slightly in the afternoon. A few days later, on Tuesday, 29 October, the New York stock market experienced its most devastating day ever: by the end of it, over 16 million shares had been unloaded (or at least recorded – many more transactions certainly went unrecorded at the time) and all the gains of the previous twelve months were wiped

◀'Lost all on the stock market. . .':
an eloquent plea at the time of the Wall Street crash.

out. It was not until mid November that the market stopped falling, for a while at least. The crash was over, but the worldwide slump which it heralded was about to begin.

The immediate effects of the crash in London were far less dramatic than might have been expected. There was little if any panic selling, and share prices for the most part held firm, although some investors had to sell securities to repay loans to bankers and others. What became very evident to bankers was the rapidity with which short-term loans to brokers, with collateral in the form of securities, could become unrecoverable when the underlying assets were unrealisable, and one direct consequence of this was a decrease in the amounts lent by bankers to members of the Stock Exchange and hence a general weakening in the links between the stock market and the money market.

However, although the Wall Street crash was not echoed by a similarly drastic fall in the London market, there was little cause for rejoicing in the House and what the *Financial Times* used to describe as a 'dull' or 'muted' tone prevailed. By 1931, Britain was in the throes of a deep financial crisis, which ultimately saw the collapse of Ramsay MacDonald's minority Labour government and the formation in August of a National government, led by MacDonald but dominated by the Conservatives.

The House was briefly cheered by this news, but it was soon to be shaken by an event which had a lasting impact on the stock market – Britain's final departure from the gold standard. Ironically the last act was played out on Saturday, 19 September, the first Saturday since the war on which the House was open – and indeed was frenetically busy as the run

'Britain Off the Gold Standard' – the Daily Express, *21 September 1931.*

Daily Express

NO. 9,790.   MONDAY, SEPTEMBER 21, 1931.   ONE PENNY.

BRITAIN OFF THE GOLD STANDARD.

LAST NIGHT'S DECISIONS BY THE GOVERNMENT

| No More Gold To Be Sent Abroad. | Stock Exchange Closed To-day. | Bank Rate Up To Six Per Cent. |

THE PRIME MINISTER running into 10, Downing-street on his return from Chequers last night for consultations in connection with the crisis.

BUSINESS AS USUAL.

"THE INTERNAL POSITION OF THE COUNTRY IS SOUND."

THE GOVERNMENT announced last night that following the week-end demoralisation of the international money market:—

The Gold Standard is suspended from this morning.

The Stock Exchange will not open to-day.

GOOD NEWS.

THIS MORNING'S pronouncement from Whitehall is good news.

Nothing more heartening has happened in years.

Never mind how it came about.

Don't waste time in reviling the foreigner or in moaning about the humiliation of events.

The fact remains that at last we are rid of the gold standard—rid of it for good and all.

To future historians it will seem incredible that we should ever have been chained to an arbitrary metal, and that our financial standing in the world should have been at the mercy of unscrupulous and panic-stricken foreign investors.

Now our export trade will have its chance to grow, because the £ will be at its correct level and not an artificially sustained one.

It is true that for a time we shall have to purchase much of our foodstuffs from abroad ; but there is such a surplus of food commodities in the world, and since we are the one great importing country we shall be in the position to protect ourselves against excessive prices.

While we are doing this we can stimulate our own agriculture to the greatest degree, and, by taking our eyes away from New York, from Berlin, from Paris, we can go ahead with plans for a self-sustaining Empire.

We repeat that whatever the difficulties and embarrassments of the moment, this morning's news is good.

It is the end of the gold standard and the beginning of real recovery.

DRAMATIC 'PHONE CALL TO CHEQUERS.

WHY THE PREMIER HURRIED TO LONDON.

FATEFUL MOVES.

FRANCE AND U.S. TO HELP THE POUND.

DISCUSSING CREDITS FOR BRITAIN.

"Daily Express" Correspondent.

WASHINGTON, Sunday, Sept. 20.

Franco-American co-operation to prevent the collapse of sterling will be forthcoming, it is believed in Government circles here.

MISS BONDFIELD ILL.

Miss Margaret Bondfield, Minister of Labour in the last Government, became suddenly ill during the week-end and was removed to a London nursing home.

She is suffering from a general nervous breakdown, caused by overwork. Miss Bondfield is fifty-eight years old, and at the age of thirteen started work as a teacher in a board school.

LATE NEWS.

---

on sterling was at its height and the jobbers in the Consol market had to cope with a flood of selling. During the day Sir Archibald Campbell, Chairman of the Stock Exchange Committee, and his deputy were requested to attend at the Bank, where they were informed by the Deputy Governor, Sir Ernest Harvey, that leaving the standard was now inevitable.

It was decided that the House should be closed on the following Monday; however what was described by an authorised clerk at the time as 'a rip-roaring market' took place in the street, fuelled by fears of inflation similar to that in Germany. On Wednesday the 23rd the Exchange was once more open for business, but all bargains had to be effected for cash, and bargains for the account, contangos and options were banned as they had been during the war; it was three months before all these restrictions were finally lifted.

The market continued to fall and did not begin to look up until the summer of 1932. Many firms cut back on numbers and imposed salary cuts and other harsh measures: on 30 September 1931 Sheppards told its staff that 'with real regret' the partners had decided to 'call upon the staff to share with them in the reduced earning capacity of the firm ... As from November 1st all salaries will be reduced by approximately 10% ...' Staff at Phillips & Drew fared even worse, their salaries being cut in the same year by a quarter, while Lancelot Hugh Smith, the autocratic head of Rowe & Pitman, ordered his partners to forgo port with their lunch, unless visitors were present.

THE RISE OF THE UNIT TRUST

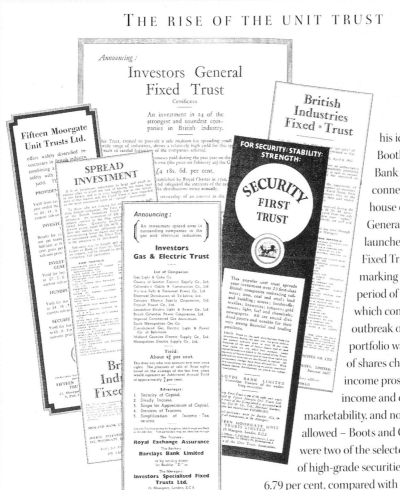

1930s advertisements from the Investors Chronicle *for investment and unit trusts*

In 1931 a London stockbroker, W.B. Burton-Baldry, visited the United States to look at the development of 'fixed trusts' there, and decided that the idea might play well in Britain. This was a brave decision considering the circumstances at the time, barely a year after the Wall Street crash and with the world still in the grip of economic depression. Burton-Baldry discussed

his idea with George Booth, a director of the Bank of England who had connections with an issuing house called Municipal General Services. M&G launched the First British Fixed Trust in April 1931, marking the first step in a period of rapid expansion which continued until the outbreak of war in 1939. Its portfolio was rigidly composed of shares chosen on the basis of income prospects, security of income and capital, and marketability, and no deviation was allowed – Boots and Commercial Union were two of the selected shares. This spread of high-grade securities provided a yield of 6.79 per cent, compared with the 4.34 per cent available from $2\frac{1}{2}$% Consols.

Stockbrokers initially opposed the idea, fearing the loss of private clients, but the trust got off to a good start and, helped by the recovery of the market and the favourable stance of the Bank of England, was soon followed by a number of others including Save and Prosper, the National Group and Allied Investors. By 1939 there were fifteen management companies operating between them eighty-nine trusts (the forerunners of today's unit trusts and open-ended investment companies), with a total value of around £80 million.

CLEANING UP THE NEW ISSUE MARKET

One good outcome of this unhappy period was the clean-up of the new issue market. The dodgy or downright fraudulent company promoters were weeded out: financial crisis was accompanied, as usual, by a flight to quality. Foreign issues, apart from those in the Empire, were severely curtailed by Treasury restrictions, and there was a pronounced shift in the market towards domestic issues. Those which came to market were usually sound, including household names such as Crosse & Blackwell, Cow & Gate and Great Universal Stores. Two methods of issuing which gained popularity in the mid-1930s – before the market began a new decline at the end of the decade, as the threat of Nazi Germany became more apparent – were offer for sale and a private placing of the shares with a Stock Exchange introduction. In the first, the shares were issued by the issuing house itself, after buying them from the company, rather than by the company. Private placings, in which expensive press advertising was avoided by brokers selling the shares to favoured City connections, were a popular method especially in cases where companies wanted to raise smaller amounts of capital. Permission to deal had to be obtained first from the Stock Exchange, and the broker usually approached investment trusts and insurance companies; normal practice was to arrange with jobbers to sell them, or give them an option on, blocks of shares.

Cazenove was particularly prominent in this field, gaining experience in company finance which was to stand the firm in good stead after the Second World War, but not everyone appreciated private placings, despite the obvious attractions of lower costs. Investors felt aggrieved that they did not always get a reasonable opportunity to purchase shares dealt in this way, and a private placing in 1935 by Cazenove of Bristol Aeroplane stock just before a government announcement of the expansion of the RAF – which enabled the chosen investors to make a nice profit – led to a protest widespread enough for the Committee to set up a sub-committee to examine the question. Vested interests, those of the larger brokers who specialised in placings, predictably won the day, led by a chorus of opinions such as that expressed by Fred Pitman of Rowe & Pitman: 'the agitation . . . had come from sources of which too much notice need not be taken.' The Committee, after consideration of the sub-committee's report, decided against a change in the rule book but did state that it was 'desirable' for issues, especially those of Ordinary capital, to be accompanied by a prospectus or offer for sale 'unless from a public standpoint the necessity or advantage of a private placing is indicated by the circumstances.' Private placings continued to grow in popularity in the years before the Second World War.

Most firms still obtained the bulk of their income from normal commission business. James Capel & Co., while acting as broker for a number of investment trust issues during the 1920s and 30s, relied heavily during this period on its connections with West End banks such as Coutts (with whom the firm had family connections dating back to the eighteenth century), Drummonds and Hoares. Two Capel partners would call on these banks every

THE WAR LOAN CONVERSION, 1932

When the depression was at its height in the summer of 1932, Mullens, Marshall, the Government Broker, was involved in one of the biggest financial operations ever undertaken by the government. This was the mammoth task of converting £2,000 million of 5% War Loan to 3½% War Loan, inherited from the First World War. The Chancellor of the Exchequer at the time was Neville Chamberlain, although the conversion had been planned by his predecessor Philip Snowden.

Rumours were flying round the City as early as March, and the conversion was finally announced on Thursday 30 June, immediately after the announcement of a fall in the Bank Rate from $2\frac{1}{2}$ per cent to 2 per cent. The Stock Exchange was opened specially on the following Saturday, and holders were given the option of repayment in cash, provided that they stated their intention by the end of September. A War Loan Conversion Publicity Bureau was set up by the government to urge the public to convert. Eddie Gosling and Edward Cripps in Mullens were responsible for persuading the City to accept the vast amount of stock: the financial climate was such that investors were happy to be guaranteed even 3½ per cent, and eventually £1,920 million was converted out of the original £2,000 million, saving the government an immediate £23 million.

Government Stationery Office workers carrying the printed War Loan conversion scheme forms in Harrow, 1 July 1932.

morning, the senior partner himself usually doing what was referred to as 'big West', taking in Coutts and the Pall Mall branch of Barclays – answering at the same time any investment queries from the banks' clients. The scale of the business they obtained in this way compensated for the fact that, by dealing for these clients, the firm was sharing commission with the bank, and it also brought large and prestigious accounts.

Despite the increasing use of the telephone and a measure of early automation these walks around the City and the West End, calling on major clients, remained the most important part of a broker's day, at least at partner level. Senior people in the firm would usually get in at around ten, look at their mail and then call on clients until midday, when they would return to their offices and give any business to the dealers. After lunch and a quick look in to the office to see that deals had been carried out, they left for home.

Personal and, still better, family connections were all-important. Nicholas Davenport, a left-leaning journalist who called his autobiography *Memoirs of a City Radical*, saw this at first hand during his not very happy days with Rowe & Pitman, where he was recruited to provide economic analysis largely ignored by his colleagues: 'Lancelot Hugh Smith, the head of Rowe & Pitman, had royalty among his friends, his clients and even his relations. He was the father figure of the great Smith clan which had brothers, nephews and cousins entrenched in the merchant banks, investment trusts and other financial institutions throughout the City. All the immense Stock Exchange business of the Smith clan poured through Rowe & Pitman. In addition to this bread and butter business, the firm floated many company issues and handed out underwriting to the life insurance companies and banks whose business it handled.' Not surprisingly, the firm's profits were substantial, and Davenport notes that the 'fabulous incomes' of the partners enabled them to 'live in great style with town and country houses . . . many of them hunted in the shires.'

THE RISE OF THE INSTITUTIONAL INVESTOR

As the 1930s progressed, insurance companies were becoming increasingly important clients. They had far more money to invest than even the richest private investor: in 1935, 54 per cent of their total assets of £1,587 million were in Stock Exchange securities, of which

Mr Blennerhassett and the Yo-Yo

BEWARE OF YO-YO
It starts as a hobby and ends as a habit

…KE WARNING by the fate of Mr.
…nnerhassett, as worthy a citizen as
…y that ever ate lobster at Pimm's, or

…led putt at Walton Heath. "Sound
…n, Blennerhassett!"- they said in
…rogmorton Street, and "Nice people
… Blennerhassetts!" was the verdict
…er the tea-cups and in the local
…nis-club.

…t Yo-Yo got him, and now ……..
…e day Blennerhassett brought his

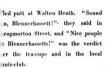

saw the Yo-Yo being played. The tricks
it could do in the hands of the expert!
Up and down the string it spun, and
back and forth: round in fast flying
circles: hopping and burring along the
floor: lying still as a dead mouse and
then suddenly returning to life—the
embodiment of eccentric speed.
Blennerhassett, ever responsive to the
"Gimme's" of his young, bought the
children one each. At home that
evening, with that deprecatory condes-
cension so familiar in parents, he
offered to give them the first lesson.
Strangely enough the Yo-Yo was recal-

SOLE DISTRIBUTORS TO THE TRADE
For the only genuine all British
Yo-Yo tep made from selected kiln-
dried Canadian maple.

CHEERIO 99

Yo-Yo
NOVELTY SALES SERVICES, LTD.,
10, DANE STREET, LONDON, W.C.1.
Telephone : Chancery 8673.

citrant. It sulked. First it would and
then it wouldn't. But the Blennerhassett
blood was up. The dinner-gong rang
unheeded. The children suggested,
implored and cried but Blennerhassett
kept on. He was determined to make
that little devil do its stuff.
The nurse took the children to bed.
Mrs. B. took herself to bed. But
Blennerhassett toil-d on at Yo-Yo.
Came the dawn, and he was still there,
dishevelled and wild-eyed, with the
Yo-Yo string still dangling from his
trembling fingers. They tried to part
him from it; but it was no use; and

eventually poor Blennerhassett was
taken away.

To-day he is happy in a quiet place in

the country, and under sympathetic
surveillance he practises Yo-Yo tricks.
His old friends at Pimm's miss him at
lunch and three-quarters of a certain
golf foursome have had to find a
stranger to make up their quorum.

*So beware of Yo-Yo which starts as a
hobby and ends as a habit.*

However, in case you feel
immune you can buy a
Yo-Yo at any good toy shop
or store. The price is
. . . . But you have been warned.

Part of the offending advertisement from the Evening
Standard, *26 May 1932.*

The summer of 1932 saw the craze for yo-yos at its height, but one member of the House had no reason to participate. This was Mr W.L.R.P.S. Blennerhassett, who was much put out by an advertisement for the toy in the *Evening Standard*, headed 'Beware of the yo-yo.' This featured a 'Mr. Blennerhassett, as worthy a citizen as any that ever ate lobster at Pimm's, or holed putt at Walton Heath', who had become completely obsessed with the yo-yo and had to be 'taken away', presumably to an asylum. The stockbroker did not relish the ragging and ribaldry to which he was subjected in the House after the advertisement appeared, and, despite an apology by the newspaper, he insisted on suing the manufacturers, Novelty Sales Services Ltd. The case, heard in the summer of 1933, produced much amusement as Sir Patrick Hastings, K.C., interrogated the plaintiff, asking him whether it was not true that Blennerhassett was an accepted 'funny name', which had been used by both W.S. Gilbert and Mark Twain in a humorous connection? Wasn't the Stock Exchange the home of practical jokes? Poor Mr Blennerhassett replied that because of the low state of the market 'I was the first joke that had happened for a long time.' The jury was in fits of laughter for much of the time, and despite the evidence of an alderman who claimed that Mr Blennerhassett might have been thought to have contravened the rules against advertising, the judge eventually dismissed the case 'with costs.'

▲ *Picture map of the floor of the Stock Exchange, by Rex Whistler, published in the* Financial News, *November 1933*

about half were in gilts. Insurance companies were notoriously suspicious of ordinary shares; during the First World War (and again in the Second), they patriotically put almost all their new money into government securities. By the outbreak of the Second World War their total assets stood at over £1,750 million, of which about half were in Stock Exchange securities and the rest in 'non-market assets' such as mortgages, real property and cash. It was to give them some ammunition in their dealings with the qualified accountants and actuaries staffing institutional investors such as these, and the growing number of investment and unit trusts and pension funds, that a few stockbroking firms, often with considerable reluctance, began to employ actuaries and statisticians – only later to be known as analysts.

A LOOK BEHIND THE SCENES

A recognition of the needs of the public, already stimulated by the Hatry scandal, began to grow as the 1930s progressed. Advertising by members was still forbidden, but in November 1933 the *Financial News* published a 32-page investors' guide to the Exchange, with a foreword by Sir Archibald Campbell, which provided a good deal of information on its workings as well as a delightful map of the floor of the House by the artist Rex Whistler. The jobbers' positions were represented by pictorial symbols: top-hatted gentlemen riding on steam trains to depict the Home and Foreign Rails markets, natives with spears dancing round a statue of Rhodes in the Kaffir market, while the Statue of Liberty presided over the 'Yankees.' An overview of the Exchange, written by 'Midas', gives a vivid picture of the House at work:

'At first, all visual impressions are swamped by one overwhelming feature – the noise. Experienced "House" men will claim that they need to do no more than go in at any of the doors and listen for a minute or so in order to gain a really accurate idea of what the markets are doing.

'To the untrained listener the noise will probably sound like nothing but a senseless babel: and by way of assistance to a more intelligent appreciation of its quality I can only suggest that when markets are active the resultant sound may be compared to the steady hum of a dynamo; and that when things are "quiet" the noise will be considerably greater, much more uneven, and punctuated at frequent intervals with choruses of laughter or snatches of popular songs, usually of a bygone age.'

Midas comments that it is not easy to gain an impression of the Stock Exchange as a whole, partly because during business hours it is too full of people, and also because 'the building has never been conceived and executed as a whole, and proportioned accordingly.' He continues with a detailed description of each of the different markets, the pitches of the dealers, or jobbers, round each pillar with lists pinned up above their heads of the stocks in which they deal, and the wooden stands 'resembling diminutive pulpits' in which the waiters sit, dressed in the Stock Exchange livery of top hat trimmed with gold braid and dark blue suit with red facings and gold buttons.

The guide included a complete list of broking firms and their partners as well as articles dealing with the technicalities of arbitrage, making a new issue, bargains and settlement. It had an introductory piece, 'A House with many markets – but only one standard of honesty', by Sir Stephen Killik, senior partner of the family firm of Killik & Co., a member of the Committee and a future Lord Mayor of London.

In the same year, 1933, the Committee for General Purposes published its first official booklet, *The Work of the Stock Exchange,* also by Killik, of which 5,000 copies, priced at one shilling, were printed.

▶ *A Stock Exchange Waiter*

There was still no officially recognised training or entrance examination to stockbroking, but lectures on Stock Exchange law and practice were provided by various colleges including the City of London College, one of whose lecturers, F.E. Armstrong, published in 1934 a popular text book, *The Book of the Stock Exchange*, which was in its third edition by 1939.

This gradual acknowledgement of the existence of a general public outside the charmed circle of investors personally known to members did not, however, extend to allowing women, who had gained full suffrage in 1928, to become members. Three years before that, in 1925, the daughter of an Irish stockbroker, Oonagh Mary Keogh, was admitted to the Dublin Stock Exchange; reports of this in the *Financial Times* alarmed the London Exchange into taking legal advice on their own position, and they were doubtless much reassured to learn that in the opinion of their solicitors they were free to admit or exclude anybody, male or female, as they wished. Further publicity, a decade later, about a woman broker in Bradford (who employed a male clerk) led to an intrepid woman, Mrs Mab Gosnell, applying for membership in London. This was refused, after some discussion, and she accepted the decision with regret, acknowledging that 'such an innovation has difficulties which time may or may not remove.'

Another possible innovation which exercised members at this period was a compensation fund. Members of the investing public had, indeed, been urged in the *Financial News* guide to 'submit to the Committee any charge or claim' they might have against a member, and were assured that they would have such claims 'fully and impartially investigated', but there were no arrangements to guarantee compensation if fraud was discovered or if a firm defaulted. Banks made good any losses resulting from fraud by their own employees, but there was considerable resistance to the idea of a fund both from jobbers, who did not have direct dealings with the public anyway, and from the more prudent brokers who, not unreasonably, felt that they would be subsidising those of their fellow-members who were less cautious and failed to carry out basic checks on their staff and clients. By the summer of 1938, however, the idea had been agreed in principle: the cost, estimated at £20,000 a year, would be met by subscriptions that were voluntary for existing members, compulsory for new ones. War intervened before the scheme could be carried out, and it was not until 1950 that the Stock Exchange Compensation Fund was established to make good any loss caused by the 'failure, death or negligence' of a member.

The Exchange showed no signs of relaxing its restrictions on numbers, composition (the ban on German nationals was still in force) and activities of members. Membership remained fairly constant at around the 4,000 mark, but there was a considerable shift in the balance between brokers and jobbers. In 1918 there were slightly more jobbers, as there had been before the First World War, but twenty years later there were 2,491 brokers and only 1,433 jobbers. Jobbers came under pressure in the inter-war period as outside firms and banks competed, often successfully, for their business; like brokers, they were restricted as to the number of clerks they could have on the floor of the House, which limited the possibilities of expansion. Sometimes the smaller ones formed market partnerships, informal alliances to deal in a specific security, which prevented the business by-passing the Exchange altogether, and a 'country' jobbing firm, J.W. Nicholson of Sheffield, was by 1939 acknowledged to be among the largest firms of jobbers in Britain.

Complaints in the House about country jobbing were equalled by continual grievances over bucket-shop activity and 'share-pushing.' In 1935 the *Daily Mail* claimed that the public had been swindled out of at least £10 million by bucket-shops, and the following year the City of London Police formed a special squad to investigate their activities. R.P. Wilkinson, the Deputy Chairman of the Stock Exchange Committee, sat on several government committees aimed at preventing fraud, the most effective of which was the Bodkin Committee which reported in 1937, noting the increase of private investors since the first war, mostly comprising 'clergymen, widows and spinsters.' The inadequacy of existing criminal law to protect these vulnerable members of society was cited in all the committee reports, and their work eventually bore fruit in the shape of the Prevention of Fraud (Investments) Act, which was passed in 1939 but did not come into effect until 1944. This enforced licensing of outside dealers by the Board of Trade tightened up the regulations for prospectuses and forbade house to house hawking of shares, as well as confirming the restrictions on advertising. Penalties were stiff – a maximum fine of £500 or two years' imprisonment or both – and the Act did eventually succeed in forcing bucket-shops out of business

The clouds of war

By 1937 officials of the Exchange had accepted the fact that war was inevitable, and had begun to draw up plans accordingly. It was clear that bombing was likely to be an immediate danger in London, and a meeting was held in July 1937 to discuss how best to cope with air raids. However the majority of members and many of their clients remained sanguine, and it was not until September the following year, when Hitler's aggression towards Czechoslovakia became clear, that the markets began to weaken. After Neville Chamberlain's return from his meeting with Hitler in Munich on the 28th and his speech from Downing Street announcing 'peace with honour', there was a rush of brokers and their clerks into Throgmorton Street and a tumult of opportunistic after-hours deals. The following day the feeling in the House was that 'the war is over', and later the Exchange sent a congratulatory message to Chamberlain.

However, the officials were less sanguine than some of the members, and continued to hold discussions with the Bank and the Treasury on what the Exchange should do if and when war did break out. Various sub-committees (optimistically characterised as 'of a non-permanent nature') pondered specific issues such as settlement and clearing, and one subject was considered of over-riding importance – whether or not the Exchange should move right out of London. Many members established emergency addresses, often in the private houses of the firm's partners, to which they moved essential staff, books and papers; this was the first time for over a hundred years that they were allowed to operate from offices more than a quarter of a mile from the Exchange. After much discussion the Managers, who were especially concerned about the extensive glass roof over the trading floor, agreed in June 1939 to take an option to lease nearly 20,000 sqare feet on the first and second floors of the Denham and Pinewood film studios in Buckinghamshire. This would provide an ample trading floor with accommodation for jobbers and their staff, while brokers were to make their own arrangements to occupy houses or offices nearby.

The move, however, never took place, as it soon became evident that communications between Denham and the City were far from adequate even in peacetime, and proposals for special trains came to nothing. Although 120 jobbers agreed to go, the Consol market flatly refused to move far from the Bank of England, the majority of whose operations remained in Threadneedle Street; the Denham plan was finally abandoned, and the option assigned to the Ministry of Supply in November 1940, because the necessary 'close and constant touch between all parties' could not practicably be maintained.

When war was finally declared on 3 September 1939 the Exchange, helped by the experience of the first war, was well prepared. The markets had been increasingly inactive over the previous year and the dwindling business was accounted a blessing because it had 'reduced open accounts to a minimum.' On 31 August 'Autolycus' of the *Financial Times* reported that 'the general attitude of the House is one of a calm waiting upon the course of events with . . . a feeling of surprise at the way in which stocks and shares were being absorbed.' On 1 September the House was closed 'until further notice' and the settlement of open bargains suspended. The closure was initially because of the mass evacuation by train of London schoolchildren and blind people and consequent transport difficulties, and the House re-opened six days later on Thursday the 7th. (An outside market had, unsurprisingly, already started operating.) The plans were smoothly translated into action: sales and purchases for the pre-war account were to be settled by 21 September, all trading was to be for cash and immediate delivery, and government debt and stocks were subject to minimum prices.

THE CITY UNDER FIRE

When the air raids on London started in earnest in September 1940 the Managers constantly renewed their warnings about the dangers to the House, and a careful watch was kept on the upper floors and roof, by 'fire-spotters' drawn from members and staff, for any fires started by incendiary bombs. Klaxons were sounded throughout the building if there was any danger. Air-raid shelters were arranged for up to 760 people 'within the triangle' of the Capel Court site, and a further eighty at 26 Austin Friars – these were for Exchange officials, staff and tenants, and it was stated plainly that they were not to be used by members or clerks. An emergency fire station, known as 36 'Y', was established within the Exchange, with a Watchroom and living accommodation in the basement; the equipment – two fire engines and two heavy trailer pumps, with a couple of old London taxis to tow them – was parked in Shorter's Court.

On the night of 29 December 1940 a clutch of incendiaries, which were soon extinguished, fell on the flat roof of the Exchange. This was the night of the greatest fire in the City since the Great Fire in September 1666. The House also suffered blast damage on several occasions from near misses – in October 1940, all the windows on the Throgmorton Street side were shattered by the blast from a parachute mine that destroyed the Dutch Church in Austin Friars and the offices of several Stock Exchange firms.

Trade was, of course, drastically affected. Telephone trading between offices was encouraged, as it lessened the likelihood of injuries if the floor should be hit. The market in fact kept open throughout the war; the floor of the House was closed for one day in 1945 because of damage from a V2 rocket, but trading continued in the basement. All settlement was for cash: the Settlement Department was closed, as it had been during the First World War, but its staff were redeployed within the Exchange as far as possible. British overseas investments suffered heavily, declining between 1939 and 1946 by more than £1,100 million, but while the Exchange could play no role in the international securities market, it co-operated with the government in efforts to remove any competition for the funds required for the successful prosecution of the war. It ceded to the Treasury the right of vesting any new issue – if it did so the Stock Exchange would not. A new issue needed approval from both Council and the government's Capital Issues Committee (CIC), which was not granted unless it was deemed to be in the national interest; and in placing new securities, the Committee warned members that they must take 'all possible steps' to avoid any brake on the subscription to government loans.

As the war progressed the House began to chafe against these restrictions, and the Committee, while supporting the principle, was driven to complain to the Treasury that non-approved issues were frequently made privately, on what was dubbed the 'grey market', but official action was rarely taken against the offenders, giving rise to a 'large . . . uncontrolled outside market.' In 1944 the Treasury finally responded, removing controls on issues of under £100,000 and taking steps to ensure that non-approved issues did not take place outside the Stock Exchange.

The drop in the Exchange's income was fierce. The Managers at first waived the subscriptions of members and clerks joining the Forces, as they had done in the last war, but this meant a loss of around £250,000 a year, which was compounded by falling rents, departing tenants and difficulties in producing price lists because of the stringent rationing of newsprint. Eventually, and with some reluctance, an annual fee was charged from 1942 onwards of ten guineas per member, and this was continued throughout the war. A minor innovation was the decision in 1942 to allow two firms, Haley & Co. and A. Sherriff & Co., to employ women as settling clerks, but this privilege was withdrawn in 1946.

◄A view from St Paul's Cathedral just after the end of the war.

THE FORMATION OF THE COUNCIL

By 1942 nearly all members – under the 1904 rule – were proprietors, few holding any substantial number of shares, which greatly reduced conflicts of interest. Opinion swung in favour of a single governing body, and in July, a joint committee was established, which considered the question under three main headings: the constitution, the financial implications of the transfer of assets, and possible incorporation by charter. In September 1944, it was decided that from 25 March 1945 the Committee for General Purposes would cease to exist and would be replaced by a Council consisting of the nine Trustees and Managers *ex officio* as foundation members plus thirty ordinary members chosen by ballot. The financial arrangements and the question of incorporation would be decided after the war.

▲ *Service of*
Thanksgiving held in
the Stock Exchange,
14 May 1945.

The first meeting of the new Council, on 24 April 1945, under the chairmanship of Sir Robert Pearson, bravely confronted the looming demands of the post-war world. A possible rebuilding scheme was discussed – 'by modern standards our present buildings are out of date', stated Sir Robert roundly. Of more immediate anxiety was the whole question of the Exchange's 'image.' The *Daily Express* had recently conducted an investigation into the public attitude towards it, in which the answers to the question 'Do you consider that the Stock Exchange performs a useful service in the life of the community?' made melancholy reading: yes, 29 per cent; no, 33 per cent; don't know, 38 per cent. A lot of people 'think of us as an awful glorified Monte Carlo or else a gathering of bookmakers', noted one Council member, an idea 'derived from the bucket-shops which can advertise.' The Socialists (although few in the City as yet seriously envisaged their return to power) were 'dead against the Stock Exchange' and Labour's policy included the vague but menacing promise to 'control private investment.' The appointment of a Public Relations Officer was even mooted, one member asserting that he knew of two firms who had taken this step, after which everything 'went comfortably.'

The end of the war in Europe was marked by a double Bank Holiday on 8 and 9 May, Tuesday 8 May being Victory in Europe (VE) Day. (A few members did come in to the City on the first day, just in case.) A Thanksgiving Service was held in the Exchange on Monday 14 May, conducted by the Rector of St Margaret's, Cornhill, with three hymns and music provided by the Grenadier Guards. There was no community singing. Some 1,250 members and over 1,000 clerks were still in the Forces, and 228 names were subsequently added to the Stock Exchange War Memorial.

The Birth of the Modern Market 1945–1965

A FTER VE DAY, 'LASSITUDE PREVAILED IN THE MARKETS', noted the *Financial Times* – partly because of the political situation in Russia, partly because of the impending election, fixed for 5 July. The Stock Exchange had prohibited any 'dealings in majorities' ahead of general elections some years before the war, but this rule was largely disregarded and the odds on the return of Churchill and a Conservative government were short: hardly any members seriously contemplated a Labour victory, and the most pessimistic computations on the floor of the House predicted a majority of thirty seats for the Tories.

Because of the necessity to collect the votes of men overseas in the Forces (nearly three million were still abroad), the result was not declared until 26 July, when 'the City, with the nation, was shocked by the political landslide' as Clement Attlee gained a majority of 147 seats. The immediate result was that prices were heavily marked down as members contemplated the 'bogy' of nationalisation of steel, railways and other stocks. Worse still was

the possibility that, under a socialist government known to be hostile to the Stock Exchange and almost everything it stood for, the securities market itself might wither away as alternative methods of financing the economy were developed. At home there were the twin threats of the provincial stock exchanges in the field of company shares, and the discount houses which were dealing in increasing amounts of government debt directly with banks and institutional investors. Abroad, the New York Exchange was now the centre of what was left of the international securities market. Although the House itself was relatively unchanged, returning members found the market more edgy and less ebullient than it had been before the war.

The Stock Exchange therefore entered the era of peace in a defensive frame of mind. Members were keen to be free of wartime controls, and to see the resumption of traditional forms of trading such as the fortnightly account, contangos and options. The Committee had approached the Treasury even before the end of the war, in March 1945, for permission to abandon the cash trading which had been mandatory since the beginning of the war, but it was not until nearly two years later, in December 1946, that account trading was allowed. In any case the Exchange had to re-start the Settlement Department, which had been closed during the war, and train new staff, and the department was not working properly until

DEVALUATION DAY, 1949

*I*n the autumn of 1949 a business recession in the United States, resulting in a substantial reduction of American purchase of British goods, and a decline in UK gold and dollar reserves, triggered the devaluation of the pound against the dollar from $4.03 to $2.80. This was announced by the Chancellor, Stafford Cripps, in a radio broadcast to the nation on the evening of Sunday, 18 September 1949. The Stock Exchange was closed on Monday the 19th but a lively market took place in the street, which provided enough business for the FT Index to rise from 108.2 to 110.1, with gold shares doing especially well. This impromptu trading was lambasted by Aneurin Bevan in a debate in the House of Commons as 'the obscene plundering that went on on the Monday in Throgmorton Street.' Despite the initial reaction of the House, prices soon began to fall as other countries around the world followed sterling in devaluing their own currencies.

A lively market in the street on Monday, 19 September, when the Exchange was closed because of devaluation.

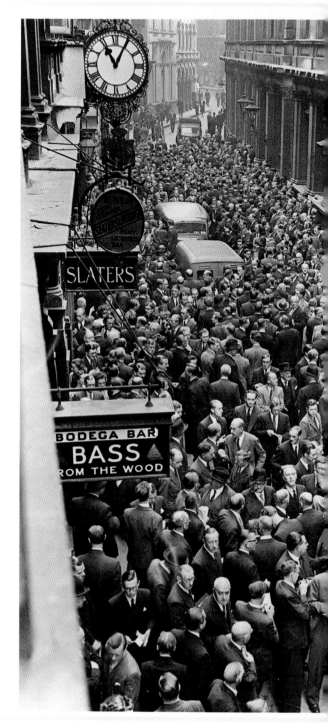

January 1947. Contangos were allowed from April 1949, with the explicit guarantee of the Stock Exchange that they would not be used for 'speculative purposes'; the Bank of England was firmly against the re-introduction of options, and the Council decided to leave the question alone for the time being. Although non-members used them, and there was a small but vociferous group in the House anxious for their restoration, the use of options was not finally approved by a vote of the entire membership until May 1958, when it was hoped to restore flagging business by their renewal. The Bank of England was still against them, but for once the Council decided to go against its wishes.

The new Council had many other issues to contend with in the immediate post-war period. The Cohen Committee, set up by the government in 1943 (with R.P. Wilkinson, chairman of the General Purposes Committee, as a member) to examine the possibilities of reforming company law, reported in July 1945 just before the results of the election were known; its work finally resulted in the 1948 Companies Act. The report itself was staunchly in favour of limited liability, viewing it as necessary for the economic health of the country, and the Act enforced the consolidation of company accounts, paving the way not only for the 'cult of the equity' but, ultimately, for a significant increase in shareholder power.

Nationalisation

Of more immediate concern was the question of nationalisation, or what was frequently referred to as the 'socialisation' of industry. It was apparent from the King's Speech in Parliament in August, within a few weeks of the new government taking office, that nationalisation would proceed very rapidly. The Chancellor, Hugh Dalton, announced that the Bank of England would be the first to be taken over, followed by the coal industry; also that capital controls on new issues and exchange controls would remain as they had been during the war. In fact the nationalisation of the Bank of England was a low-key, even symbolic affair, merely a curtain-raiser to that of industry. The Bank retained its operational independence and, more importantly, its authority in the City, so that the government was effectively precluded from direct jurisdiction over the clearing banks. Changes in lending policy, for example, were effected via the Bank.

Within the next six years the coal, iron and steel, railway, electricity and gas industries had been taken into public ownership. A major source of discontent was the way that compensation was calculated, in particular the question of whether all classes of shareholder should receive compensation which would roughly maintain their income. This was especially contentious at the time of the nationalisation of the railway companies, when the government abruptly switched from its previous complicated valuation system to one based on market prices. This decision provoked an angry response from the Council of the Stock Exchange, who blandly declared to the government in December 1946 that share prices were not a suitable basis for valuation, as they were the result of 'hope, fear, guesswork' among other considerations.

The cost to the government of its entire nationalisation programme, including that of the iron and steel industry which took place after the general election in February 1950 had returned Labour to power with a majority of just six, was £2,150 million, a huge increase in the National Debt. For the stock market, the programme brought mixed fortunes. Many of its traditional markets were lost, but the announcement of each succeeding takeover and of its vesting date initiated a flurry of trading activity which helped to keep the Stock Exchange alive. Institutional and private investors actively rearranged their portfolios; the former had been virtually obliged to buy government securities during the war and now took the opportunity to consider a different distribution. This marked the beginning of the so-called 'cult of the equity'. George Ross Goobey was a prime mover in this regard: as the pension fund manager for Imperial Tobacco in Bristol, he persuaded the company to move its funds out of gilts and into equities from 1948. Ross Goobey's argument, that company dividends would rise in real terms, which met with much initial scepticism in the City, was soon proved right, as rising inflation eroded the return on gilts; he said at the time that industrial shares were so cheap and so varied that he felt 'like a child in a sweet shop.' However, it took more than a decade for the so-called 'reverse yield gap' to appear – it was a long, gradual process.

There was also a modest amount of new issue business, although the provisions of the Companies Act of 1948 made the whole process more complex, which favoured the merchant banks who were large enough to be able to employ staff with the necessary skills and experience. Increasingly, brokers came to act in co-operation with the issuing houses, rather than compete directly with them on unequal terms. They were still used for the smaller issues, usually under £1 million, which the merchant banks disdained. Placings and introductions, although popular with issuers, were increasingly discouraged by the Council because of their exclusion of the general public, and in December 1958 it was ruled that at least 25 per cent of an issue of shares, and 20 per cent for fixed interest securities, had to be available in the market at the time of a placing. Public offers with a full prospectus were most favoured by the Council, and the brokers who dominated the new issue market in the 1950s were Cazenove, Hoare & Co, Panmure Gordon, Rowe & Pitman, Greenwell and Joseph

TO THE MEMORY OF THOSE MEN WHO WENT OUT FROM THIS HOUSE AND DIED FOR THEIR KING AND COUNTRY

1914 1918

▲ *King George VI,*
Queen Elizabeth and
Princess Margaret at
the London Stock
Exchange to mark the
150th anniversary of the
laying of the foundation
stone, 23 May 1951.
John Braithwaite,
Chairman of the
Council, stands on the
King's right.

Sebag. All six of them were brokers to the offer for sale of United Steel in 1953, the first steel company to be de-nationalised under the Conservative government elected in 1951.

Just before the end of the war, public relations were starting to become increasingly important – partly because of the professionalism of the institutions, partly because of the large and growing numbers of private investors, with both constituencies expecting a higher level of information. Contact with the world outside the House was at first maintained via Francis Cooke, the Secretary of the Share and Loan Committee, who sat wreathed in clouds of tobacco smoke at a desk which at one point held a picture of Stalin; but in 1947 Major Harrison, the Managing Director of the London Press Exchange advertising agency, was appointed 'in an

▲ Left. to right: Mary
Crook, Joan Cressall
and Gillian Evans, the
first three Stock
Exchange Guides,
photographed in
November 1958.

◄ Sir John Braithwaite,
Chairman from 1949 to
1959, painted by
Anthony Devas.

advisory capacity' for matters of advertising and publicity. At his suggestion the House was, exceptionally, opened to the public on Saturday mornings during the Festival of Britain in 1951, when some officials, members and clerks showed visitors round. Another PR exercise of this year was the preparation of a booklet on the workings of the Exchange, initially intended for parliamentary candidates at the October general election. Written within a week and published in four days, its 10,000 print run was quickly exhausted, and a second edition of 20,000 was produced a year later.

THE VISITORS' GALLERY

In November 1953, a visitors' gallery was opened (seventy-five years after such a bold step had been advocated by the report of the Royal Commission). Five years later three trimly uniformed Gallery Guides were appointed; there was a rapid turnover, because many of them swiftly found husbands among the members, who were urged, not always effectively, to curb their instincts for noisy horse-play, and in particular to refrain from throwing paper balls up at the gallery. By this date the Exchange was slowly becoming accustomed to being in the public eye. A film, *My Word is My Bond*, was commissioned in 1958 and shown in a small cinema next to the gallery, and the House featured in several television programmes (over which the Council exercised as much censorship as it was able). A panel of lecturers, seventy strong, was assembled to respond to the increasing demand from all over Britain for information about the workings of the Exchange.

THE BRAITHWAITE ERA

A moving spirit behind this new attitude to publicity was John Braithwaite. He had joined the Committee for General Purposes in 1937, the third partner of Foster & Braithwaite to serve on it; he became Chairman in 1949 and over the next decade, until his retirement in 1959, he put his stamp firmly on the Council and the Exchange as a whole. He was a virtually full-time, although unpaid, chairman (he was knighted in 1954) who took his role very seriously, and was especially enraged by any of the – at this time quite frequent – assertions that the House was some sort of 'top people's' betting shop. When Herbert Morrison in 1950 said that 'most working people regard its work tolerantly as being rather in the same category as horse racing', Braithwaite (whose wife was at the time campaigning on behalf of Morrison's party) fired off a furious reply, emphasising the valuable contribution of the Exchange in the field of public finance, and finishing with the assertion that 'every ignorant attack upon the Stock Exchange or upon the City of London is itself a damaging attack upon the national credit.'

His ten-year reign saw the establishment in 1950 – after a series of scandals involving members which attracted considerable and unwelcome attention – of a Compensation

THE BANK RATE TRIBUNAL

*O*n 19 September 1957 Bank Rate was sensationally raised from 5 per cent to 7 per cent – a level not seen since 1920. This sharp rise was imposed as a crisis measure by a Conservative government faced by a spiral of rising wages, costs and prices. Almost immediately rumours began to circulate in the City that a leak had led to after-hours trading of gilts on the previous day, the 18th, and the Parker, or 'Bank Rate', Tribunal was set up a few months later to investigate the affair.

The mixture of fact, information, guesswork and rumour that sustains the movements of money rates and share prices in the City has rarely been revealed so clearly as it was by this Tribunal. It had to establish whether there was any truth in 'allegations that information about the raising of Bank Rate was improperly disclosed' ahead of its move upwards on 19 September 1957, and if so, whether use had been made of such disclosure 'for the purpose of financial gain'.

For the first time in its history the Stock Exchange published turnover figures in gilts on the relevant days, revealing aggregates of sales and purchases of government stock as £21.5 million on 18 September and £18 million on the morning of the 19th, before the announcement of the change. Particularly notable gilt sales had been made by Royal Exchange Assurance, the British Match Company and Lazards – on the boards of all of which sat Lord Kindersley, who as a member of the Court (Director) of the Bank of England had known of the planned rise a couple of days before it took place.

The public inquiry into the affair was chaired by Lord Justice Parker. The tribunal heard evidence on oath from 132 witnesses, cross-questioned, often very harshly, by a team of lawyers headed by the Attorney General, Sir Reginald Manningham-Buller (whose hectoring style here and elsewhere gave rise to the nickname 'Bullying Manner'). In addition to the principal witnesses – Lord Kindersley and W.J. and J.H. Keswick – those who gave evidence included journalists, a stockbrokers' clerk and his typist wife, and various makers of small deals in the gilts market including a gentleman who 'had a flutter' from time to time instead of doing the crossword puzzle on his train to work in the morning.

The tribunal's 32-page report, published in January 1958, accepted the testimony of Lord Kindersley that he had only known of the sales made by the companies in which he held directorships after they had taken place, although he did admit to having tried, without success, to deter Morgan Grenfell from a proposed debenture issue and a simultaneous rights issue for Vickers. It was evident that he had made no personal financial gain, and matters rested there. It remained for Harold Wilson to remark in Parliament the following month that the tribunal had 'quite fortuitously provided the country with a valuable insight into many other questions of national concern. One of the impressions which many people have formed is the essentially amateurish way in which vital decisions affecting our whole economic well-being are taken - the "old boy" network, the grouse moors, "Nigel was very depressing"...'

◄ *Messengers leaving the Bank of England with news of a change in Bank Rate.*

Fund, financed by members' subscriptions and designed to compensate members of the public 'who have entrusted to Members of the Stock Exchange money or securities for investment or redistribution and [who] have suffered loss as a result of a failure.'

Braithwaite was a tireless campaigner for the reduction of stamp duty, which at 2 per cent on every transaction was a continuing scapegoat for periods when business was poor, but he was also anxious not to rock the City boat. The cautious negotiations of the Stock Exchange with the Treasury and the Bank of England in the early years after the war established the pattern of this complex relationship for many years. Effectively, the market resigned itself to various restrictions in return for which it was allowed to maintain self-regulation.

Braithwaite's attitude is nicely summed up in a note he made for the Council after an unsuccessful attempt in 1951 to get the Bank of England to re-open debate on the thorny subject of rebate of commissions, which was to drag on for the next twenty years: 'It is in our interest to use our freedom to act as we please only in such a way that we do not run the risk of losing it.' The Exchange kept the Bank informed of 'changes that we contemplate, that would have any impact on public policy, and we receive their advice upon such changes, which is given normally after contact with the Treasury, sometimes after the matter has gone to the Chancellor himself.' It was not a question of formal approval or disapproval, he emphasised, but 'merely a verbal expression of opinion' on which the Exchange was free to act as it wished – but such 'informal control is much to be preferred to formal or statutory control' such as was in place in New York, where the Securities & Exchange Commission had been set up by Congress in 1934 as a result of the Wall Street crash. The Bank, Braithwaite said, had 'a warm and understanding attitude towards the Stock Exchange and all its problems.'

John Braithwaite retired in 1959 at the age of seventy and the Exchange presented him with a new Rover car to mark the occasion. It was a splendid year for the stock market. The return of the Conservatives at the October election with an increased majority was greeted the following day by some of the most frenzied dealing ever experienced, with the steel market exceptionally active; the FT Index rose by 6 per cent from 268.6 to 284.7, the equivalent of over 300 points in today's FTSE, and the ensuing boom put tremendous pressure on the Exchange's settlement system. More good news came at the end of the year when it was announced that the Trustee Act was to be amended to allow up to 50 per cent of trust funds, previously confined to fixed income stocks, to be invested in equities. Business was indeed booming, and relief at the Tory victory was reflected in the jump in price of a Stock Exchange nomination from £175 in March 1959 to nearly ten times as much in November.

Plans for rebuilding

Numbers had fluctuated sharply since the end of the war. A market boom starting in August

1954 checked the post-war decline in membership, and for the first time for some years the new members elected, in the year to March 1955, balanced those who left through death, business failure or retirement. Ventilation in the House was inadequate, old-fashioned speaking tubes were still in use between different areas and floors and there was a grievous shortage of telephones, for which members were frequently forced to queue. Some departments, such as the Clearing House, were too small and were regularly overwhelmed with business, yet there was a good deal of wasted space. A modern building, with more letting space, might be 'both structurally possible and economically self-supporting', as Braithwaite optimistically put it in 1956.

The Surveyor to the Exchange, G.J. Buckingham, had whiled away the tedious hours of fire-watching during the war by roughing out designs for a new building. He produced a detailed plan in 1948 and conditional approval was given by the planning authorities the following year, but, although this remained in force, building restrictions in the City prevented a start being made for some years after the end of the war. It was also feared that the expense involved might provide 'a handle for those Socialists who were critical of the Exchange.'

THE END OF DUAL CONTROL

An added complication was the question of ownership. There were still nearly 4,000 proprietors who, while they had no powers over the Exchange as an institution, did own the building and were at this juncture reluctant to spend the necessary amounts of money to rebuild or substantially improve it. Eventually a scheme was agreed which involved converting the 20,000 outstanding shares into 40,000 4 per cent annuities, initially redeemable in March 1953 but later extended to 1958. Thus the building and the business were together valued at £4 million. All non-members had to surrender their shares and accept annuities by March 1948; one share in the Exchange was issued to each member, but they had no value and had to be given up when membership ceased. This scheme was accepted by a good majority, the Committee for General Purposes and the Committee of Trustees and Managers were finally wound up in March 1948, and the Council took over all responsibility for both the transaction of business and the administration of property and assets.

The advent of a Conservative government in 1951 removed the anxiety about potential Labour criticism, but by that time the internal finances of the Exchange were in no state to allow building to begin: interest charges on the annuities issued to the proprietors when they were bought out in 1948 were proving a heavy burden, and falling membership naturally meant a decreasing income from subscriptions, while members expected an increasingly high standard of service now that they were the 'owners' of the Exchange. Eventually things were put on a more favourable footing by an agreement with the Inland Revenue that the Exchange should be taxed as a mutual organisation rather than a commercial business, which allowed considerable savings in tax.

There now remained only one significant obstruction in the way of rebuilding – to find sufficient space to allow the market to continue while the work was in progress. After a vigorous search, which included consideration of the possibility of using the Royal Exchange and a building in Coleman Street, the solution was to purchase three adjoining freeholds on the Threadneedle Street side of the site, including buildings owned by the Post Office. The decision to rebuild was announced to members in March 1961, although demolition work on the old building did not begin until 1966.

THE CROWDED HOUSE

By the time that the decision was taken there were under 3,500 members, but with clerks and 'blue buttons' probably as many as 8,000 people had access to the floor. Conditions in the House were uncomfortably crowded, although this was not always seen as a disadvantage. Rival jobbing firms were 'literally a matter of a few feet away' – as one of them described it, 'nudging elbows a lot of the time'; lip-reading was a valuable skill, enabling those who could practise it to pick up information, from colleagues and often from rivals, among the hubbub. The location of your pitch was vital: if you were close to where the leading brokers passed, even though you were not a large firm, this brought opportunities to quote a price and form a judgement about the business. Pitches were small enough – the best ones were by one of the pillars, but they could consist of 'just a small board of perhaps 24 inches by 12 inches hung on the wall, and somewhere to stand probably four feet away from there. . . ', and if a firm was moving, or amalgamating, there was hot competition to grab a better vantage point.

While the House was in process of rebuilding and the market floor moved to the Post Office building, the small gilt jobber Charlesworth & Co. had a tiny cramped site which turned out to be a positive advantage: '. . . we had Wedd [Jefferson] on one side of us, and Akroyd [& Smithers] on the other, and to get from one to the other, everybody had to pass us. We were fully aware all the time of what was going on, and we were rarely caught out when there was a change in the market. We started dealing large in shorts [short-dated government bonds] and things like that which we'd never dealt in before, and we were doing very well because anybody who was passing our pitch, almost had to brush past us, and it kept us on our toes the whole time.' There were still plenty of jobbing firms consisting of just one partner and an office manager, who would frequently 'undo their book' on another jobbing firm, so that there were only between twenty and thirty firms actively trading, about a third of the overall number.

Nevertheless, the plight of the jobbers was becoming more marked during the 1950s and 60s. A major factor was that the institutions wanted to deal in large amounts of stock, increasing the jobbers' need for capital. Successive Stock Exchange committees looked into this position but the Council repeatedly refused to allow them to employ outside risk

▲ *The floor of the house in the 1950s*

capital, thus driving some out of business and some into mergers. Durlachers, for example, merged successively with Bone Oldham in 1960, Bradford & Paine in 1963 and Kitchen, Baker, Mason in 1965, in each case increasing its capital base and extending its dealing capabilities into new areas, finally in 1968 merging with Wedd Jefferson (which had taken over Hadow & Turner in 1962) to form Wedd Durlacher. There were also some mergers between brokers, banding together in the face of the growing complexity of taxation and auditing requirements, the demands of the institutional investors and a need for capital which, if less pressing than that of the jobbers, was still important. Management accounting, with which many firms were quite unacquainted (in one firm it took the form of the senior partner, on his annual departure in August to shoot grouse, assuming that 'enough money for the year' had already been made) gradually became the norm during the late 1950s and early 60s, partly because of the Council's need to be able to scrutinise firms' finances more closely after the establishment of the Compensation Fund.

Professional skills

Although 'good connections' were still vitally important to most stockbroking firms, large or small, the twin catalysts of increasing need for specialist skills – especially research and analysis – and early mechanisation meant a considerable widening of recruitment. The leader in the research field was undoubtedly Phillips & Drew, which was the first broker systematically to employ actuaries and which, during the 1950s, specialised in forecasting company profits and providing comparative analysis of different shares and sectors. Under the active leadership of the senior partner Sidney Perry, himself an actuary who was determined to employ only the best qualified people, the firm took the unprecedented step in the early 1950s of ruling that no partner was allowed to bring in a relative. By the middle of the decade over four-fifths of its business was with institutional investors, including many of the pension funds which mushroomed in the post-war period.

James Capel similarly built up research capabilities so that it was able to offer clients one of the earliest daily breakdowns of the asset values of investment trusts, and brought in additional partners to extend its coverage of specialised services such as Australian shares and European securities. This expansion led in turn to a more formalised management structure, so that by 1959 the partners were working in groups with specific responsibilities and staff assigned specifically to each group, a pattern that was also adopted by Sheppard & Co. and some of the other larger firms.

The growing demand for investment analysis put pressure on companies to disclose more information, and in August 1964 Lord Ritchie of Dundee, the broker who became chairman of the Council in succession to Braithwaite, wrote to the chairmen of all publicly quoted companies urging them to disclose more information about themselves. The Exchange itself had remained highly secretive and reluctant to issue information about its own business, despite

HOSTILE TAKEOVER

The late 1950s and the 1960s were marked by some epic takeover struggles, notably the landmark battle for control of British Aluminium by Alcoa and Tube Investments – a battle which was won by the latter in the stock market – and one of the most fiercely contested, the bid by ICI for Courtaulds in late 1961 and early 1962, which was the largest in the UK up to that date. ICI's initial bid, announced on 18 December 1961, valued Courtaulds at £180 million, rocking the City by its size and audacity, as companies this size were not in those days viewed as legitimate targets for a hostile bid.

Courtaulds went all out to evade ICI's clutches, trumping increased bids from ICI with various sophisticated defence tactics, including promises of dividend increases of up to 10 per cent over the next two years, a cash distribution out of profits within three years, a £40 million capitalisation issue and the creation of a £40 million investment trust. Courtaulds shares rose rapidly, but ICI battled on before finally, and fatally, making its bid unconditional before counting acceptances – having been advised that this would lead to a further favourable surge. It did not, and on 12 March 1962 ICI had to concede that its bid had failed with acceptances of only 37.4 per cent. The widespread publicity attracted by the whole affair depicted Courtaulds in the light of a brave David defeating a predatory and ruthless Goliath, paving the way for a decade of acquisitions by the company under the autocratic leadership of Sir Frank Kearton as he tried to salvage Britain's foundering textile industry.

'Every shareholder should resist their iniquitious, invidious, immoral bid until the offer goes up at least five bob . . .' A press cartoon during the battle for Courtaulds.

▲ *Lord Ritchie of Dundee, Chairman 1959–65, painted in his Privy Councillor's uniform by Edward Halliday.*

the fact that Braithwaite had, while Chairman, frequently urged the benefits of fuller disclosure. The *Daily Official List* provided prices at which bargains had been done on the previous day, and some details of the numbers of bargains, but its information was incomplete as the 'marking' of bargains was entirely voluntary and bargains at special prices were frequently omitted. The report of the Radcliffe Committee in 1959 simply noted that the provision of Stock Exchange information (like that of the Bank of England and most other City institutions) was 'inadequate', and it was not until September 1964, a month after Ritchie's request, that the Exchange began to publish monthly figures of turnover by value and number of bargains in five different sectors, including equities and gilts with a life of over five years. Meanwhile, in November 1962 the *Financial Times* had launched the FT-Actuaries Index, which was an All Share Index of the market capitalisation of the largest companies, and the flow of available market information began to gather pace.

Increasing mechanisation helped in this respect. The Exchange, which had installed a Hollerith punched card system for use in the settlement process in 1949, acquired its first computer, an IBM 360 (prompting criticism for being 'unpatriotic' in failing to choose a British make) in 1964, which made cost savings estimated at £42,600 annually. It was used for, among other functions, the centralised delivery which the Exchange had begun to provide for members the previous year, and which was followed in 1966 by a central stock payment scheme. By this date the old building was in process of demolition, much lamented, in spite of its many inconveniences, by most of the members who felt, in the words of one of them, that the move was 'like leaving home.'

A STOCK EXCHANGE GALLERY 1

Sir Derrick Mullens and Sir Peter Daniell were successively senior partner of Mullens & Co and Government Broker throughout the 1950s and early 1960s, presiding over the gilts market at a time when the Conservative government began to use monetary policy. Dick Wilkins was one of its most memorable and influential members; an exuberant figure who lived at the Savoy during the week, he had tremendous flair and helped Wedd to become one of the top three firms in the gilts market during his time as senior partner. Heading the rival firm of Akroyd & Smithers, Hugh Merriman was also a proponent of change and modernisation on the Stock Exchange Council.

Major roles in the industrial equities market were played by the astute and well-connected Esmond Durlacher ('the Emperor'), an important figure in the post-war market and senior partner of Durlacher for over 30 years; and by Sir Nigel Mordaunt ('the Baronet'), who specialised in the brewery market, and was the head of Bone Oldham, one of the clutch of jobbing firms which merged with Durlacher in the 1950s and 60s. Lewis Powell was senior partner of C.D. Pinchin & Co., which specialised in electrical and engineering stocks. Cazenove partner Charles Purnell ('the Rook'), the firm's senior dealer for many years, was a powerful force in the equity market, much respected by the jobbers.

Non-gilt jobbers included George Lazarus of Lazarus Brothers, who dominated the volatile and competitive post-war market in South African gold mine shares. Equally important in the stores market was Sydney King, a bullying, hard-nosed jobber who was the number two in Smith Brothers. The senior partner of P.A. Duke & Co., Percy Duke, was one of the best known and remembered 'characters' of the old House. Always dressed in striped trousers and wing collar, Duke was the subject of innumerable anecdotes, usually centring on the hectoring of his juniors.

Equally unwilling to suffer fools gladly was the fiery Kit Hoare, senior partner of Hoare & Co., whose bushy eyebrows struck terror into the hearts of his subordinates. He was an aggressive and successful broker with real market flair. At Cazenove, Sir Antony Hornby was senior partner from 1954, a generous man of strong views and a brilliant new issue broker. His colleague Peter Kemp-Welch, approachable and humorous, brought in prestigious new clients and did much to help the firm become more professional during the post-war period; the steadfast Godfrey Chandler was another outstanding Cazenove broker. Sebag owed its position as a leading corporate broker almost entirely to Sir Jock Gilmour.

Jock Hunter, senior partner of Messel, was a voice of progress within his own firm and also on the Stock Exchange Council. Other firms which benefited from vigorous and far-sighted leadership were Vickers da Costa, where Ralph Vickers pioneered a profitable Japanese business in the early 1960s, and Strauss Turnbull whose Julius Strauss was the undisputed king of the early Eurobond market.

▶ *The dome of the old House is dismantled, 1966.*

10

The Stock Exchange Tower 1966–1979

THE WORK OF DEMOLISHING THE FOUNDATIONS OF THE OLD STOCK EXCHANGE building took the contractors several months, and it was not until January 1967 that the site was cleared and the work of building the new Exchange, designed by Professor Lloyd Llewelyn Davies and Fitzroy Robinson, could begin. The Queen Mother laid the foundation stone on 14 November 1967. Building was scheduled to take place in three phases. The first involved building a new Post Office and the main tower, which affected the floor very little. In the second, the four lower floors of the tower were turned into brokers' boxes, telephone rooms and a temporary floor. This was in use for nearly three years while the final phase, including the construction of the permanent floor, took place. The new building was opened by the Queen on 8 November 1972, although the floor was not in use until 11 June the following year.

This new City landmark, taking its place among a cluster of tower blocks which were radically altering the London skyline during the 1960s and early 1970s, presented a strong

◄ *The Stock Exchange Tower under construction in 1969 – a coloured etching by Richard Beer.*

contrast with the old House. It was twenty-six storeys and 321 feet high, with a floor slightly smaller than its predecessor but with no pillars; jobbers (who had been asked to choose between three different types of pitch) had rings of seats inside which their clerks sat. At the top were Council and administrative offices, and the middle floors were let to member firms. It was a major achievement of the chairmanship of Sir Martin Wilkinson.

INCREASING SIZE OF PARTNERSHIPS

During the years of rebuilding the preoccupations of Council and members were gradually changing. Discussion of issues such as advertising, nationality (members still had to have British nationality), rates of commission and the admission of women rumbled on without reaching any new conclusions. However, as firms grew by amalgamation, usually in order to be able to provide the services increasingly required by institutional investors, the Council agreed in 1967 to allow them an unlimited number of partners. This was now possible because the new Companies Act of that year permitted partnerships to comprise more than

THE STOCK EXCHANGE WAS REBUILT
BETWEEN 1966 AND 1972

OPENED BY HER MAJESTY THE QUEEN
ON 8TH NOVEMBER 1972

▲ *Queen Elizabeth II
opening the new
building, on
8 November 1972.*

◄ *The Stock Exchange
Tower.*

twenty. It led to the formation of even larger firms – by 1969 Wedd Durlacher and Sheppard & Chase each had thirty partners.

However, there was no relaxation in the rules that each partner had to be a member, and could not pursue any other occupation or have any other unlimited liability. A limited partnership scheme, under which outsiders were allowed to provide up to a third of a firm's capital, was introduced in 1966 but was not successful, largely because banks, insurance companies and other financial institutions, who might have been keen to provide backing, were specifically excluded from doing so. Finally, in 1969, the Council agreed to allow both broking and jobbing firms to become incorporated and to accept institutional shareholders, although there was still unlimited liability for working directors. Even so, jobbers found it more and more difficult to make a profit and by 1970 they constituted only 13 per cent of the membership, which represented a fall from 20 per cent a decade earlier.

INVESTING OVERSEAS

As communications improved so did the chances of international investment. The Stock Exchange certainly missed out on some possibilities in this field, most notably the booming Eurobond market which largely by-passed the Exchange because of its rules which insisted on the deal going through the market – ensuring that the jobber got his turn – and on commissions being paid by both buyer and seller. However, members were becoming increasingly aware of the potential benefits of international expansion. Among the first to

155

THE POSEIDON AFFAIR

Poseidon 'braves' say it's £200 a share

AFTER 10 weeks or more of half-fact, rumour, and sheer tittle tattle, the **Poseidon** wonder was finally confirmed yesterday as the mining marvel a few brave souls have believed all along.

And though the company finally spoke up on what it has found at Windarra, in Western Australia, the message from the crowded and jubilant meeting in Adelaide was typically with a grade of 2.4% nickel. A large amount of drilling and evaluation still needs to be done on the five deposits within the Poseidon claims.

And on the basis of these calculations it is reckoned Poseidon may be capable of producing 50,000 to 60,000 tons of nickel a year by 1975.

The Daily Express *trumpets the 'mining marvel', 20 December 1969.*

The Australian nickel booms of 1968–70 provide a wonderful example of stock market rumour, hype and excitement. In the autumn of 1969 Poseidon was quoted at 20s 9d among the little regarded 'marks' on the inside page of the *Financial Times*. Then rumours of its making the richest nickel discovery in history sparked a renewed attack of nickel fever, following the Western Mining excitement in the previous year. (The importance of the discovery at Windarra Prospect in the centre of Western Australia was that it indicated a possible new source of mineral reserves miles away from the traditional areas of Kambalda and Carr Boyd Rocks.) The market had been flat for months and the Poseidon news was seized on joyfully, the share price almost trebling overnight on 29 September 1969 to 59s 6d. It went on rising, with particularly frantic bidding in City streets and pubs after the market closed at 12.30 p.m. on Christmas Eve.

Early in the New Year saner spirits realised that Poseidon's market value was greater than that of many large British industrial companies, without an ounce of the metal having been extracted, but it continued to boom, reaching its peak at £124 in February 1970. However, the $94\frac{1}{4}$ per cent rate of short-term capital gains tax at the time meant that many UK investors were effectively locked in to their investment. By the end of the year the shares stood at £19.

open offices overseas – with permission from the Exchange – were brokers Spencer, Thornton & Co. in Brussels in 1962 and Vickers da Costa in Luxembourg the following year. In 1967 Cazenove, which already had strong ties in California, took an even bolder step and became the first London firm to buy a seat on an American exchange, on the Pacific Coast Stock Exchange in San Francisco for $50,000. The main attraction for Cazenove, apart from gaining a presence in one of the fastest-growing areas of the US, was that the Pacific Coast exchange allowed split commissions between members, thus enabling the London brokers to receive compensation for US orders channelled through US brokers.

This move required changes in Stock Exchange regulations, as well as approval from the Bank of England, and other firms rapidly took advantage of Cazenove's pioneering work, encouraged also by the sterling devaluation in November 1967.

Joseph Sebag and Rowe & Pitman both purchased seats on the Pacific Coast exchange, the latter avowedly to give their clients 'a better service at a better price.' Just how much better was realised by one of the partners when he learnt to his surprise that on one of their first deals the client was charged just £18 commission whereas the previous week he would have had to pay £78. W.I. Carr joined the Hong Kong Stock Exchange and James Capel purchased a seat on the Midwest Exchange in Chicago, at the same time announcing its intention to apply for associated membership of all other regional stock exchanges in the USA. Nervousness about Capels' jobbing activities in Chicago and the blurring of traditional boundaries between broker and jobber provoked a *cri de coeur* from John Robertson of Wedd Durlacher Mordaunt, who wrote to the Chairman of the Exchange: 'I cannot visualise the Council allowing our brokers to be "market makers" in European shares or our jobbers to deal directly with non-members, unless we want to have a complete "free for all." Our peculiar system is envied by many foreigners and if we disturb this basic principle we may lose out on the enormous possibilities which undoubtedly exist for us.'

The New York Stock Exchange was still at this date closed to foreign membership, as was London. An application by an American firm, Hallgarten & Co, in 1968 to become a member of the London Exchange was viewed favourably by the Council but heavily outvoted by the committee which vetted applications, on the grounds that competition from 'financially more powerful' US firms would be damaging to British brokers.

Going Nationwide

An early experiment in expansion in Britain was made by J. & A. Scrimgeour, who in August 1967 took over four provincial firms and opened branches in thirteen towns, to acquire what was virtually a nationwide network which could compete on more equal terms with provincial brokers who had lower overheads and operated under a more relaxed system than that imposed on London firms, including the ability to act as both broker and jobber. It was not, however, particularly successful.

THE ASSET STRIPPERS

In the 1960s, an entrepreneur began operating in a way which struck terror into the heart of British boardrooms and which was ultimately credited with 'unleashing the power of the stock market.' Jim Slater started his working life as an accountant with the Leyland Group and spent a period of convalescence in reading everything he could find about stock market investment. He wrote a successful share-tipping column (under the pseudonym 'Capitalist') in the *Sunday Telegraph*, and in 1964 went into business with Peter Walker, a young Conservative MP. Many supposedly 'family owned' companies – such as an early victim, Cork Manufacturing – were found by Slater Walker's assiduous research methods not to be so: the families had often sold off the shares over the years and remained as minority share-holders, defenceless in the face of a determined assault by a predatory purchaser. The Slater Walker method of operation was to pick out companies trading on the stock market which were valued at less than their assets were worth, acquire their shares and, having gained control, 'strip the assets', such as property or under-performing parts of a group, by selling them off – often for more than they had paid for the entire company in the first place.

This was widely, if mistakenly, held to be a method of making industry more efficient, and successive governments turned to Jim Slater for advice on industrial restructuring. Slater Walker's asset stripping activities undoubtedly helped the strong bull market of the late 1960s, but they were looked at askance by many members and others in the City, who felt that it was becoming a sourer, more edgy place in which to work. The widespread anxiety about bid practices led the Stock Exchange and the Bank of England to appeal in 1967 to the Issuing Houses Association to review the informal takeover guidelines issued some years earlier. The subsequent investigation led to the publication of a new Code on Amalgamations and Mergers and the formation, in March 1968, of the Panel on Takeovers and Mergers, on which both Bank and Stock Exchange were represented.

The panel's work suffered an early setback in the 'Gallaher affair' just four months later, when it condemned as an infringement of the new code share dealings by Cazenove and the merchant bank Morgan Grenfell to further the takeover of Gallaher by American Tobacco. This was firmly denied by both parties; the Stock Exchange Council accepted that any breach of the code had been unwitting and took no further action, prompting fears that the panel would prove useless in practice. However, largely as a result of the Gallaher affair the panel was strengthened and given new powers, and moved from its original cramped premises in the Bank of England to better accommodation in the Stock Exchange building itself. A new and tougher Takeover Code was issued in 1969, and members accused of offences against it quailed when summoned into the formidable presence of the panel's Chairman, Lord Shawcross, and Director General, Ian Fraser of Warburgs. Its subsequent history was a success which went some way towards appeasing those non-City people who were suspicious of the efficacy of self-regulation.

INSIDER TRADING

One aspect of the stock market which remained shadowy for many years, and where self-regulation did prove inadequate, was the difficult area of insider trading. While officially frowned upon, it was certainly practised, but any large-scale activity was usually fairly evident. The Council investigated all cases where leaks, sometimes through carelessness but more often deliberate, allowed profitable share deals to take place by a small group of those in the know, often ahead of the announcement of a takeover bid. Most cases were not proven: only a handful were proved, and in these instances the culprits were reprimanded or occasionally suspended. In the spring of 1973 the Exchange and the Takeover Panel together recommended that insider deals should be made a criminal offence, but it was not until June 1980, after a considerable amount of further investigation and discussion, that this was effected. Even then, the difficulty of obtaining proof meant that there were very few convictions.

DOMESTIC MATTERS

Meanwhile there were several important internal events. In February 1970 a new system, the

◀ *A view of the floor in the Stock Exchange Tower in 1980, by Boyd Evans.*

Market Price Display Service (MPDS) was introduced and became immediately popular. At the touch of a button, brokers could have direct access to a continuously updated visual display of the middle prices of some 700 leading securities. It was a computer-driven system using closed circuit television techniques, the first real-time computer system to be undertaken by the Council. The initial annual subscription fee for members was £500 plus £50 for each individual TV display unit, while non-members paid £1,000 per annum.

TALISMAN

A much more ambitious scheme was Talisman (Transfer Accounting and Lodgement for Investors, Stock Management for jobbers) which revolutionised the whole business of settlement. The Council agreed to it in early 1974; its basic function was to set up a depository (known as Sepon) for holding all stock passing through the market in course of settlement, which was a radical change from the cumbrous and expensive 'paper-chase' ticket-passing system which had operated almost unchanged for over a century. Talisman was to be available to brokers and jobbers throughout the country, and was the first time that a service of the Exchange required compulsory input, via a computer, from subscribing members. Its design proved far more expensive and difficult than originally envisaged, requiring, as well as many extra staff and complex computerisation, various changes in legislation, prin-

THE COLLAPSE OF ROLLS-ROYCE

The stock market shuddered in November 1970 at the sudden and unexpected news that Rolls-Royce, one of the show-pieces of British manufacturing industry, was in difficulties and would be given a rescue package of £60 million of public funds, to mitigate the soaring costs of developing an aero-engine for the Lockheed Tri-Star. The share price fell from 11s 6d to 7s 9d at the news, and worse was to follow. On 4 February 1971 a receiver was appointed and shares were temporarily suspended at 7s 6d.

The market, like the general public, could hardly believe that such an old-established firm as Rolls-Royce could collapse, and the affair proved a dilemma for a Conservative government which had declared its unwillingness to bail out failing companies. It was nationalised under an emergency Act of Parliament – the government emphasising that the defence aspect of the company's work necessitated such a move, and that its overall policy of non-intervention remained in force – and became Rolls-Royce (1971) Ltd. on 23 February.

By that time, dealings had resumed (having continued unofficially during the two days of 11 and 12 February when the Exchange was closed to implement decimalisation) and a flurry of buying ensued until dealing was finally suspended before the new company came into being, when they closed at 18.5p in the new decimal currency (about 3s 8½d).

Anxious workers at the Rolls-Royce factory in Derby, 6 February 1971.

cipally in order to allow the transfer of securities by book entry. There was considerable opposition to it from members and within the Council itself – at one point the consultants McKinsey were called in to report on the mushrooming costs. However, the tide of computerisation was running against the objectors, and Talisman's champions managed to prevent the project being axed. It was finally implemented in 1979 and worked well until Crest was ready to take on settlement (see page 193).

This new technology, however, did nothing to assuage the desires of the increasing numbers of members who conducted business overseas and who felt that they were being most unfairly handicapped by the Exchange's insistence that they must abide by the rules of the London market while so doing. The Council was finally obliged to agree, and in February 1973 made a landmark amendment to the rules which allowed the overseas organisations of broker firms to act as 'market makers' in the USA and Canada, and jobbers to open offices there.

External pressures were likewise the stimulus for some long overdue changes in the rule book. The examination by the Monopolies and Mergers Commission into professional services made it uncomfortably likely that fixed minimum commissions would come under scrutiny. Although Edward Heath's Conservative government, elected in June 1970, was less hostile to the City than its predecessor, the Exchange reluctantly conceded that some alterations to what were clearly restrictive practices would have to be made. The 1971 report of

▶ The first women members to be elected to the Stock Exchange in March 1973. In the centre is chairman Sir Martin Wilkinson, flanked by his deputies George Loveday, who succeeded him as chairman in May 1973 (left), and Kenneth Crabbe.

the Monopolies Commission ominously noted the frequent connection between restrictions on advertising and on price, and the Council decided to put the question of advertising to a vote, hoping to deflect attention from commissions. Predictably, opposition was strongest from the smaller firms, who were nervous about their inability to match the financial expenditure of the larger ones; but eventually, after various unsuccessful half measures, press advertising was permitted at the end of 1973, and this was extended to television and direct mail three years later.

Two other barriers to fall in this period were the prohibitions on women and foreign-born members. The report of the Monopolies Commission recommended the admittance of both. When the rule banning foreign-born members was originally introduced during the First World War, the bogeys had been the Germans – now, the Americans were more to be feared. Peter Swan of Phillips & Drew expressed to the Council his apprehension that 'while a foreigner may no doubt pass his exams – he may come from a country that does not have the same standards as we have built up in the City.' Membership was cheaper in London than in many other countries, especially the US, and 'an influx of Americans' would almost certainly take business away from recognised London firms, with the result that we 'may begin to lose our sovereignty.' Many agreed with him, but the rule was finally repealed in 1971.

Even more painful to some members was the thought of a woman member of the House. Federation had not brought any very great advantages to British brokers or jobbers, but many had hoped that it might be the preliminary to nationwide amalgamation. The negotiations were long and difficult, centring around country brokers' unwillingness to give up dual capacity and London's desire to ban provincial members from direct access to the floor of the House. The debate was enlivened by an exchange of letters in *The Times* in the summer of 1971. Graham Greenwell, much annoyed by an editorial in the paper condemning as 'irritating and out of date' the refusal to admit women, stoutly defended the position which he said embodied 'the wishes and past experience of members.' Both the Baltic and the Stock Exchange, he claimed, were 'in essence . . . private men's clubs and not business institutions and wish to remain so', and he castigated the 'doctrinaire' teachings of the female sex, 'from which our country has been suffering.' This letter was refuted by the Chairman, Sir Martin Wilkinson, who replied the next day that it was 'totally untrue' that the Stock Exchange regarded itself as a private men's club, and that it did indeed perform a public service 'whether or not it exists to do so.' Philip Greenwell, Graham's son, then entered the lists with the claim that the reluctance to admit women was 'just another example of resistance to change of any kind . . . only too prevalent in this country today.' If the Exchange was a private club, he had never been able to find either the dining room or the card room, he said, adding for good measure that the writer of the original letter had been elected to the Exchange 'nearly fifty years ago.'

AMALGAMATION

The problem was finally resolved in March 1973 when the London Stock Exchange formally amalgamated with the other eleven exchanges in Britain and Northern Ireland, after which the new entity was known as The Stock Exchange. Among these other bodies there was a total of thirteen women members, so it was obvious that they could no longer be barred in London; additionally there was not, and never had been, anything in the constitution of the Exchange to keep them out. Anxious to avoid any direct confrontation, the Council – by twenty-four votes to five – finally agreed to accept applications from women members for the year beginning in March 1973. The first to be elected was Mrs Muriel Wood, who had made two previous unsuccessful applications, the first in 1966 under her maiden name of Bailey and in 1972 in her married name. Within a few months women clerks were allowed on the floor, and by the end of 1973 there were twenty-seven women members, fourteen of them in the 'London unit' of the new amalgamated Exchange.

In 1968 the Council had reduced what had become a proliferating number of committees, revised their duties and re-organised the various departments of the Exchange: Finance, Quotations, Membership, Services and Public Relations. The work of the Council and committees continued along broadly similar lines. There were many routine functions such as interviewing candidates for membership, scrutiny of firms' accounts, rulings on exceptions or exemptions to quoting requirements, disciplinary questions and arbitration on disputes between member firms other than the most minor which were dealt with by the Honorary Market Officials – respected and recently retired members who operated from a tiny cubby-hole adjacent to the floor. Beyond this, the Council was primarily concerned with policy, and was led by a chairman and two deputies, one of whom – by practice rather than rule – was a jobber and one a broker. These three formed an executive committee which met every day with the Secretary-General (later the Chief Executive) and the Secretary of the Council in attendance, in a morning session known as 'Chairman's Room.' This committee had only limited constitutional powers, but was enormously influential in steering the Exchange's business.

163

By 1972 there were 900 staff, annual revenue was approaching £5 million and the property of the Exchange was valued at £16 million. It was clear to several members of the Council that the administrative burden was becoming too great for a part-time, somewhat amateur body. Britain's membership of the EEC was a further complicating issue. In November 1972 the Council approved the formation of an advisory committee with the remit of studying these and other issues faced by the securities industry, to be chaired by Nicholas Goodison, who had joined the Council in 1968.

The committee was strongly influenced by the recent Baines report on local authorities and its proposals were based on much the same philosophy as that of Baines – that the Council must ensure 'that the machine works but . . . should not be required to operate it.' What was needed was 'the directional and management skills appropriate to any large organisation.' The committee's report, advocating wholesale reorganisation, was adopted by the Council in October 1973.

Ultimate authority was to remain in the hands of the Council, who would essentially be concerned only with deciding policy and ensuring that it was carried out. A Chief Executive would be appointed with direct responsibility for the management of the personnel, assets, finances and equipment of the Exchange, reporting directly to the Chairman and with the heads of the executive departments as his immediate subordinates. The numerous standing committees in each department were pruned, and a Planning Committee to look at specific problems and opportunities and a Chairman's Liaison Committee, including representatives from all users of the market, were established.

THE FIRST CHIEF EXECUTIVE

After a considerable search, in October 1974 the Council appointed to the key post of Chief Executive Robert Fell, a top-level civil servant who had previously been head of the Export Credits Guarantee Department. Fell became a member of a new small Executive Committee of the Council, which met weekly and consisted of the Chairman, Deputy Chairmen and the chairmen of the standing committees: he was not a member of the Council itself. Among his first tasks was to visit the various provincial 'units' of the amalgamated Exchange, to bring them more closely in touch with London while efforts were being made to develop services – especially settlement – countrywide, as a cement for the recent union. Fell was also anxious to develop links between the Council, by now under the chairmanship of George Loveday, and government ministers: this was a new idea to the Exchange which had been very good at 'minding its own business' and had tended to ignore the outside world unless forced into a response to external events.

By the time of Fell's arrival the Exchange was facing one of its most serious crises. In 1972 stock market levels had peaked throughout the world, but from then on all the major economies were in decline, and a two-year bear market, culminating in the crash of 1974, was under way. During these years the stock market came under intense political and economic pressures which included a sterling crisis, the Egypt-Israeli war in October 1973 and the resulting oil price hikes, spiralling inflation, the secondary bank crisis and the collapse of the property market. Industrial action by the coal miners and the 'three-day week', introduced to save fuel at the end of 1973, triggered the final crash. A general election in February resulted in a hung Parliament: Heath was unable to form a government and Wilson returned to Downing Street with a minority government. By the summer prices appeared to be in free fall, and the FT Index went under 200 with a devastating psychological effect on the market.

Other pressures on the beleaguered Exchange were technological. In 1969 a computerised dealing system known as Instinet had been launched in the US, and rumours of a British counterpart soon began to circulate in the market. In August 1972 the Accepting Houses Committee confirmed members' fears by announcing that the merchant banks were combining to produce Ariel – the Automated Real-time Investments Exchange Limited, which would be available to institutions on subscription and guaranteeing their anonymity. The Council was sufficiently unnerved by this threat of direct competition to announce drastic cuts in commission rates, although those projected by Ariel were still substantially lower. At one point the Exchange even considered buying Ariel, but negotiations foundered and it was decided that the best method of minimising its impact was to press ahead with the development of a system to record prices of deals instantaneously, and a further communication system through which brokers could inform institutions of their interest in lines of stock. This ultimately resulted in Topic (Teletext Output of Price Information by Computer) which, despite resistance from the larger firms of brokers who felt it would unfairly benefit the country jobbers, was successfully installed in March 1980, a year after Talisman had finally gone on line.

THE MARKET IN DECLINE

In the event Ariel failed to take its expected market share, partly because by the time it came into operation in February 1974 the market was in steep decline. During that year every firm on the Exchange suffered to a greater or lesser extent. Institutional business dropped, many private clients stopped investing altogether, firms' profitability shrank and partners had to call on their personal capital to cover expenses. In some cases clients went bankrupt, without warning, so that unlimited liability held new terrors. Some firms ceased trading, many merged and six, including some long-established ones such as Chapman & Rowe and Mitton, Butler, Priest & Co. (ironically the first broker to be incorporated, in 1970, in order to attract outside capital), were hammered. The Exchange moved swiftly to tighten up both scrutiny of members' accounts and their capital requirements, and in 1975 sole traders were banned while corporate members were required to keep a minimum margin of £200,000. The membership profile had altered dramatically – broking firms declined in number from

165

A RECORD EQUITY OFFERING

Sir Thomas ('Tommy') Gore Browne, Government Broker, 1973–81.

The sale to the private sector of 66.8 million shares in British Petroleum in June 1977 was at that date the largest single share sale ever. The genesis of the sale was two years earlier, when the Bank of England acquired a 20 per cent share of BP in its bail-out acquisition of Burmah Oil, on top of the 48 per cent already owned by the government. The finance controller of BP, Quentin Morris, realised that this hefty stake could lead to problems in the future, and that a sale of the ex-Burmah stock would be of enormous benefit to the company.

The main problem was one of size. The shares were worth £564 million, equivalent to one-fiftieth of all shares held by British investing institutions, and many people in the City predicted that the whole thing might turn out to be a gigantic flop.

With the assistance of the US investment bankers Morgan Stanley, it was decided to conduct the sale internationally, with sales on Wall Street at the same time as on the London market – not a straightforward procedure in view of the many differences in practice between the US and UK markets. The launch date was fixed for Tuesday 14 June, and five brokers – Mullens, Cazenove, Hoare Govett, Rowe & Pitman and J. & A. Scrimgeour – were authorised, along with ten merchant banks, to conduct deals. The brokers were led by Tommy Gore Browne, the Government Broker, and the bankers by David Scholey of Warburgs. Five US investment banks, including Morgan Stanley, were also involved. 'Operations rooms' were set up in Mullens' offices at 15 Moorgate and in Britannic House, BP's London headquarters, organised by Quentin Morris, now inevitably known as 'Q'.

A week before the sale, the fifteen dealers had sent in the names of the 782 client institutions which wanted to bid and allocations were made. By the afternoon of 13 June price recommendations were made by the dealers and sent to the Bank of England where a price of 845 pence a share was set by the Governor, Gordon Richardson, with the advice of the Government Broker. A last-minute hitch took place when it appeared that some members of the cabinet were objecting to the sale, and Richardson was summoned to 10 Downing Street, from where he rang Gore Browne to ask about the possibility of a 24-hour delay. The latter replied that with so much at stake, the launch would have to be postponed for several months. Finally, at 8.45 in the evening, the Governor gave the go-ahead. The agreed price was entered into the prospectuses, and the sale went off as planned the next day. By the afternoon of the 14th this all-time record issue was fully underwritten. A week later it was announced that it had been nearly five times oversubscribed.

168 in 1973 to 129 in 1975, jobbers from 31 to 16 in the same period, and the numbers of London members dropped from 3,536 to 3,390.

The finances of the Stock Exchange itself were grievously affected, by the falling levels of subscriptions and fees for services and initial listings, lack of rental income as offices in the new building fell vacant and could not be re-let, and the mounting expenses of Talisman. By Christmas 1974, things were grim indeed – there had been a large number of staff redundancies, bonuses were cut, and many members were considering whether to cut their losses and leave the market altogether. Some of the traditional Christmas merriment, such as the singing of 'Oh, for the wings of a dove' by Eric 'Ginger' Baker arrayed in his Eighth Army khaki shorts and pith helmet, took place as usual, but people's hearts were not in it.

The collapse of Burmah Oil on the last day of 1974 was another shattering piece of news for the market and prompted a further fall in share prices on 2 January, the first day of trading in the new year. The FT Index reached its low point of 146 on 6 January. However, the action of some of the larger institutional investors, who began a programme of aggressive buying concerted by the Joint Investment Manager of the Prudential, Edward Hatchett, went some way to restoring confidence. During the second week in January business began to pick up rapidly and the estimated value of quoted private sector shares rocketed within eight weeks from £17,000 million to £35,000 million. The FT Index rose to 300, and the bull market lasted until the spring of the following year.

The finances of the Exchange improved along with the market, and in April 1978 it initiated a market in traded equity options, originally available on the shares of ten leading companies. It showed no interest, however, in the possibility of a futures market and members were largely apathetic, if not definitely hostile, towards the nascent London International Financial Futures and Options Exchange, or LIFFE, which was being discussed in the late 1970s and finally began operations on 30 September 1982.

COMING EVENTS . . .

On 3 May 1979 a Conservative government was returned to power under Margaret Thatcher; on 23 October two announcements which would have a profound effect on the stock market were made. The first said that all remaining exchange controls were to be removed immediately. The other news was disquieting. Two years earlier, the Office of Fair Trading had placed the rule book of the Stock Exchange on the register of the Restrictive Practices Court, and the threat of a court hearing had been impending ever since. The Council had lobbied fiercely against the OFT's decision, and had hoped that the new Conservative government would overrule it – but now the market learned that it was to stand. Some of the more prescient in the City appreciated the importance of these two decisions, which combined to light the fuse that would detonate the Big Bang.

Big Bang
1979–1986

*B*Y THE MID-1970S THE REGULATIONS UNDER WHICH THE STOCK EXCHANGE operated were coming under severe pressure, which increased sharply after the abolition of exchange controls in 1979. International capital markets were now completely freed as far as London was concerned: domestic investors could look to overseas markets and London firms began to regard foreign firms as serious competition, while many international markets, such as that in South African gold shares, simply bypassed London altogether.

The New York Stock Exchange had already been deregulated on 1 May 1975, 'Mayday', and the abolition of fixed commission rates there had led to the emergence of a number of large, very profitable investment banks which were now eyeing London voraciously. London firms were hobbled by the Stock Exchange rule book and were quite unable to compete internationally: if they wanted to expand abroad they still had to abide by the London rules, although the change to Rule 60 in 1970 and the 1973 concession allowing brokers' overseas branches to act as market makers in the US had alleviated the position.

Some further relaxation had, despite the weight of those in favour of the *status quo*, already begun. Fixed commissions, although ostensibly set in stone, were in practice subtly eroded by 'free services' such as extensive research provided to favoured clients. Even the

▲ *Sir Nicholas Goodison, Chairman 1976–88*
painted by Tom Phillips RA

separation of capacity, dating back to 1909 and much vaunted as a measure to protect investors, was to some extent diluted by the 'put through' rules where brokers matched business on the basis of market prices and were able to control both sides of the deal. However, the basic uncompetitiveness of the London market *vis à vis* its overseas, and particularly at this date American, rivals, remained, and many feared that unless radical changes were made London could be sidelined.

The Council of the Stock Exchange, under the chairmanship of Nicholas (later Sir Nicholas) Goodison, held many debates on these issues in the late 1970s and early 1980s. One possibility was to allow firms to establish international dealerships which would be allowed to trade in international equities, but this foundered on the question of what, exactly, was an international equity. As overseas investors could, post-1979, deal in BP or ICI shares, such shares were in effect international equities, and it was obvious that freedom to trade them would affect the domestic market.

Despite the pressures for deregulation – one of the most forceful and powerful of whose advocates was Goodison himself – there was still a strong resistance to change within the market and on the Council. The Exchange provided a charmed circle inside which a very reasonable living was to be made; the commissions viewed as high by some merchant banks and institutional investors were not considered at all unreasonable by those who charged them, and had the extra advantage of ease – no negotiations over the terms of a deal were necessary. This was especially true of the gilt brokers who enjoyed a virtual monopoly in their market, and there was also some support from users. International or global business was still in its infancy in the 70s: although a few of the larger brokers had business in the US, Australia and South Africa (the latter a popular destination in the winter), the majority of members, particularly the smaller firms, openly feared the foreign competition to which deregulation would expose them.

THE THREAT OF COURT ACTION

Soon, however, events would force the Exchange's hand. In 1976 the Restrictive Trade Practices Act, which had previously only applied to the manufacturers of goods, had been extended to include service industries, which at that time were coming under fire from various consumer groups. In the three months before the new provisions of the Act came into force it was possible to seek exemption. Successful applications were received from the legal and medical professions, and from Lloyd's and other organisations, but the Stock Exchange did not apply – perhaps because its Council or its legal advisers considered that the Exchange, as a market, would not be involved.

Whatever the reasons for this omission, once the new provisions of the Act were in force the Exchange's fate seemed to be sealed. In 1978 Sir Gordon Borrie, Director-General of the Office of Fair Trading, announced that he intended to submit the Exchange's 'Agreement' – the Deed of Settlement, Rules, Notices and Code of Dealing – to the Restrictive Practices Court on the grounds that it was prejudicial to public interest. The committee under David LeRoy-Lewis which had prepared the detailed evidence to the Wilson Committee in 1977, was immediately reconstituted as the Restrictive Practices Committee and began work on the Exchange's defence. The chief restrictions which were likely to be challenged by the court were the minimum commission rates, the ban on overseas members and the single capacity rule prohibiting brokers from trading on their own account; but a major problem for the committee was that the OFT refused to single out any particular rules, insisting that the rule book as a whole should be considered by the court.

After the election in 1979, Goodison made a direct appeal to the new Trade Secretary, John Nott – a former merchant banker – asking him to halt the court action and approach the whole matter in a different way. A court case, Goodison believed, was entirely wrong – if the verdict went against the Exchange, the rule book would be struck out but there was nothing in the legislation to say that the OFT, or indeed anyone else, had to suggest an alternative to it; the result would be a complete free-for-all and a disorderly market. There was, however, a disinclination in the new Conservative government to be seen to be doing something which favoured the City, and Nott, like his successor John Biffen (who had himself acted as a consultant for a stockbroking firm), refused. However, the Exchange did manage to wrest some concessions from the government, including an amendment to the Act which allowed a stay of execution of nine months in the event of an unfavourable judgement.

In 1980 the Wilson Committee, which had been appointed to look at the way British industry was financed, and in particular to examine the growing power of the pension funds, published its report. The general tenor was favourable to the Exchange and the report expressed doubts as to whether the Restrictive Practices Court was the appropriate forum in which to settle the matter, but the government did not agree. Wilson pointed out in the debate on his report in the House of Commons that there was no 'corpus of law' on which a court could base a verdict, but that it was a case of 'what works best in the interests of the market, industry and all who are served by the institutions involved.' Nigel Lawson, then Financial Secretary to the Treasury, replied that, while sympathetic to the difficulties, the government had made up its mind – and that it was convinced that to 'change course now might well take a great deal longer and prolong the uncertainties which are making life difficult for the Stock Exchange.'

The hands of the Stock Exchange were indeed tied. Once the matter had been referred to the court it was *sub judice*: there could be no open discussion or debate and voluntary reforms were impossible. The Restrictive Practices Committee continued to prepare the Stock Exchange's defence, and in March 1981 filed a 'Statement of Case' with the court, covering 181 'restrictions.' The case was unlikely to be heard before 1984; meanwhile the Chairman continued to lobby the government and the Bank of England to consider some more acceptable forum than a court of law, one suggestion being the Monopolies and Mergers Commission.

Two years later, in 1983, there was a breakthrough. After the general election in June, Cecil Parkinson succeeded Lord Cockfield as Trade and Industry Secretary, and was anxious to see the reform of the Exchange. Even before the previous election in 1979 he had sought legal advice about how to bring the action to an end and produce the desired reforms by negotiation, only to learn that primary legislation would be necessary – which Nott had ruled out.

Almost immediately after the 1983 election, Parkinson met the new Chancellor, Nigel Lawson, and the Governor of the Bank of England, Gordon Richardson, at 11 Downing Street. Richardson revealed that he, the previous Chancellor Geoffrey Howe and Arthur Cockfield had been having talks on the subject, but these had been interrupted by the election. Richardson was keen to see some progress before his imminent retirement from the Bank, Lawson was equally keen and Parkinson was already *parti pris*. The main problem was one of timing – the judge who was scheduled to hear the case after both sides submitted their pleadings at the beginning of October, refused to adjourn it unless the government had issued a statement in the House of Commons saying that it would introduce the relevant legislation. The House was due to rise for the summer recess in five weeks and by the time it

reconvened in October, it would be too late and the legal juggernaut would have begun its unstoppable roll.

THE PARKINSON-GOODISON AGREEMENT

Goodison had already been in touch with the new Trade & Industry Secretary to press for urgent action, and the two men now met in Parkinson's office with nobody else present. Parkinson asked Goodison what he could offer in return for the suspension of the case. Goodison volunteered the abolition of fixed commissions in stages, by the end of 1986, and various constitutional changes including places on the Council for non-members (who would be approved by the Bank of England), but emphasised that the final decision would have to be made by the Stock Exchange Council. There was also the vexed question of the separation of capacity. The Exchange still clung to the view that this provided a measure of consumer protection, and it seemed to some people to be absurd to scrap it, especially as Lloyd's was currently engaged in implementing it.

The Bank of England also favoured single capacity at this date, and Goodison said he would do what he could to preserve it, while acknowledging the strength of the 'link' argument, which was largely based on experience in the United States, where there had always been dual capacity. This claimed that if brokers were to be able to survive in the new competitive environment of negotiated commissions, they would want to match as high a percentage of buying and selling orders as possible within their own firm. If a complete match could not be achieved, they would deal with the balance either by taking the surplus for their own account, or selling short to ensure that both sides of the bargain were fulfilled. If brokers could take stock for their own account, jobbers would insist on being able to deal directly with the public – and single capacity would no longer exist.

After the meeting between Goodison and Parkinson there followed almost a month's intensive debate conducted under conditions of stringent secrecy – within the Exchange, discussion was restricted to members of the Council, and the Cabinet knew nothing of the plan, although Mrs Thatcher was kept informed by Parkinson. Non-Council members, while obviously aware of the overall position, were unaware of the meetings between Goodison and Parkinson, and some of them doubted whether the Council would be able to bring matters to a satisfactory conclusion.

One of the reasons for their doubts was the composition of the Council, whose 40-odd members comprised a wide range of people with vested interests, very few of whom were active participants at the top level in the market. The small firms usually had a senior partner on the Council, but senior and more able partners of the big firms were too valuable to spare. Eventually there was a meeting to discuss the position between senior partners and Goodison, at which for the first time the views of those who were active market participants were expressed. They made it quite clear that, in the words of one of them, 'although single capacity was wonderful consumer protection, anyone who thought that it could survive negotiated commissions was living in cloud-cuckoo-land.'

A 'CHOICE OF RISKS'

For the Council the crunch had come at a special two-day meeting on Thursday 21 and Friday 22 July. Goodison began by outlining the position sympathetically but firmly, telling Council members that the Cabinet was going to debate the issue on the following Tuesday, 26 July, and that the Council had to 'make the choice of risks.' If they continued with the law case there was the risk that minimum commissions would be shot down, and perhaps that single capacity and membership restrictions would go too. Barriers to membership, he said, were an important part of the OFT's case, and the major risks of going to court were that 'we would be under the attention of the OFT for ever' and that an unsuccessful outcome would lead to a disorderly market. Exemption from the case by the government carried, he thought, a smaller risk, but they were undoubtedly 'navigating in uncharted waters.'

There was frank and lengthy discussion of all the issues involved, although all the members were agreed that the future development of the Exchange had effectively been frozen while under the threat of the court case, and that a wholly disproportionate amount of time, money and resources had been expended on preparations for it. (Costs within the Exchange amounted to well over £1 million, including legal fees, and the special committee charged with responsibility for the defence case had been sitting virtually non-stop since the original reference had been made.) On the second day, after Goodison had insisted that everyone who had not spoken on Thursday should now do so, the resolution was passed unanimously (with three members assenting *in absentia* and one unable to be contacted because he was 'in a caravan in Germany') that the Chairman could tell the Secretary of State that the Council accepted the proposals he had put forward.

The agreed package of reforms largely met the OFT's case: minimum commissions would be abolished by December 1986, the Council would include lay members to represent the interests of the users of the market, and lay members would form the majority on a new appeals committee which would adjudicate on the case of anyone refused membership.

'IT'S LIKE SELLING THE FAMILY SILVER'

"Mr Kinnock! Would you care to buy some Georgian silver, antique family furniture and an old painting ? "

Cartoon from the Daily Express, *13 November 1985.*

*T*hese words summed up the feelings of Lord Stockton (the former prime minister Harold Macmillan) as he contemplated Margaret Thatcher's series of privatisations which did much to shape the stock market in the 1980s and early 90s. The Conservative government gave different reasons for the programme at different times, ranging from increased efficiency to the fact that a smaller public sector would allow them to reduce taxes (which they did); its result was that by the end of the 1980s one in four

The Times, acting on leaked information, published a critical article about the agreement on the morning that Parkinson was due to announce it to the Cabinet, which led to further anxious discussion there, but consensus was finally reached after the inevitable sub-committee – which finally included almost the entire Cabinet – had been hastily assembled to modify Parkinson's draft statement.

When the announcement of what came to be known as the Parkinson-Goodison agreement was made on 28 July, it was the subject of a good deal of criticism and hostility, but the Exchange could spare little time to analyse outside opinions. In mid August the Council began detailed discussions as to how to dismantle minimum commissions. Goodison needed a 75 per cent agreement from members, and had to persuade them that his decision was the right one. Some undeniably felt betrayed, but an Extraordinary General Meeting on 11 October overwhelmingly supported the decision of the Council to accept the conditions on which the court action would be stopped. The government promoted the Restrictive Practices (Stock Exchange) Bill through Parliament and it received Royal Assent the following spring, on 13 March 1984.

A WHOLLY NEW MARKETPLACE

The taking of these momentous decisions in 1983, after years of debate within the Council, meant that just three years were left in which to formulate and implement an entirely new method of working for the securities market. The introduction of new dealing and settle-

families owned shares, although nearly two-thirds of the 11.5 million shareholders had shares in only one company, sometimes the one they worked for.

The first really big privatisation was British Telecom in November 1984, when the sale of 50.2 per cent of the business by the government for some £4 billion created the biggest company on the London Stock Exchange. The share price rose by 90 per cent within twenty-four hours of the issue, and about a billion shares changed hands on the first day.

Like most of the ensuing sales, this one was promoted by an energetic advertising campaign – an expensive one too, at nearly £12.5 million – but the one that most took the public's fancy featured Sid, who was the pivot of a £20 million campaign in the sale of British Gas two years later. Sid – who never appeared in person, just as the target of increasingly fevered endeavours to locate him to tell him about the sale – was the centrepiece of the vast British Gas issue in December 1986, aimed at a target of over four million shareholders. It raised £5.4 billion, and was four times oversubscribed.

The privatisations carried out between November 1979 and December 1991 raised in all over £46 billion, selling varying percentages of the shares of, among others, British Petroleum, Ferranti, British Aerospace, Cable & Wireless, Jaguar, British Airways, Rolls-Royce, and the steel, water and electricity companies.

ment systems, using a range of new technology, was recognised as an imperative, and if single capacity were to be abolished there was the need for a new form of investor protection. One set of uncertainties, the outcome of the court case, had been replaced by another – the implementation of a new system based on negotiated rates. The time scale of three years, which seemed generous to those not involved, was in fact quite severe, and meant that the mechanics of change would have to be devised without delay.

In September 1983 the senior partners of member firms were approached by the Chairman and asked to comment on the way in which the fixed rates might be abolished. Goodison suggested a range of alternatives, including the introduction of negotiated rates by class of security, following the example of the US where commissions on larger bargains were reduced in stages, or the adoption of a single specific date on which negotiated rates would take place across the board.

The publication of a short but incisive paper by the Capital Markets Committee – a Bank of England 'think tank' chaired by Martin Jacomb – further underlined the strength of the 'link' argument. By April 1984 it was evident that the only practical method of dismantling the minimum commission structure was not in steps, which would have resulted in a general destabilisation of the market, but all at once – in a so-called Big Bang. (The first person to use the phrase 'Big Bang' in this connection was Douglas Dawkins, a deputy in the Bank of England to David Walker, who had joined the Bank from the Treasury and was the Executive Director there responsible for the equities market.)

◄ Cartoon from the Financial Times, *15 January 1984.*

OUTSIDE CAPITAL

The question of outside capital was closely related to the whole issue. Since 1969 this had been allowed up to a maximum of 10 per cent for any single outside investor, which had proved too low to be really attractive; the Exchange during the 1970s had remained deeply reluctant to allow banks and other financial institutions to get a foothold in the market and undermine the separation of broker and jobber. However, the spiralling costs of staff, equipment and offices meant that both brokers and jobbers were hard pressed to retain their business, let alone expand it, and many firms were dangerously under-capitalised because of the increasing size of transactions. In 1982 the level of a maximum holding was raised to 29.9 per cent, and some financial institutions were quick to make a move. Security Pacific Corporation, an American bank based in Los Angeles, was first out of the starting blocks – taking a 29.9 per cent stake in the broker Hoare Govett a year before the deal with the government was announced – but in July 1983, once it was appreciated that fixed commissions would go and (by most) that single capacity would surely follow, the real 'feeding frenzy', as Wall Street termed such buying sprees, got under way. In early 1984 the Exchange ruled that members could deal in dual capacity and without fixed commissions, in overseas shares.

The world's well-capitalised banks now saw the way forward to entering the London brokerage business, which had hitherto been closed to them. The brokers and jobbers – the firms numbered by this date 225 – knew that their capital, for the most part, would not be adequate in the brave new open-to-all world which the stock market was about to enter. Matches could be made between capital and know-how to provide London with the muscle to compete in the big league of securities centres with New York and, by this time, Tokyo. Strategic planning for the future, frustrated by the years in which the threat of legal action had hung like a miasma over the Exchange, was suddenly astir as the various firms eyed each other and brokers and jobbers began to receive increasingly importunate advances from prospective buyers.

In April 1984 the Exchange issued a discussion paper recommending to members the abolition of the 29.9 per cent limit on outside capital, which speeded up the acquisition process. The paper also outlined the new shape of the market. As the trading system itself was to be overthrown, a new system was necessary, and the chosen replacement was a scheme by which all Exchange firms would become broker-dealers able to trade on their own account as well as to 'broke' securities as before. This was known as the 'competing market-maker system', formulated on the US model of the National Association of Securities Dealers Automated Quotation system, or Nasdaq, a screen-based market organising the shares of hundreds of the securities of American companies throughout the US. It was chosen by London in preference to the New York Stock Exchange's system where specialist companies matched trades and, sometimes, intervened on their own account.

It was decided that prices would be quoted on an electronic screen and deals would be fixed either on the floor or by telephone. This would allow for far more market-makers than the current limited jobbing sector. Prices were to be disseminated via the Stock Exchange Automated Quotation system (Seaq), to be developed over the next two years to cope with the large numbers of deals which London expected under the new system. Seaq was grafted on to the Exchange's successful Topic information network and much work was done on a system of public reporting of deals which would yet not make the market-makers' 'books' too transparent to the competition. In addition, Seaq International was introduced shortly afterwards to offer an attractive marketplace for foreign securities. The trinity of Seaq, Topic and Talisman – which was adapted to allow settlement by firms in their new capacities – would form the electronic heart of the new regime.

It was evident that the gilt-edged market would also have to be completely reshaped. Well before the period leading up to Big Bang, the Bank of England had been discussing with the Exchange possible improvements to the gilts market, which had at one time seemed in danger of competition from international broker/dealers accustomed to different methods of dealing in government debt, and from London's recently established financial futures market, LIFFE. During the 1970s, when government borrowing soared, the Treasury had been irked by the rates the institutions had to pay on high volumes of gilts business, and Mrs Thatcher was now determined to cut the cost of government debt. While appreciating the virtues of the current orderly market in gilts, dominated as it was by the two large jobbers, the Bank was also worried that the 'paper system' was vulnerable to surges in turnover. The discount market already played a significant role and it was entirely possible that the Exchange might lose its share unless it was able to make significant improvements in the facilities it provided.

THE INTRODUCTION OF THE FOOTSIE

Sir Nicholas Goodison launches LIFFE's new FTSE 100 futures contract, 3 May 1984.

The first major UK share index appeared in 1935, when the *Financial News* introduced its 30-Share Index of industrial equities, concentrating on the most actively traded shares irrespective of their market capitalisation. This later became the FT 30-Share Index.

In February 1984, the FT 30 was largely superseded by perhaps the most useful of all indexes, the FTSE 100 Index, soon to be familiarly known as the Footsie 100. This was designed by the Stock Exchange (who would have preferred it to be named the SE 100), and consisted of an aggregation of the minute-by-minute share price movements of 100 leading companies. Its main purpose was to provide a 'real-time' index for the futures and traded options markets, and LIFFE immediately announced plans to trade a financial futures contract based upon it. This was launched on 3 May 1984, and at the same time London's first stock index options were traded on the Stock Exchange, both markets being opened on the first morning by Nicholas Goodison.

CHANGES IN THE GILTS MARKET

By early 1984 plans for what was referred to as a Central Gilts Office were well advanced, based on a system developed jointly by the Bank and the Exchange and known as the book entry transfer system for gilt-edged securities, or BET. The Bank insisted that BET should be open to non-members, to which the Exchange agreed. However, the Central Gilts Office was designed for a single capacity marketplace, and approaching deregulation required a more radical change.

With much input from Eddie George and his department in the Bank, an entirely new gilts market structure was designed, once again on the American model. The new system replaced the two major stockjobbers, or market makers, with twenty-seven primary dealers who continued to make a market in gilts but could also deal directly with their investment clients. The twenty-seven were chosen by the Bank from a list of over thirty applicants and were together capitalised at around £700 million – a striking contrast with the capital of the three major gilts dealers in the 'old' market whose joint capitalisation was about £100 million. Several large financial institutions including Schroders, Union Discount and the American securities house Drexel Burnham Lambert, withdrew their applications before the final choice was made, apprehensive – rightly, as it turned out – that the market, with a turnover of £262 billion of stock in 1985, did not have the potential to grow fast enough to provide an adequate return on a seven-fold increase in capital. Inter-dealer brokers, or IDBs - who also came to play an important part in the equity market – provided the mechanism through which the primary dealers were able to trade anonymously with each other and unwind the positions they built up by dealing with their investment clients. The IDBs were thus providers of crucial liquidity in the market, ensuring that the stock could move swiftly from buyer to seller.

THE RUSH TO BUY

All these innovations and prospects provided the courtships that took place in the run-up to Big Bang with enough excitement, intrigue and unexpected twists to furnish the plots of several novels. Both the Bank of England and the Treasury were anxious that some major British-owned conglomerates would emerge, and the Bank acted in the role of 'facilitator'; David Walker conducted many private talks with the principal people involved and would-be partners were able to meet privately on neutral ground in Threadneedle Street, away from the eyes of the gossipmongers in the Square Mile.

It was obvious that the jobbers, being so few in number, would be the main prizes, and indeed the first match to be made was in November 1983, when Akroyd & Smithers, the largest jobber, announced that it would be joining with Mercury Securities, part of the merchant bank S.G. Warburg, in an alliance that had been quietly planned for some time in anticipation of the move towards deregulation. Then Mullens, the Government Brokers, and Rowe & Pitman joined the group, which became Mercury International (now S.G.Warburg Group).

Next to give up its independence was Wedd Durlacher Mordaunt, which, after considerable negotiation with the merchant bank Kleinwort Benson, was finally bought, together with the broker de Zoete & Bevan, by Barclays in March 1984. It was grouped with Barclays' own merchant banking arm to form Barclays de Zoete Wedd (BZW). The firm advising Wedds was Phoenix Securities, run by John Craven, which then enjoyed, in the words of its

FAREWELL TO THE GOVERNMENT BROKER

*T*he appointment in April 1981 of Lord Cromwell as Government Broker was a popular one, and his death in a riding accident in August the following year was a devastating blow to Mullens & Co. and to the City as a whole. The second Government Broker, Roger Daniell, who would in the normal course have succeeded him, had only been in this post for eighteen months and the Bank of England felt that a more senior figure should be chosen. It was decided that the new Government Broker would come from outside the firm for the first time since the stockbroker Benjamin Cole was named as Broker to the Commissioners for the Reduction of the National Debt in July 1786.

Nigel Althaus, the senior partner in Pember & Boyle, took over as Government Broker and senior partner of Mullens & Co. in October 1982. He was a well-known City figure, whose father and grandfather had both been senior partners of Pember & Boyle before him – his father, Frederick Althaus, was Deputy Chairman of the Exchange and President of the International Federation of Stock Exchanges. By this time, however, the events leading up to Big Bang were already in motion, and the impending changes to the gilts market were obviously going to make the position of Government Broker impossible to sustain in a dual capacity firm. After various possibilities had been considered, it was decided that Nigel Althaus and his dealing partner, Kenneth Hill, would join the staff of the Bank of England. The Bank would do its own dealing in the market, and the long connection between Mullens & Co. and the Bank came to an end on 21 March 1986.

Sir Nigel Althaus, Government Broker entering the Bank of England, March 1986.

founder, 'two happy years' handling over twenty of the thirty or so major Stock Exchange marriages which took place at the time.

NatWest bought Bisgood Bishop, a medium-sized jobber, and the broker Fielding Newson-Smith, and later acquired another broking firm, Wood Mackenzie, from Hill Samuel. The Midland Bank acquired the broker W. Greenwell with the intention of building a strong gilts operation, which it did. Lloyds was the only one of the High Street banks to decide against forming one of the new strategic alliances, on the grounds that the risks were too great, but started up its own gilts operation which was later closed.

Most of the UK merchant banks were more cautious than many other suitors. Their culture was entirely different, and they did not understand the volatility of the business; one was even quoted as saying that 'bankers used to despise stockbrokers.' They never called on a broker – senior partners were sometimes summoned to the banks' offices – and 'you didn't even know jobbers.' Yet if they stood aloof, they risked being left behind as the new, integrated securities houses took over their traditional roles of managing corporate issues, and no one knew whether, in the reorganised City, companies would continue to retain, as in the past, both a merchant bank and a stockbroker (or brokers). If many chose to use just one adviser, the merchant banks who had not taken the plunge would be in danger of being edged out of the marketplace because of a lack of distribution capacity. This capacity was absolutely critical, and at the time was possessed only by Cazenove, Hoare Govett and Rowe & Pitman at the highest level in really big transactions.

Warburgs chose the integration route; Morgan Grenfell hesitated, then bought two smaller firms, the jobbers Pinchin Denny and brokers Pember & Boyle, but closed them down within a few years. Some, like Lazards, decided not to participate at all.

Overseas buyers were also prominent, with Americans, who had long been eyeing the British stock market, in the vanguard. Purchases by US firms included Citicorp's acquisition of the two brokers Vickers da Costa and Scrimgeour Kemp-Gee, and the discount house Seccombe Marshall Campion. Chase Manhattan bought brokers Laurie Milbank and Simon & Coates, while Security Pacific upped its stake in Hoare Govett to 100 per cent. Merrill Lynch, the 'thundering herd', bought a small gilts jobber, Giles & Cresswell, and Shearson Lehman bought the broker L. Messel. One American firm, Prudential-Bache, gained permission from the Stock Exchange to start a new brokerage which was run by some of the former partners of James Capel: it also bought the discount house Clive. Other US firms decided, rather than making acquisitions, to strengthen their existing operations by major recruitment and investment – this sensible and ultimately much more successful route was taken by Salomon Brothers, Morgan Stanley and Goldman Sachs.

European banks were not so immediately acquisitive. Their primary interests were Eurobonds and international equities; the bulk of UK domestic equities was little regarded by them, and most of the important shares were already being turned into international equities on the over-the-counter market provided by M.J. Nightingale & Co. Gilts were a

GOING IT ALONE

The Senior Partners' room, Cazenove & Co.,
in 1990. From left: Anthony Forbes,
John Kemp-Welch, Stephen Carden, Rae Lyster.

The only major broking firm that stood proudly independent at the time of Big Bang, refusing the many and lucrative offers which it received, was Cazenove. Realising from the beginning of the 1980s that change was bound to come, it had spent the intervening years, under joint senior partners John Kemp-Welch and Anthony Forbes, in a major internal reorganisation designed to prepare itself for the new City. As other firms were taken over or merged, its future was the target of what *The Times* described as 'the same kind of fascinated curiosity with which Europe watched the later careers of Louis XVI and Marie Antoinette.' However, Cazenove stood firm. As it turned out, it was a wise commercial decision. The majority of Stock Exchange firms, both brokers and jobbers, lost their identity within a few years

different matter because they had an established international market and fitted better with Eurobond fixed interest stocks, and two Swiss banks joined the scramble for primary dealerships. The Union Bank of Switzerland bought Phillips & Drew, Crédit Suisse bought the small broker Buckmaster & Moore. No German bank bought a British broker or jobber.

Within eighteen months of the announcement of the agreement, all the major jobbers and eighteen out of twenty of the top brokers had entered into partnerships. The total figure for the takeovers – when over a hundred Stock Exchange firms changed hands within not much more than a couple of years – can probably never be accurately assessed, but it certainly ran into hundreds of millions: one estimate puts it at over £1.5 billion. The biggest single deal was Warburg's triple purchase which cost *in toto* some £200 million. Prices were high – usually based on multiples of between ten and fifteen times earnings (in the form of taxed profits), which were particularly healthy in the long bull market.

What were the purchasers actually buying? Skill, expertise, knowledge, obviously. Few assets changed hands, and most of the partners withdrew their cash interests before the sale. Effectively, these hefty sums were an entry into the marketplace, something that could be termed 'goodwill' in an ordinary balance sheet. The main beneficiaries were, naturally, the current partners. Many received a million pounds or more, some several millions. Some firms did make gifts of money to recently retired partners and to the next layer down within the firm – the so-called 'marzipan layer', above the cake but below the icing – in recognition both of their work to date and of the fact that they did not have the reward of a partnership to look forward to. Much of the purchase price was paid out as 'slow money', in instalments with legal agreements, or 'golden handcuffs' to ensure that key personnel stayed in place at least for the duration of the payment schedule.

PROPERTY BOOM

The vast sums spent on acquisition were matched by almost equally huge amounts spent on recapitalisation and providing the market makers with expensive new electronic equipment, including a highly sophisticated dealing desk for each person engaged in dealing, marketing and research, supporting between £20,000 and £30,000 worth of screens and telecommunications systems. Huge dealing floors were necessary, leading to a property boom not only in City developments such as the Broadgate Centre near Liverpool Street station, but well beyond its limits - Salomon Brothers, unable to find adequate space in the Square Mile, leased the huge Victoria Plaza building near Victoria station and fitted out a 55,000 square-foot dealing area. Some moved across the Thames to the south bank – unimaginable a year or two earlier – while others awaited the confirmation of the link at Bank station with the Docklands Light Railway before announcing their decisions to move to the 8.8 million square feet of offices planned at Canary Wharf in the Isle of Dogs Enterprise Zone.

In June 1985 the members voted to allow the extension of corporate ownership of firms from 29.9 per cent to 100 per cent, starting in March 1986. This change effectively introduced the large international firms to full membership of the Stock Exchange. The predominant holders of the shares, however, remained the individual members, who contributed only a small proportion of the Exchange's revenue. A second motion, designed to make it possible for individual members to sell their shares (presumably to corporate members) by splitting each share into five and permitting the sale of four, foundered. However complete corporate membership was achieved at the end of the year, when it was agreed that each member would be compensated for the loss of proprietary rights by the sum of £10,000 at the age of 60 – a crucial decision taken at an Extraordinary General Meeting in November, when the necessary majority of 75 per cent was only just achieved.

Right up to the changeover firms were still seeking space on the floor, but within a few weeks they had all gone, retreating to their newly equipped dealing floors: only the traded options market remained. The empty spaces were a poignant symbol of the new order. The corporate lifestyle, while offering excitement and sometimes rich rewards, was subject to pressures of ruthless competition unimagined by brokers and jobbers of an earlier generation.

LAST DAY – FIRST DAY

❝ The old Exchange has been lying in state all week,' said the *Financial Times*, and Friday 24 October 1986 saw its funeral, a funeral accompanied by a 'rowdy Irish wake', a few tears and more than a few drinks. A pantomime horse whose rear end concealed a junior clerk, was cheerfully kicked around the floor, followed by chancellor Nigel Lawson's puppet from the TV programme *Spitting Image*, which served not only as a focus for good-natured jeers but also as a timely advertisement for the full listing of Central TV, scheduled for the following week.

The Government Broker, Sir Nigel Althaus, was mobbed, and shaving foam and toy guns added to the furore. The close of business at 3.30 p.m. was marked by a lusty chorus of 'Auld Lang Syne' as members departed to ready themselves for the new era beginning the following Monday.

On the Monday, 27 October, the City was all agog to try out the new system, having had a successful dress rehearsal nine days earlier. At 7.30 a.m. everything went well, but there was a surge of requests to look at pages of Topic at 8.25 and four minutes later the system reached 100 per cent capacity (12,000 requests per minute). Bells rang, red messages flashed on the screens and Seaq had to be suspended ('Seaq and ye shall not find' quipped 'Lex' in the *Financial Times*).

Order was partially restored by 9.40, but there was only limited access to Seaq, and trades could not be reported within the five minutes allowed. There were no price quotes from Nasdaq and the government securities price dissemination system was switched off.

The overwhelming feeling among market makers was relief that it was the Topic equipment, not their own, that had failed. Tuesday was better, although when the North American prices system came on stream, coinciding with a 'debugging' programme being run by the Stock Exchange, there was another shut-down.

By Friday, after user access had been restricted to particular parts of the system and some of the minor services cut out altogether, the position was greatly improved. The Footsie had closed up 9.1 at 1586.2 on the Monday: by Friday evening it was at 1632.1, up 55 points on the week. By this time only a third of business was being transacted on the floor – within another week, it was deserted except for the traded options market. The City had embraced a new, deregulated way of life.

Ready to trade on the morning of 27 October 1986.

◀ *The vast trading floor of Warburgs.*

▼ *The deserted trading floor of the Stock Exchange.*

A STOCK EXCHANGE GALLERY 2

Sir Thomas ('Tommy') Gore Browne became Government Broker in 1973 and had to grapple with a period of change and volatility in the gilts market: he was an inventive holder of the office and earned much goodwill in the City.

Influential figures in the market during the 1970s and 80s included George Nissen, a Deputy Chairman of the Stock Exchange Council from 1978–81 and senior partner of Pember & Boyle from 1982–86, and the economist Gordon Pepper of W. Greenwell & Co. Andrew Rutherford was the head of Grieveson, Grant, a firm which was a major broker in both gilts and equities and which had significant international interests.

Akroyd & Smithers owed much at this period to three men who were among the most influential gilt jobbers and pushed the firm into its prime position in this market. Brian Peppiatt had a pronounced market 'flair' and was in charge of the firm's government stock operations from the mid-1960s to mid–1980s. David LeRoy-Lewis, a powerful thinker, also took a leading part in the affairs of the Stock Exchange Council, and Tim Jones was a popular figure who ran Akroyd's short business (inevitably dubbed 'Jones the Short').

Michael Marks, today (2001) the executive chairman of Merrill Lynch Europe, started as a 'blue button' with Smith Brothers and rose to be its head – a man greatly liked and respected throughout the market and the City. Another jobber, Brian Winterflood, after a brief period as a broker, progressed steadily up the ladder at Bisgood Bishop, becoming its managing director from 1981–86; he ultimately set up the flourishing business Winterflood Securities.

This was a period when corporate broking came of age, with three dominant firms: Cazenove, Rowe & Pitman and Hoare (later Hoare Govett). In Cazenove, Luke Meinertzhagen, a major City figure, operated in the new issue sphere; David Mayhew, who began on the sales side, later became an outstanding practitioner in the field of takeovers and mergers. Julian Martin Smith (a member of the well-known Smith clan) became senior partner of Rowe & Pitman in1970; Bill Mackworth-Young and Peter Wilmot-Sitwell urged the firm to modernise and were jointly responsible for much of its success in the fields of corporate equity and fixed interest stocks. Richard Westmacott presided over Hoare Govett as an effective chairman from 1975–90. Dundas Hamilton, senior partner of Fielding, Newson-Smith, was Deputy Chairman of the Stock Exchange Council from 1973–76. Two of his books, *Stockbroking Today* (1968) and *Stockbroking Tomorrow* (1986), spanning the eras before and after Big Bang, are among the clearest expositions of the stock market.

Equities Powerhouse
1987–2000

THE CRASH OF OCTOBER 1987 WAS THE MORE SHOCKING in that it was, like the physical storm which preceded it, almost entirely unexpected. The bull market that had been in evidence for more than four years roared on after Big Bang, confounding those who had predicted disaster. Share prices leapt by 46 per cent in the first seven months of 1987 after a rise of almost 25 per cent the previous year, recent privatisation issues boosted the trend and investors welcomed the greater depth of the new market and its lower transaction costs. By September 1987 client business in British equities was over £1.1 billion a day (£0.6 billion in 1986) with another £0.8 billion of deals being made between the thirty-five market makers. The reorganised gilts market also experienced a significant rise in business and lower transaction costs.

The overall rate of commissions, when charged, remained at 0.45 per cent; for big institutional deals of between £250,000 and £1 million, rates were 0.25 per cent compared to 0.31 per cent before Big Bang. A quarter of all deals were done net, so the overall commission was 0.33 per cent. Nigel Lawson had halved stamp duty at Big Bang, in order to give the new regime a good start, and in 1987 the Bank of England calculated that, excluding the settlement cost, a major institutional deal worth £500,000 would have cost 0.9 per cent to 1.1 per cent of its value to effect post Big Bang, almost 50 per cent less than the previous 1.8 per

HELPING SMALL BUSINESSES

Debbie Moore, founder of Pineapple Dance Studio, on the floor of the Stock Exchange on the day the company went public, 5 November 1982.

The Unlisted Securities Market (USM) was opened by the Stock Exchange in November 1980, partly in response to the recommendations of the Wilson Committee in that year, to help smaller companies obtain a market for shares which did not meet the requirements of a full listing. The new market, which imposed simpler and less expensive listing conditions, began trading the shares of just eleven companies, mostly oil and technology. It soon flourished, helped by high-profile launches such as those of the dance studio Pineapple, and during the 1980s it brought 817 companies to the market

and raised £47 billion. However most of the issues took place before the 1987 crash, in which the smaller companies which were listed on the USM suffered the most.

In 1990, largely because EC regulations meant that the distinctions between the two had been eroded, the Exchange combined the USM with the Third Market, its other small company forum, which itself had been scarred by the 1987 crash just after its launch. However, this move failed to stem the loss of business – ironically, one of the reasons for this was that in 1991 the Stock Exchange made full listing much easier.

The establishment of a rival marketplace for small companies, OFEX, which was set up in the spring of 1995, and government disapproval of the planned closure of USM, combined to lead the Exchange to a rethink of its small company strategy. In June 1995 it successfully launched AIM – the Alternative Investment Market. The principal difference between AIM and its predecessor, the USM, is that companies quoted on AIM are required to appoint a nominated adviser, who decides whether a company is suitable for the market, and a nominated broker, is a member of the Exchange, who provides a means for investors to buy and sell the company's shares.

cent.

Tremors in Wall Street

By October 1987 Wall Street was beginning to show signs of trouble. The US trade figures for August, published during the week before the crash, had been worse than expected for the third month running, bank lending rates were rising and during that week the Dow Jones Index lost a total of 235.48 points, wiping nearly ten per cent off the total market value. But this news was overshadowed in Britain by the hurricanes which struck southern England during the night of Thursday 15 October, leaving nineteen people dead and a swathe of destruction in their wake. Roads and railway lines were blocked, phone lines were down and few people could get into the City. The Stock Exchange was open, but Seaq was down, telephone lines were erratic and eventually the FTSE Index was suspended.

On Monday the 19th, the screens turned red within a couple of hours of the market opening, and Seaq was twice switched for short periods to 'fast', meaning that market makers could not be held to the prices they were quoting. The FTSE 100, which stood at 2301.9 at the close of business on Friday, plummeted to 2052.3 by the end of the day, and on Wall Street the position became even worse over the next few days – 'the bears were running rampant.' Black Monday in London gave way to an even blacker Tuesday, with the FTSE falling by a record 250.7 points in a day to 1801.6, representing a loss of £43.7 billion in share values on top of the loss of £50 billion the previous day. Some market makers ceased trading altogether for a while, but those who did continue to answer their phones, and honour their commitment to continue trading in bad times as well as good, later found that they gained much goodwill from having done so.

The newer recruits in the City, who had never known anything but a rising market, were stunned. By the end of the week they felt even more shattered as they reckoned up the loss on the five days of trading – the price of equities, reflected by the FTSE, had fallen from 2301 to 1795. The crash had come at a particularly unlucky moment in London. Most of the major institutions had heavy underwriting commitments, including the ill-fated BP privatisation – at the time the world's largest ever equity offering – whose preliminary details had been released on Thursday, the day of the storm. The government was selling its remaining 31.5 per cent stake in the company, which was making a simultaneous issue to raise £1,500 million. On Black Monday the Chancellor, Nigel Lawson, came under fierce pressure to pull the issue; he staunchly refused, but did agree to repurchase partly paid 120p shares if they should fall to 70p (in the event they opened at 90p on the first day of trading, 30 October, and closed at 85p, leaving the underwriters with paper losses of £700 million).

Alliances crumble

In the aftermath of the crash, it began to be evident that the vast jump in capacity and the

189

reduction in commissions of the deregulated market were having effects that had been concealed by the boom, and in the next twelve months some of the alliances that had been greeted with such euphoria and golden showers of money, started to unravel in the face of rising staff numbers, spiralling salary levels and falling revenues, as well as, in many cases, irreconcilable culture clashes. Closures and cutbacks, with inevitable redundancies, swept the City. W. Greenwell closed its equities business in January 1988; Morgan Grenfell stunned the City at the end of that year by closing down its whole securities business with immediate effect. Chase Manhattan ceased its equities business in 1989. Seven of the gilt-edged market dealers out of the original 29 shut up shop, and Citicorp axed its equity business, Citicorp Scrimgeour Vickers. Other firms such as Phillips & Drew announced heavy losses, while Shearson Lehman openly regretted its purchase of L. Messel. Barclays held on to BZW until 1997 before selling it, leaving only one of the major alliances, HSBC/James Capel, still in existence – its name was changed in 1999 to HSBC Investment Management. The British groups, so strongly promoted at the time of Big Bang, were mostly subsumed into European investment banks.

These shakeouts, and the disappearance of old and respected City firms which had often taken decades to build, received widespread and unwelcome publicity, although some firms did prosper, notably the independent Cazenove. The market itself recovered remarkably quickly from the crash, and the rash of bids and management buy-outs which had begun in the mid-1980s continued until almost the end of the decade.

The Stock Exchange as an institution changed radically as a result of Big Bang. A major development was the merger with the recently formed International Securities Regulatory Organization, or ISRO. This had been set up by overseas dealers and banks in a bid to keep international bond dealing outside the market regulation of the Stock Exchange, a potential schism which was eventually averted by the amalgamation of the two bodies shortly after Big Bang, following an agreement to form a single exchange in London which would oversee the trading of both international and domestic securities, under the name of The International Stock Exchange. The merger was overseen by a committee made up of equal numbers from the London Exchange and ISRO, chaired by Goodison with Stanislas Yassukovich, the head of Merrill Lynch in Europe, as his deputy.

COMPETING IN A GLOBALISED MARKET

Once the voting rights of individual members had been bought out, signifying the beginning of corporate control, the first phase of the revolution of Big Bang was over. International firms now had a recognised place in the London market, which was able to compete successfully in the increasingly globalised business of securities trading, and the market in foreign equities rocketed. By 1990, the Exchange was listing foreign companies' shares with a market value of £1,288.3 billion, representing over 60 per cent of all quoted securities in London. The shift of power to the major international figures in the financial marketplace was virtually complete.

The merger with ISRO was only one facet of the massive changes in the regulation of UK financial markets which took place in the 1980s and early 90s. As a result of various scandals in which investors lost money at the hands of those supposed to be looking after their funds, the Department of Trade and Industry had commissioned Professor Jim Gower of London University to look into the whole question of investor protection and the regulating and policing of financial services. His final report, which was published in 1984, made a series of complex recommendations, many of which took the US Securities and Exchange Commission as their model. The Thatcher government, however, was keen that the financial sector should maintain a measure of self-regulation, though conceding that an umbrella organisation should oversee the self-policing, and it was in order to enshrine this doctrine that it embarked on the road towards the 1986 Financial Services Act (FSA).

THE FINANCIAL SERVICES ACT

The Act initiated the Securities and Investment Board (SIB), which as the regulator of last resort presided over a number of self-regulatory organisations (SROs) and attempted to ensure that they drew up proper rule books and enforced compliance with the rules on their members.

One of these SROs was the Securities Association, formed to take over part of the regulatory role of the Stock Exchange. The Exchange's Compensation Fund, which in 1986 ceased to allow open-ended claims and limited compensation for any one claimant to £250,000, was wound up in 1988 and replaced by a scheme operated by the Securities Association covering the whole industry. The Association had no easy task. By 1989 there were 391 corporate members, of which 248 were British; almost all the firms, of whatever nationality, were engaged in diverse businesses such as Eurobonds and financial futures as well as trading equities and gilts. The size, diversity and novelty of their operations, as well as the inexorable development of technology, made regulation increasingly complex.

HUGH SMITH AT THE HELM

In November 1988 Nicholas Goodison was succeeded as chairman of the Exchange by Andrew Hugh Smith, senior partner of the stock-

▶ *Sir Andrew Hugh Smith, Chairman of the Stock Exchange 1988–94, by Susan Ryder.*

broking firm Capel-Cure Myers. Among his immediate concerns were the governance and organisation of the Exchange, where he suggested reforms which were strongly backed by the new independent Council members who had been brought in at Big Bang. He also briefly considered a possible merger with LIFFE, a project which had come to nothing in 1987. LIFFE once more decided to maintain its independence, but in March 1992, after two years of tortuous negotiations, it purchased the London Traded Options Market from the Exchange for the nominal sum of £4, marking the end of trading on the floor.

Internal reorganisation was achieved more easily. The Council agreed to stand down and a new board structure was implemented in the autumn of 1991, reflecting a balance of the various constituents who used the Exchange's market, and the 1802 Deed of Settlement was replaced by a Memorandum and Articles of Association. The Board also decided to trade under the name of The London Stock Exchange. In 1989 the Chief Executive, Jeffrey Knight, had resigned after twenty-two years with the Exchange; he was succeeded by Peter Rawlins with a brief to manage the business and play a more pro-active role in developing policy, including a rationalisation of the cumbrous system of committees and sub-committees.

Hugh Smith and the new Board had also to tackle the intertwined issues of the portfolio of services that the Stock Exchange provided to its members and the technology used to deliver them. While its function of supervising members and their relationships with clients had been taken over by the Securities Association (which merged in 1991 with the Association of Futures Brokers and Dealers to become the Securities and Futures Authority, or SFA) the Exchange was still responsible for listing and information services, trading and settlement, and there was now a growing need to devise a new electronic settlement system.

The Taurus affair

Talisman was completely reliable, but increasingly became too slow to process the huge new volume of trades which had developed since Big Bang, and at the same time the Exchange was under pressure from both government and Bank of England to introduce an up-to-date electronic settlement which would meet the international standards set by the Group of Thirty. Work had in fact begun back in 1981 on a successor to Talisman known as Taurus – Transfer and Automated Registration of Uncertified Stocks – but this was put on hold three years later during the run-up to Big Bang. Planning had been restarted in 1987, and Taurus was initially scheduled to become operative in 1989. The crash of 1987 did have one beneficial side effect: the downturn of business allowed Talisman to catch up with the huge backlog of unsettled transactions which had mounted up since Big Bang, but even so the delays in the crucial and expensive settlement process were estimated to be costing members something like £200 million a year in 1989.

Taurus was an exceedingly complex and sophisticated system, but that was not the real reason for its ultimate failure. It tried to satisfy the different, and in many cases irreconcilable, demands of too many constituents – banks, finance houses, registrars, members, private investors, custodians. Delays and difficulties proliferated and so did the number of Exchange sub-committees struggling with its intractable problems under the umbrella of Siscot, the steering committee, chaired by Patrick Mitford-Slade, which represented the interests of the whole industry.

Member firms became increasingly alienated as they spent hefty sums but were still left in suspense over what systems they would ultimately need to have in place to be compatible with Taurus. Eventually, in March 1993, the Stock Exchange gave up the struggle. It cancelled the entire project and wrote off the huge costs involved (in the region of £75 million, besides an estimated £320 million invested by member firms); 350 staff were made redundant, and the Chief Executive, Peter Rawlins, resigned. Hugh Smith asked the Bank of England, which had become increasingly worried about the risks posed by unsettled transfers, to start afresh, which it did by means of a specially composed task force, headed by one of its Executive Directors, Pen Kent, and including two members of the Stock Exchange Board.

The system put in by the Bank – which had long experience in settling transfers in the National Debt – was known as Crest. Crest focused on the requirements of financial institutions (which were already equipped with the necessary electronic systems), and was operational in August 1996. The final transfer from Talisman was successfully made the following year, without the loss of a single security. Rolling settlement, which the Bank had long been urging, replaced the old fortnightly 'book' in phases: ten days in July 1994 and five days a year later.

The whole Taurus episode dealt a devastating blow to the pride and the reputation of the Exchange. The portfolio of services to members, comprising all the elements of a trade from the beginning of a deal to its final settlement, had been broken: one of its most important functions had been removed in the most public, long drawn out and humiliating of circumstances. But events were moving too fast in the City for the Exchange to be able, even had it wished to do so, to spend time licking its wounds. Hugh Smith, who was widely acknowledged to have done an excellent job of holding the bruised organisation together, took on the role of Chief Executive in addition to his chairmanship until the appointment of Michael Lawrence, formerly the Finance Director of Prudential Assurance, in February 1994.

Sequence

In the wake of Taurus, the immediate preoccupation was first to rebuild morale, and secondly to take a fresh look at the services provided to the members, including the provision of a new trading system. Dissatisfaction among the market makers with Seaq had been swelling since the 1987 crash, and at the beginning of the 1990s the Exchange made various efforts to solve the problem, such as SAEF (the Stock Exchange Automated Execution Facility), none of which was successful. In October 1993, just seven months after the demise

◀ *Sir John Kemp-Welch, Chairman of the Stock Exchange 1994–2000*

of Taurus, the Exchange launched a new three-year, six-phase scheme to replace all its existing trading and information systems, known as Sequence. The oversight within the Exchange of this huge project was soon afterwards assumed by Christine Dann, a former head of the Birmingham Stock Exchange, who was appointed Director of Business Operations in March 1994. Sequence was developed in partnership with Andersen Consulting, which was given the brief to modernise, rationalise and run the Exchange's computer programmes. There was a faction on the Board, including representatives of some of the biggest and most powerful market makers, that felt it would be cheaper and more effective to buy the Nasdaq system. However Hugh Smith, who felt that to take the Nasdaq route would be effectively to hand over to the US a significant degree of control of the Exchange, successfully forced through agreement to the Sequence alternative.

Market participants were consulted throughout the development of Sequence, which was the biggest and most complex computerisation in Europe at the time, but not allowed, as they had been with Taurus, to swamp it with their varying demands. It was completed on time in 1996 and, at a cost of just over £80 million, under budget.

STRATEGY AND GOVERNANCE

Hugh Smith – who was knighted in 1992 – was succeeded as chairman in July 1994 by John Kemp-Welch, who had been joint senior partner of Cazenove since May 1980 and had come onto the Board of the Exchange as one of the early non-executive directors in October 1991. One of his first priorities was to commission a rigorous strategic review of the whole of the Exchange – what it was, where it was going and what was expected of it by its owners, members and users.

The Board took a weekend away in autumn 1995 and a further day the following spring to consider the resultant report, 'Marketplace to the World', and confirmed that the purpose of the Exchange was to 'provide a dynamic portfolio of regulated markets' where intermediaries could bring together issuers and investors 'on a basis that was attractive and cost effective.' The public affirmation of its intentions was helpful in quieting much of the adverse press comment querying the role of the Exchange, which had lingered in the wake of the Taurus affair.

Kemp-Welch also asked his two deputy chairmen, Ian Salter and Ian Plenderleith (an

Executive Director of the Bank of England who was appointed Government Broker in 1989), with the assistance of the Secretary of the Exchange, Keith Robinson, to carry out another review, this time of the governance of the Exchange with particular reference to its decision-making processes. They sought the opinions of members and users, and reported after four months, recommending further streamlining of policy and rule-making to reduce the number of committees – at that time twenty-three – by adopting a much flatter structure. They suggested having two main committees, one for primary and one for secondary markets, as well as four of the existing sectoral advisory committees, each of which would give much greater weight to input from practitioners than had been the case since the switch from Council to Board in 1991. Each committee was to be chaired by a Board member. They also noted that while discussions on ownership of the Exchange were not felt to be appropriate at that moment, they were by no means ruled out for the future. Their recommendations were approved by the Board in the summer of 1996.

By this time the six phases of Sequence were complete. Part of the restructuring involved the Stock Exchange's information system Topic, which from the early 1990s had to face strong competition from other information providers such as Reuters, Extel and Bloombergs, all of which sold their products in substantial international markets and had correspondingly substantial investment programmes. Recognising its inability to compete on these terms, the Exchange took the decision to move out of the direct provision of information terminals and concentrate on the wholesale distribution of information to market participants. This was achieved by the sale of Topic's customer base to two other information vendors, ICV and Telekurs, in December 1994. Sequal, the Exchange's trade confirmation service, was sold two years later.

ORDER-MATCHING

From the start Sequence had been planned to support order-based trading, to replace the traditional method in which the trades of all stocks on the Exchange were effected by matching quotes, with market makers displaying the prices at which they were prepared to deal. Even so, the final transition from a quote-driven market was not accomplished without considerable friction, which came to a head in the autumn of 1995. External pressure for the change was coming – once again – from the Office of Fair Trading, which still felt that some of the Stock Exchange's practices were restrictive, and from potential competition from electronic systems such as Tradepoint or Reuters' Instinet.

There was a wide diversity of opinion on the question of a centrally matched order-book. Many of the large firms were hostile to the idea: they were comfortably aware that they were the only ones with enough capital to play a major role in the new, deregulated City. However, there were some strong forces for change besides the regulatory and technical considerations. One was the growing demand for reduced costs in the trading process; the large insti-

THE SINGLE REGULATOR – THE FINANCIAL SERVICES AUTHORITY

*A*fter Labour won the election in May 1997, the new Chancellor, Gordon Brown, wasted little time before tackling some major City issues. Within a week the Bank of England had been given independence and soon after that Brown proposed that a single regulatory body should be responsible for all UK financial institutions.

The Financial Services Authority (FSA) is now established in Canary Wharf. Its nucleus is the former Securities and Investments Board (SIB) with the addition of banking supervision. Under the provisions of the Financial Services and Markets Act, it will replace the nine self-regulatory organisations (SROs), each of which had its own staff, rule book, and procedures. The Authority is run by a thirteen-member board appointed by the Treasury; its chairman and chief executive, until 2002, is Howard Davies, former deputy governor of the Bank of England.

A structure of civil penalties has been put in place to combat 'market abuse', replacing the former – largely ineffective – criminal penalties for insider trading and market manipulation. The Authority is able to impose unlimited fines and lifetime bans on City workers who contravene its rules.

tutional investors were already forcing the market to price its execution service down to an uneconomic level. The major US investors – who by this date owned some 10 per cent of the UK equity market by value – complained about the 'adversarial' nature of the competing market-making system. It was also becoming apparent that the return on capital from market-making was dismally low: one estimate put it at just 1 to $1\frac{1}{2}$ per cent. This was barely viable, and indeed was usually carried out in order to further other activities such as underwriting, derivatives dealing and proprietary trading.

After some fierce debate, the Board decided in November 1995 that the Exchange would definitely go ahead with order-matching for the most liquid stocks, and the market makers, some with considerable reluctance, fell into line, on the clear understanding that they would be closely involved in the implementation. To achieve this, Kemp-Welch initiated a steering committee, of which he was chairman, early in 1996, which was composed half and half of Board members and practitioners. Together they hammered out the details of the new system, to which resistance was further diminished by an alteration of the stamp duty regime for UK shares agreed by the Chancellor, Kenneth Clarke, which provided exemption to any member firm wishing to commit capital and act as a principal. Without this change, warmly welcomed by the Exchange, it would have been even harder to gain the agreement of the market.

One Stock Exchange casualty was Michael Lawrence, who had ruffled feathers throughout the City and whose handling of the order-book situation caused further ructions. In early 1996 the Board decided that he would have to go. Once again the Chairman had to assume the role of Chief Executive during the search for a replacement: this time the Board chose Gavin Casey, the former Chief Operating Officer of Smith New Court (which had been acquired by Merrill Lynch in 1995), who took up his new role in August 1996.

Under Sets (Stock Exchange Electronic Trading Services) which went live in October 1997, member firms display bid and offer orders on major stocks to the market on an electronic order book (market makers continue to handle the other listed securities, over 3,000 in all). When the prices match, orders are executed automatically on-screen, while orders as yet unmatched remain on the order book until they are either executed against a new incoming order or deleted. Once the market became accustomed to the new way of trading, Sets continued to increase its market share, and by mid-2000 was accounting for around 50 per cent of all trading in FTSE 100 shares.

LONDON AND EUROPE

Internationally, the 1990s saw major progress as London's market, less encumbered with regulation and providing a depth and liquidity often lacking in other European markets, attracted a large and growing share of international business, especially in the shares of large European companies. In 1993 the value of trades on Seaq International topped that of those on Seaq for the first time. The approach of the euro directed the attention of investors towards the continent of Europe, and mutual funds experienced a surge of interest in pan-European stocks. Pensions were another important factor: the UK was significantly ahead of most of Europe in pension provision, and in Germany in particular the state pension system was coming under increasing pressure, with mutual funds, again, eager to cater to the new demand from companies setting up individual pension schemes. The 'cult of the equity' was beginning to take hold in Continental Europe.

The other European stock exchanges – over 30 in all – were alarmed by London's growing international supremacy. The direct result was that a process of deregulation and rationalisation began on the continent from the late 1980s onwards, with the exchanges of Paris, Madrid and Milan all opting for versions of a Big Bang, while the six German exchanges joined forces to become the Deutsche Börse, under the leadership of the Frankfurt Exchange, in 1993. It was clear enough that competition would intensify – indeed, the Germans explicitly stated that their ambition was to overtake London to become the leading equities market in Europe. Both investors and intermediaries told the Stock Exchange that they wanted an efficient, pan-European marketplace. The Exchange believed that the answer must lie in consolidation, and in July 1998 the Exchanges of London and Frankfurt announced a strategic alliance: they would start work immediately on setting up a common 'access package' to allow the shares of the top 300 European companies to be traded on either exchange. They also planned to harmonise market rules, and, eventually, to build a single electronic trading system.

In May 1999 the six next biggest continental exchanges – Paris, Madrid, Zurich, Milan,

Amsterdam and Brussels – signed an agreement with London and Frankfurt to work together towards the creation of a single platform for trading the top 300 stocks in Europe. Less than a year later, in March 2000, the stock exchanges of Paris, Amsterdam and Brussels announced a full merger of their three markets as Euronext – the first such merger between exchanges of different countries, which sent a clear signal of their joint determination to become the central marketplace for European equities.

The established exchanges were by now facing growing competition in the US from both online brokerages such as Charles Schwab and Instinet, and the multiplying numbers of electronic crossing networks or ECNs. It was the success of electronic share broking systems in the United States that prompted both the New York Stock Exchange and Nasdaq in July 1999 to announce plans for demutualisation – they wanted to be able to raise sufficient funds to improve their technology to compete. In the same month the London Exchange, too, announced plans to change its ownership structure.

Demutualisation

Big Bang, and the consequent demise of the trading floor on which members met each other face to face almost daily, had killed almost all the 'clubby' aspects of the London Stock Exchange. One, however, remained – it was still a mutual organisation, owned by its members. Mutuality had become a serious hindrance to decision-making in the fast moving post Big Bang world of securities trading – the difficulties in pushing through Sets being just one example. What securities traders and investors want is delivery of cheap and efficient trading, and if they do not find that in an exchange, they can choose to migrate elsewhere. The Board decided that in order to be able to fulfil the requirements of its users, the Exchange should demutualise.

In order to do this the agreement of 75 per cent of members was needed and this was comfortably achieved at an Extraordinary General Meeting on 15 March 2000, when 298 member firms voted to end its 199 years of mutual ownership and turn it into a shareholder controlled company – by far the most sweeping change since Big Bang, and perhaps the most important decision taken in the Exchange's history. Each member firm received 100,000 shares, which could be sold or added to although initially no firm was allowed to hold more than 4.9 per cent of the equity. The Exchange had no immediate plans to seek a stock market listing so the shares can only be bought or sold on a matched basis, managed by Cazenove. The prospectus showed that the Exchange had net assets of £211.3 million, of which £201.1 million was in cash and investments, and many shareholders were in line for windfall gains if they sold their shares. The Exchange promised to pay dividends which would be 'three to five times covered by earnings' – which had been rising sharply as the bull market of the last years of the century roared on and it consolidated its position as the leading market in international equities.

Kemp-Welch, who was knighted in 1999, announced that he would retire the following year, and did so in May 2000. He had been at the head of the Exchange for just under six years, a period in which it successfully overcame a host of challenges from both without and within, and during which it had made significant progress in developing, regulating and delivering its markets as well as managing its own business.

A STILLBIRTH AND A FAILED BID

Kemp-Welch's successor as chairman was Don Cruickshank, former Oftel regulator and author of a highly critical report on UK banking. Within a couple of weeks of his appointment, rumours which had been swirling around the City for some months were confirmed: the London Stock Exchange and the Deutsche Börse announced plans for a full merger of their cash markets in equities and derivatives products. The new market was to be named iX-international exchanges. At the same time, it was announced that the merged exchanges would seek a long-term relationship with Nasdaq.

In London, there was immediate hostility to the proposal, particularly from some of the private client brokers. Users of the Exchange criticised plans to split the blue-chip and high-growth markets between London and Frankfurt, and there was widespread anxiety over issues such as listing rules, regulatory differences between the two countries and the cost of moving from Sets to the German trading system, Xetra. Shareholders felt that none of these concerns were adequately addressed by the offer document which was published in mid-July, and the increasingly negative publicity opened the way for a surprise hostile bid from OM, the Swedish

◀ *Cartoon from the* Guardian *26 May 2000.*

technology company which runs the Stockholm exchange.

OM's initial £803 million cash and share offer was dismissed by the Board of the Exchange as 'derisory', but it forced the LSE to postpone the vote on the iX merger, and provided ammunition for the growing numbers of shareholders who opposed the Frankfurt deal. That plan itself collapsed in September; both sides withdrew, and after a highly charged AGM, at which the Board came in for some furious criticism, chiefly from retail firms, Gavin Casey resigned as Chief Executive. Despite an increased offer by OM, the Swedish company ultimately failed in its bid, managing to secure the commitment of only 6.7 per cent of the LSE's shares by the expiry date in November: the shareholders had demonstrated uncompromisingly that they were, currently at any rate, unwilling either to sell the Exchange or see it merged with a competitor.

AT THE HEART OF THE CITY

The Exchange has from its earliest days showed a remarkable ability to survive changing circumstances – war and peace, bull markets and bear markets, regulation and deregulation, right wing and left wing governments, scandals and triumphs. It approaches its two hundredth anniversary after one of the most eventful years in its history, with many questions unanswered and further changes inevitable. In January 2001 a new Chief Executive, Clara Furse, was appointed. Cruickshank has pledged to continue to strengthen the Exchange's position, and certainly does not rule out future integration. Meanwhile it remains a truly international Exchange at the heart of the City of London.

▶ *The high-tech revolution: Jonathan's Cyber Café,*
set up at the Stock Exchange to celebrate the tenth
anniversary of Big Bang, October 1996.

FURTHER READING

Unpublished Stock Exchange papers, including Committee and Council minutes dating from its origins until, in most cases, the mid-1950s, are lodged in the Guildhall Library. Papers after this date, to which I have had unrestricted access, are retained by the Stock Exchange.

David Kynaston's PhD thesis, 'The London Stock Exchange, 1870-1914: An Institutional History' (London University, 1983) is a further rich source of information and comment. Published works on the Stock Exchange and the City of London and its markets number many hundreds. This brief list covers those which I have found most useful in my research.

THE STOCK EXCHANGE
Duguid, Charles, *The Story of the Stock Exchange* (1901)
Jenkins, Alan, *The Stock Exchange Story* (1973)
Michie, Ranald C., *The London Stock Exchange: A History* (1999)
Michie, Ranald C., *The London and New York Stock Exchanges, 1850-1914* (1987)
Morgan, E.V., and W.A. Thomas, *The Stock Exchange: Its History and Functions* (1962)

HISTORIES OF MEMBER FIRMS
Hennessy, Elizabeth, *Stockbrokers for 150 years: A History of Sheppards & Chase 1827-1977* (1978)
Janes, Hurford, *de Zoete and Gorton: A History* (1963)
Kynaston, David, *Cazenove & Co.: A History* (1991)
Lycett, Andrew, *From Diamond Sculls to Golden Handcuffs: A History of Rowe & Pitman* (1998)
Reader, W. J., *A House in the City: A Study of the City and the Stock Exchange Based on the Records of Foster & Braithwaite 1825-1975* (1979)
Reader, W. J., and David Kynaston, *Phillips & Drew: Professionals in the City* (1998)
Reed, M.C., *A History of James Capel* (1975)
Sebag-Montefiore, Denzil, *The Story of Joseph Sebag & Co. and its Founding Families* (1996)
Wainwright, David, *Government Broker: The Story of an Office and of Mullens & Co.* (1990)

THE CITY AND THE STOCK MARKET
Hamilton, Adrian, *The Financial Revolution: The Big Bang Worldwide* (1986)
Hamilton, J. Dundas, *Stockbroking Today (1968)* and *Stockbroking Tomorrow* (1986)
Kynaston, David, *The City of London*, Volumes 1-1V (1994, 1995, 1999, 2001)
Littlewood, John, *The Stock Market: 50 Years of Capitalism at Work* (1998)
Reid, Margaret, *All-Change in the City* (1989)

INDEX

A

Accepting Houses Committee, 165

advertising 108, 122, 125, 153, 162

AIM (Alternative Investment Market) 188

Alley men 49, 51-2

Althaus, Sir Nigel 180, 180, 184

American securities 40, 44-5, 65, 66, 67, 71, 79, 85, 102, 104

anti-Semitism 103

Antrobus, Philip 27, 27

arbitrage 92, 105

asset stripping 158

Autolycus (Walter Landells) 107, 126

B

backwardation 14

Bailey, Francis 29

Baker, Reggie 91

Bank Charter Act (1844) 52, 60

Bank of England 7, 16, 19, 26, 37, 40, 52, 60, 64, 135, 142, 158, 172, 177, 179, 180

   and the Barings crisis (1890) 75-6

   and Big Bang 177, 179

   nationalisation 135

   Rotunda 18, 19, 29

Bank Rate Tribunal 141

Bankruptcy Act (1849) 55

Barings 29, 34-5, 44, 62, 75-6, 76

Barnard Act 15, 16, 41, 60

Barnato, Barney 80, 80, 89

Battle of Throgmorton Street 83, 83

Bevan, Gerard Lee 109, 111

Biffen, John 170-1

Big Bang 167, 174-85, 187, 190, 198

Blennerhassett, W.L.R.P.S. 121

Boer War 86

Borrie, Sir Gordon 170

Bottomley, Horatio 88, 111

BP (British Petroleum) 166

Braithwaite, Sir John 137, 138, 139, 142, 143, 148

British Shareholder Trust Ltd 104

brokers 8-10, 9, 10

   brokers' medals 28, 39-40, 40

   business dress 56

   calling on clients 120

   capital base 165, 176-7, 183

   commissions see commissions

   dual capacity 71, 92-5, 162, 172, 176

   fictional 89

   incorporation 155

   on international exchanges 157

   and jobbers distinguished 15, 32, 71

   jobbing brokers 15, 71

   licensing 9, 10, 15, 28-9, 28, 56, 73

   numbers 89, 124, 167

   online brokerages 198

   overseas branches 157, 161, 168

   partnerships and alliances 146, 153, 155, 179, 181-3, 190

   personal and family connections 120

   public perception of 71

   retirement 92

   social standing 89-90

Brokers' Relief Act (1884) 74

Brokers' Rent 74

Brown, Gordon 196

Bubble Act 12-13

bubble companies 11-12, 13, 36-7, 38, 38

bucket shops 73, 108, 125

bulls and bears 15

Burdett, Sir Henry Charles 82, 82, 84

Burton-Baldry, W.B. 117

buying-in and selling-out 55-6, 82

Byron, Emma ('Kitty') 91

C

Campbell, Sir Archibald 110, 116, 122

canal stocks 20

Capel, James 27, 27

Capel Court 23, 24

Carruthers Gould, F. 70, 71, 73

Casey, Gavin 196, 200

Castaing, John 6

caveat emptor principle 61, 112

Cazenove 28, 54, 104, 108, 118, 136, 157, 158, 166, 181, 182, 186, 190, 198

Central Gilts Office 178

challenge system 99-100

Chandler, Godfrey 149

Change Alley 10, 12, 13, 19

Charlesworth and Co. 144

Chartists 53

Clarke, Charlie 85-6, 85, 103, 104

clearing 64-5

Clearing House 143

clerks 24, 71, 89, 92, 124

coat of arms 113

Cole, Benjamin 19, 19, 180

commissions 55-6, 60-1, 73, 90, 93-4, 108, 153, 161, 168, 169-70

   minimum scale 61, 93-4, 108, 173, 174

   negotiated rates 172, 173, 175

   post-Big Bang 187

   rebates 142

   tapering tariffs 170

Committee for General Purposes 16, 20, 21, 22, 24, 26, 29-30, 40, 41, 43,

68, 72, 81-2, 96, 100, 123, 130, 143

Committee of Trustees and
Managers 24, 26, 143

community singing 85, 86, 104

Companies Acts 61, 135, 136, 153

company law reform 135

Compensation Fund 124, 139, 191

competing market-maker system 177

computerisation 148, 160-1, 165

Consols 33, 38, 60, 67, 71, 87, 95, 101

contango dealing 14, 106, 116, 133,
135

Council of Associated Stock
Exchanges 93

Council of the Stock Exchange 130,
131, 136, 143, 158, 163, 164, 173

The Course of the Exchange and
Other Things 6, 7, 28

Courtaulds 147

Crest 193

Cromwell, Lord 180

Cruickshank, Don 199, 200

D

Daniell, Sir Peter 149

Daniell, Roger 180

Dann, Christine 194

Davies, Howard 196

Dawkins, Douglas 175

decimalisation 160

defaulting members 20, 31, 56, 60, 71

demutualisation 198-9

deregulation 95, 168, 169, 170
see also Big Bang

Deutsche Bourse 197, 199

devaluation of the pound 134, 157

discount houses 133

dual capacity trading 71, 92-5, 162,
172, 176

Dublin Stock Exchange 45, 124

Duke, Percy 149

Durlacher, Esmond 149

E

English, Henry 36, 38

Erie Railroad 67

eurodollar market 155

Euronext 198

exchange controls, abolition of 167,
168

F

Fell, Robert 164

Financial Services Act (1986) (FSA)
191

Financial Services Authority (FSA)
196

First World War 95-104
ban on non-British members 103
controls over new issues 102
dealing restrictions 100-1, 105, 106
Exchange closure 98, 99
postponement of commercial
payments 98
shrinkage in value of securities
103-4
War Loans 99, 119

foreign securities 34-5, 40, 40-1, 43,
65-6, 104, 109, 127, 190

Foster & Braithwaite 61, 79, 104, 139

fraud 20-1, 88, 89, 110, 111, 113, 125

FT-Actuaries Index 148

FTSE 100 Index 178, 189, 197

the Funds 7, 15, 20, 28, 55, 56, 109

Furse, Clara 200

G

Gallaher affair 158

gambling 55, 56, 60, 67, 72

games and practical jokes 32, 37, 94

General Strike 107, 107

Gilmour, Sir Jock 149

gilt-edged securities 95, 141, 170,
177, 178-9, 180, 181-2, 187

Glasgow Stock Exchange 93

global market 155, 169, 170, 190-1

gold standard, departure from 115-6

Goldsmid, Abraham 29

Goldsmid, Benjamin 29

Goodison, Sir Nicholas 164, 169,
169, 170, 172, 173, 174, 175, 178

Gore Browne, Sir Thomas 166, 186

Gosnell, Mab 124

Gould, Jay 67

Government Brokers 19, 71, 149, 166,
180

Greenwell, Graham 162-3

Greenwell, Philip 163

Grizewood v. Blane case 56, 58

Guy, Thomas 11

H

Hall of Commerce, Threadneedle
Street 58, 58

Hamilton, Dundas 186

Hammond, William 23, 23, 24

Hatry, Clarence Charles 109-10, 111,
112, 112, 113

Hemming, John 29-30

Hoare, Kit 149

Honorary Market Officials 163

Hooley, Ernest Terah 88

Hornby, Sir Antony 149

Hudson, George 46, 50, 50

Hugh Smith, Sir Andrew 191-2, 191,
193, 194

Humphrey's Clearing House 64-5

Hunter, Jock 149

I

ICI 147
IDBs (inter-dealer brokers) 179
incorporation 73, 130, 155
industrial shares 95, 106, 109, 136
insider trading 159, 196
institutional investors 120, 122, 136,
    137, 144, 146, 167
international exchanges, mergers of
    197-8, 199
The International Stock Exchange
    190
investment analysis 122, 146
investor protection 175, 191
investors' guides to the Exchange
    122-3
ISRO (International Securities
    Regulatory Organization) 190, 191
issuing houses 118, 136
Issuing Houses Association 158
iX (international exchanges) merger
    199-200

J

James Capel & Co. 54, 118, 120, 146, 157
jobbers 8, 72, 80, 100, 153
    capital base 144, 146, 176-7, 183
    country jobbing 125
    distrust of 9, 13, 15, 39
    incorporation 155
    numbers 124, 155, 167
    partnerships and alliances 125,
        146, 179, 181-3, 190
joint-stock companies 6, 7, 10-12,
    19, 43, 95
Jonathan's Coffee-house 6, 8, 10, 13,
    14, 14, 16
Jonathan's Cyber Café 200
Jones, Tim 186

K

Kaffir market 78-80, 86, 95
Kemp-Welch, Sir John 182, 182, 194,
    194, 196, 198-9
Kemp-Welch, Peter 149
Keogh, Oonagh Mary 124
Kindersley, Lord 141
King, Sydney 149
Kitchener, Lord 85
Knight, Jeffrey 192

L

Lawrence, Michael 193, 196
Lawson, Nigel 171, 189
Lazarus, George 149
Leeman's Act (1867) 64
LeRoy-Lewis, David 186
LIFFE (London International
Financial Futures and Options
Exchange) 167, 177, 178, 192
limited liability 64, 95, 135
Liverpool Sharebrokers' Association
    45
lotteries 7, 14, 14, 42
Loveday, George 162, 164

M

McGregor, Gregor (Cacique of
Poyais) 40
Mackworth-Young, Bill 186
management accounting 146
Manchester Stock Exchange 45
market makers 161, 168, 189, 195-6,
    197
Marks, Michael 186
Mayhew, David 186
Meinertzhagen, Luke 186
membership
    corporate membership 155, 183

nationality issues 90, 103, 153, 162
nomination system 92
qualifications 70-1
size and composition 26, 104-5,
    124, 142-3, 143, 144, 155, 167
subscriptions 21-2, 30, 56, 92, 105,
    127
    women members 162, 163
Merriman, Hugh 149
mining shares 36, 44, 78-81, 156, 168
Monopolies and Mergers
    Commission 161, 162, 171
Mordaunt, Sir Nigel 149
Mortimer, Thomas 15, 16
MPDS (Market Price Display
    Service) 159-60
Mullens, Sir Derrick 149

N

Nasdaq 177, 194, 198
National Debt 7, 15, 16, 20, 36, 55, 60,
    86, 95, 136
nationalisation 132, 133, 135-6, 160
New House (Gorgonzola Hall) 74-5,
    76
new issues 104, 106, 118, 135, 136
    offer for sale 118
    private placings 118, 136
    public offers 136
    wartime issues 102, 127
New York Stock Exchange 104, 105,
    108, 114, 133, 157, 168, 198
Nickalls, Tom 67, 79
Nissen, George 186
Norman, Montagu 105, 106, 109, 110
Nott, John 170, 171

O

October 1987 crash 189

OFEX 188

Official List 6, 54, 55, 73, 148

option dealings 35-6, 116, 133, 135, 183, 184, 192

order-matching system 195-7

Overend & Gurney crash 62-4, 63

P

Pacific Coast Exchange 157

Panel on Takeovers and Mergers 158

Paris Bourse 19, 64, 79, 197

Parkinson, Cecil 171, 172, 172, 173, 174

Parkison-Goodison agreement 172-3, 174

Paxton, Harry 79, 83, 83

Pepper, Gordon 186

Peppiatt, Brian 186

Phillips & Drew 116, 146

pitches 144

Poseidon affair 156

Powell, Lewis 149

pre-allotment dealings 49, 51, 61, 66, 73

Prevention of Frauds (Investments) Act (1939) 125

privatisations 174-5, 189

proprietors and managers 21, 67, 89, 104, 130, 143

prospectuses 125, 136

provincial brokers and exchanges 45, 46, 100, 101, 104, 108, 133, 157, 162, 1640

Pryce, Captain Thomas Tannant 106, 106

Purnell, Charles 149

'put through rules' 169

Q

quotation of prices 31, 55

R

railway shares 44, 46-52, 54, 61, 66, 67, 71, 79

Rawlins, Peter 192, 193

regulation of the market 190, 191, 196

Rescounter Days 14

restrictive practices 32, 94, 161-2, 167, 195

Restrictive Practices Committee 170, 171

Ricardo, David 22, 26, 32

Richardson, Gordon 166, 171

Ritchie, Lord 146, 148

Robertson, John 157

Rolls-Royce 160

Ross Goobey, George 136

Rothschild, Nathan 19, 33, 35, 35, 37-8

Rothshilds 35, 37, 64

Rowe & Pitman 108, 116, 120, 136, 157, 166, 179, 181, 186

Royal Commission on the Stock Exchange (1877-8) 62, 69-74, 73

Royal Exchange 8-9, 9, 10, 12, 41

rubber boom 90

Rutherford, Andrew 186

S

Seaq (Stock Exchange Automated Quotation System) 177, 184, 189, 193, 197

Second World War 125-31

bomb damage 127

cash trading 133

dealing restrictions 127

Exchange closure 126, 127

Securities Association 191, 192

Select Committee on Foreign Loans (1875) 62, 65-6

self-regulation 158, 159, 191, 196

Sequence 194, 195

Sets (Stock Exchange Electronic Trading Services) 197

settlement 14, 31

problems 81-2

rolling settlement 193

Special Settlement Rule 52, 54

Talisman 160-1, 167, 177, 192

Settlement Department 65, 82, 127, 133

SFA (Securities and Futures Authority) 192

share auctions 100

share indexes 178

Share and Loan Department 82-3

Sheppards and Chase 54-5, 116, 146, 155

SIB (Securities and Investments Board) 191, 196

single capacity 170, 172, 173, 175, 176

Slater, Jim 158

Slater Walker 158

Smith, Julian Martin 186

Smith, Lancelot Hugh 116, 120, 120

sole traders 165

South African securities 78-81, 168

South Sea Bubble 11-13

'Spanish panic' (1835) 45

speculation mania 9, 11-13, 31, 72, 80

sports and games 97

SROs (self-regulatory organisations) 191, 196

stagging 49, 51, 61

stamp duty 142, 187, 196

Stearns, Joseph 44

Stock Exchange

administrative reorganisation 163, 164, 192

    centenary celebrations (1901) 86-8

    Chief Executive post 164, 192, 196

    Deed of Settlement 26, 67, 92, 192

    demutualisation 198-9

    disclosure of information 146, 148

    dual control system 72, 92, 143

    earliest premises 16, 16

    extension and rebuilding 58-60, 74-5, 143, 144, 152-3

    floor 145, 159, 185

    foundation stone 23-4, 23

    holidays 24, 55

    hours of business 24, 55

    international supremacy 197

    London/Frankfurt merger 199-200

    nationwide amalgamation 163

    public relations 73, 131, 137, 139

    rule book 30-2, 55-6, 161, 167, 168, 170

    strategic review 194-5

    submission to the City of London authorities 28-9, 60, 74

    tax status 143

    turnover figures 141, 148

Stock Exchange guides 138, 139

Stock Exchange murder 91

The Stock Exchange Official Intelligence 84

Stock Exchange Tower 152-3, 153, 155

Strauss, Julius 149

Sweetings Alley 16, 22

T

takeovers 147, 158

Talisman 160-1, 167, 177, 192

Taurus 192-3

telegraph 68

telephone facilities 68, 143

Third Market 188

Threadneedle Street Exchange 16, 30

ticker-tape 68

time bargains 15-16, 31, 36, 41, 55, 60, 96

Topic (Teletext Output of Price Information by Computer) 165, 177, 184, 195

trust funds 142

U

unit trusts 117

United Steel 136-7

unlimited liability 64, 165

USM (Unlisted Securities Market) 188

V

vetting of quoted companies 72

Vickers, Ralph 149

Victoria, Queen 84-5, 87

Visitors' Gallery 139

W

waiters 123, 123

Walker, David 179

Walker, Peter 158

Walking Race 79, 97

Wall Street Crash 114-15, 115

War Memorial 101, 106, 131

Waterloo 33

Wedd Durlacher Mordaunt 146, 157, 179

Westmacott, Peter 186

Westralian shares 80, 88

Wetenhall, Edward 23, 28

Wetenhall, James 28, 43

Whistler, Rex 122, 122

Wilkins, Dick 149

Wilkinson, Sir Martin 162, 163

Wilkinson, R.P. 125, 135

Wilmot-Sitwell, Peter 186

Winterflood, Brian 186

women in the Stock Exchange 104, 124, 127, 138, 153, 162-3, 162

Wood, Muriel 163

Wright, Whitaker 88, 89

ACKNOWLEDGEMENTS

In writing this history of the Stock Exchange, commissioned by the Exchange to commemorate its two hundred years of existence in the City of London, I have had the help of a large number of people. My first thanks are due to Sir John Kemp-Welch, Chairman during almost all the time of the book's preparation, who despite the many calls on his time willingly read and commented in detail on the manuscript and provided a wealth of invaluable information and insights into the workings of the Exchange, the market and the member firms. Gavin Casey also kindly read and commented on parts of the book. Within the Stock Exchange I have received unstinting help and encouragement from Kay Dixon, and I am also very grateful to Jane Adamek, Keeley Austin, Allan Cameron, Keith Robinson, Julia Wilkinson and Alan Wilson for all their assistance. David Kynaston, most knowledgeable of City historians, was the consulting editor for the project, and the book would have been immeasurably poorer without his constant support and advice.

The following people gave generous amounts of time in interviews and in several cases provided useful written material: Sir Nigel Althaus, Oliver Baring, Lord Cairns, Godfrey Chandler, Peter Cooke, Christine Dann, Nicholas Durlacher, Robert Fell, Sir Edward George, Sir Nicholas Goodison, Dundas Hamilton, Sir Andrew Hugh Smith, Sir Martin Jacomb, Sir Michael Jenkins, Graham Kennedy, Jeffrey Knight, Mark Loveday, Michael Marks, Claire Mascall, David Mayhew, Lord Parkinson, Brian Peppiatt, Robin Peppiatt, Alastair Ross Goobey, Ian Salter, Dan Sheridan, Sir David Walker, Richard Westmacott, Peter Wilmot-Sitwell, Brian Winterflood and Stanislas Yassukovich. Sir Nicholas Goodison and Sir Andrew Hugh Smith both read some chapters of the book and made very helpful suggestions.

I am most grateful to Bernard Attard who kindly sent me a copy of his paper on the jobbing system; to Henry Gillett, Archivist of the Bank of England, who showed me documents relating to the Hatry scandal; to Sam Chauveau for his reminiscences of the air raids in the City during the Second World War, and to Anthony Stearns for allowing me to reproduce the silhouette of Joseph Stearns. The picture research was done by Juliet Brightmore with great professional skill, enthusiasm and imagination.

PICTURE ACKNOWLEDGEMENTS
Apsley House, Wellington Museum, London/photo Bridgeman Art Library:33. ©Associated Newspapers: 121. ©Nick Baker: 176. Governor and Company of The Bank of England: 18. Reproduced by kind permission Oliver Baring, Managing Director UBS Warburg:120. British Museum, Department of Prints and Drawings: 21, 38-39. Reproduced by kind permission Cazenove and Company: 27 below right. Corporation of London Libraries & Guildhall Art Gallery: 9, 11, 12, 14, 17, 25 photo Bridgeman Art Library, 27 above, 30-31, 35 photo Bridgeman Art Library, 40 above,42,54,59, 67, 75, 83, 84, 85, 97, 106, 123, 128-129, 153 ©Richard Beer,159 © Boyd Evans. ©John N. Deacon:180. ©Estate of Anthony Devas ARAPR:138 below. ©Estate of Edward Halliday RP:148. ©Estate of Rex Whistler. All rights reserved,DACS 2001:122. ©Express Newspapers:111, 116, 156, 166, 174. HSBC Holdings plc: 27 below left and centre. Hulton Getty: 2, 15, 37, 88, 89, 96, 107, 108, 112, 119, 145, 161. Illustrated London News: 93, 94. Imperial War Museum,London: 99. ©David Langdon: 147. ©Lichfield:182. London Stock Exchange: 7, 23, 28, 29, 41, 57, 68, 69, 70, 73, 76-77, 80-81, 82, 87,101, 105,113,130-131,138 below,148,150-151 photo Burnet Saidman, 155, 169, 185 above, 191, 194, 201 photo ip studios. National Railway Museum/Science and Society Picture Library,Science Museum,London:4 7. PA News Photo Library: 162, 172, 178, 184, 188. ©Tom Phillips RA:169. Popperfoto: 115, 133, 134, 137, 138 above, 140. Powerstock/Zefa: 38, 154, 185 below. Private Collection photo ©Jonathan Shackleton, a direct descendant of David Ricardo: 26. Private Collection: 48-49. ©Susan Ryder RP. NEAC: 191. Scottish National Portrait Gallery, Edinburgh: 40 below. Reproduced by kind permission Anthony Stearns: 44. ©Kipper Williams:199. Yale Centre for British Art, Paul Mellon Collection, USA/photo Bridgeman Art Library:19.